THE REVOLUTIONARY WAR IN SOUTH CAROLINA

Profiles in Leadership

THE REVOLUTIONARY WAR IN SOUTH CAROLINA

Profiles in Leadership

STEVEN D. SMITH AND KEVIN DOUGHERTY

CASEMATE
Pennsylvania & Yorkshire

Published in the United States of America and Great Britain in 2025 by
CASEMATE PUBLISHERS
1950 Lawrence Road, Havertown, PA 19083, USA
and
47 Church Street, Barnsley, S70 2AS, UK

Copyright © 2025 Steven D. Smith and Kevin Dougherty

Hardcover Edition: ISBN 978-1-63624-485-3
Digital Edition: ISBN 978-1-63624-486-0

A CIP record for this book is available from the British Library

All rights reserved. No part of this book may be reproduced or transmitted in any form or by any means, electronic or mechanical including photocopying, recording or by any information storage and retrieval system, without permission from the publisher in writing.

Printed and bound in the United States of America by Integrated Books International

Typeset in India by DiTech Publishing Services

For a complete list of Casemate titles, please contact:

CASEMATE PUBLISHERS (US)
Telephone (610) 853-9131
Fax (610) 853-9146
Email: casemate@casematepublishers.com
www.casematepublishers.com

CASEMATE PUBLISHERS (UK)
Telephone (0)1226 734350
Email: casemate@casemateuk.com
www.casemateuk.com

Cover images: (Front) *Battle of Eutaw Springs*. (Artist, Alonzo Chappel, c. 1858, from the New York Public Library); and (Back) *Battle of the Waxhaws, May 29th, 1780*. (Print Makers H. B. Hall, J. B. Longacre, A. H. Richie, Max Rosenthal, Wikimedia Commons/the New York Public Library)

Contents

Acknowledgements vii
Introduction ix

Overview of the American Revolution in South Carolina
and the Southern Campaign, 1775–1783   1

Profiles in Leadership
Henry Laurens and Creating Change   73
Richard Furman and Charismatic Leadership   83
William Jasper and Heroic Leadership   91
John Rutledge and Crisis Leadership   97
Thomas Sumter and Transactional Leadership   105
Francis Marion and Emotional Intelligence   111
Isaac Shelby and Cooperation   121
Nathanael Greene and Strategic Leadership   131
Daniel Morgan and Team Building   139
Thaddeus Kosciuszko and Planning Branches and Sequels   145
Henry Lee and Negotiation   151
Hezekiah Maham and Innovation   157
Rebecca Motte and Leadership by Example   163
William Moultrie and Servant Leadership   169
Andrew Pickens and Personal Leadership   179

Conclusion   187
Endnotes   191
Bibliography   215
Index   225

Acknowledgements

The authors would like to thank the following individuals for their assistance and support in completing this book. First and foremost, the talented production team at Casemate, including Ruth Sheppard, Lizzy Hammond, Elke Morice-Atkinson, and Declan Ingram. Noah Safari drafted our maps. Samuel K. Fore, Curator of the Harlan Crow Library, was instrumental in getting us together to write a previous book on Francis Marion's leadership abilities leading to this most recent collaboration. We wish to acknowledge the support of wives and friends who allowed us time to devote to this book. Despite the outstanding editorial assistance of Casemate, any errors and omissions in this book remain the responsibility of the authors.

Introduction

In 2022, Steven D. Smith and Kevin Dougherty collaborated on *Leading Like the Swamp Fox: The Leadership Lessons of Francis Marion*. Smith presented the historical background necessary to understand Marion's strategic situation, and Dougherty provided vignettes that demonstrated Marion's competency across eight broad categories of leadership. *The Revolutionary War in South Carolina: Profiles in Leadership* follows this same basic concept but expands the subject matter beyond Marion to include a host of South Carolina's Patriot leaders. As in their previous volume, Smith provides the historical context and Dougherty the leadership analysis.

Marion is of course included among the 15 leadership profiles, but in addition to venturing beyond this familiar character, *The Revolutionary War in South Carolina: Profiles in Leadership* broadens the scope of its leadership inquiry to include more than just military heroes. Henry Laurens was the president of the Council of Safety. Richard Furman was the pastor of a church. John Rutledge was the governor of South Carolina. Rebecca Motte was a plantation owner. Even William Moultrie and Andrew Pickens, perhaps most familiar as soldiers, are presented in non-combatant roles: Moultrie as a prisoner of war and Pickens as a post-war civic leader. Military leaders William Jasper, Thomas Sumter, Isaac Shelby, Nathanael Greene, Daniel Mogan, Thaddeus Kosciuszko, Hezekiah Maham, and Henry Lee round out the remaining profiles.

There were many reasons why the Americans were able to defeat what at that time was a global empire with a strong, professional, and determined army and navy. That Great Britain had to defend its empire against a consortium of European powers including France, Spain, and the Netherlands certainly played a part; as did the vastness of North America, and a bit of luck on the Americans' part. We believe, however, that the leadership qualities of these South Carolinians also determined the outcome. We hope the reader agrees!

Overview of the American Revolution in South Carolina and the Southern Campaign, 1775–1783

War in the Lower Southern Colonies, 1775–1778

From the very beginning of the American Revolution, the British ministry believed there were numerous loyal subjects in the Southern colonies, who, with only support from British regulars, would flock to the King's defense. It was a reasonable assumption, especially from afar, being reinforced by colonial Loyalists in their correspondence with the mother country. While the overall British strategy was first to subdue the rebellion in the New England colonies, the British sought opportunities to regain the South and then move north. In South Carolina allegiances were regionalized early on, with loyalism especially strong in the Ninety Six District, Orangeburg, the Dutch Fork region, and Camden, where "thousands" of Loyalists awaited the royal governor's protection.[1]

Indeed, the strong loyalism in these areas worried the Provincial Congress, and the Council of Safety, headed by Henry Laurens, commissioned William Drayton to travel the backcountry to convince Loyalists to change their minds. Drayton was accompanied by religious leaders William Tennent III and Oliver Hart. Tennent was a Presbyterian and Hart a Baptist. Together and separately, they traveled throughout the backcountry through August and September 1775, preaching the gospel mixed with a message of independence. Richard Furman, another Baptist minister, also crossed the backcountry, seeking to convert Loyalists and holdouts. They had much success in some areas, raising volunteer companies to the cause. In other areas, they met much resistance, and their efforts backfired, rallying Loyalists against them. Eventually, tensions rose to such an extent that open warfare was eminent as militias from both sides gathered. Neither side, however, wanted war at that time, and at Ninety Six, Drayton convinced Loyalist Thomas Fletchall to sign a truce. On the way back to Charleston, Drayton also met with a contingent of Cherokees at the Congarees and promised them support if they refrained from taking up arms against the Whigs.[2]

Only a month later, however, an outnumbered Whig militia force was surrounded by Loyalists at Ninety Six on November 19. For three days, the Patriots were besieged, losing one man and 12 wounded while the Loyalists also lost one man, but with as many as 52 wounded. In the end, a cease fire was negotiated, and both sides withdrew.

A second Patriot expedition of 2,500 men was then sent north under Colonels Richard Richardson and William Thomson. They marched deep into Cherokee country, and on December 22, 1775, Loyalists under the command of Captain Patrick Cunningham were attacked by Thomson at the Great Cane Brake, along the Reedy River, in modern Greenville County. While only five or six Loyalists were killed, as many as 130 were captured, and many more were rounded up in the days following.[3] Throughout Georgia and South Carolina, Loyalists and Whigs began a low-level, desultory civil war, engaging in small skirmishes and raids, burning and looting homesteads.

North Carolina Royal Governor Josiah Martin and Virginia Royal Governor John Murray were among those who were writing the ministry that the appearance of British regulars would rouse the Loyalists to the King's Colors. Their advocacy eventually convinced the British government to do just that. In February 1776, the British detached an army under General Henry Clinton from Boston with another under the command of Commodore Peter Parker from Ireland to rendezvous at the mouth of Cape Fear, North Carolina.[4]

Meanwhile, encouraged by Martin, Loyalist Scots highlanders were gathering around Cross Creek, North Carolina. Told by Martin that they should be in Brunswick Town by February 15 to join up with British reinforcements, they marched east but found their road blocked by well dug in American militia at Moore's Creek Bridge. The next day, February 27, the Loyalists foolishly attacked across the bridge and were destroyed by well-aimed fire from American rifles and cannon. At the same time, other Americans forded the river and attacked the Loyalist's rear, killing or wounding some 30 Loyalists, with 850 taken prisoner, along with 13 wagons filled with guns and supplies. With the defeat, organized Loyalist resistance in North Carolina was crushed and would not recover until the British captured Charleston, South Carolina, in 1780.[5]

Off Cape Fear, Clinton's fleet waited for Commodore Parker. Atlantic storms had scattered Parker's fleet, and it wasn't until May 1776 that the entire fleet collected and rendezvoused with Clinton. Realizing that the goal of uniting with the Loyalists in North Carolina was now not possible, Clinton looked north to Virginia, but Parker had learned that the American fort on Sullivan's Island in the harbor at Charleston, South Carolina, was unfinished and vulnerable. It was a tempting target, and the combined fleets set sail for Charleston.

Major General Charles Lee had been given command of American forces in the South by the Continental Congress. Learning that the British fleet had departed the Cape Fear, Lee was confident that their objective was Charleston. Arriving there on June 4, he soon discovered that the British fleet was anchored outside Charleston Harbor.

Lee began making improvements to the defenses surrounding the town and harbor. Visiting Sullivan's Island, across the harbor east from Charleston, he saw that the unfinished fort was a "slaughter pen" and recommended that it be abandoned. Colonel William Moultrie and the South Carolina rebel Governor John Rutledge thought otherwise, and Lee deferred. The fort would be defended, and laborers from other posts were sent to complete work on it. They would not finish it before the British attacked.[6]

On June 28, nine British frigates entered the harbor and arrived before the fort. A mortar ship was brought in but was poorly anchored in such a way that its bombs fell short. To increase the range, additional powder was added to the charges, which resulted in damaging the boat and putting it out of commission. Even while they fired, though, the mortar bombs proved largely ineffective. The bombs ranged high over the fort's walls and dropped in the mud-soaked center parade ground, which absorbed much of their explosive value. Inside the fort, the Americans stood their ground and returned fire. The British ships fired solid iron shot that was absorbed by the fort's walls, which consisted of spongy palmetto tree logs and earth; the shots did little damage.

American morale soared when Sergeant William Jasper risked his life by retrieving their flag that had fallen outside the wall and then reattaching it to a standard. Soon the British ship *Bristol* lost her cable spring and exposed her aft to the fort. The American cannon fire raked her stern, causing great damage and killing and wounding nearly 100 sailors. To further thwart the British attack, the British ships *Acteon*, *Syren*, and *Sphinx* ran into each other while attempting a flanking maneuver. The *Acteon* eventually would have to be abandoned and burned after the battle. The battle continued throughout the day, until 9:00pm when the fleet finally withdrew.[7]

Prior to the battle, Henry Clinton had landed a detachment of 700 infantry on Long Island northeast of Sullivan's Island at the opposite end of the island from the fort. While the navy traded volleys with the fort, Clinton made a demonstration of crossing but was opposed by Colonel William Thomson's entrenched riflemen. Clinton soon withdrew and had no more part in the battle. In the battle of Sullivan's Island, the Americans lost 12 killed and 26 wounded. The British had 64 killed and 141 wounded, with heavy damage to many ships and one frigate sunk.

Battle of Sullivan's Island. (Artist, Johannes Oertel, 1858, Wikimedia Commons/the New York Public Library)

Among the American officers in the fort was Major Francis Marion who commanded the American left battery.[8] Besides Sergeant Jasper and Marion, the victory established another hero, that being Colonel William Moultrie, who was recognized for his command by renaming the fort, Fort Moultrie.

Elsewhere in the South, Georgia remained relatively quiet in 1775 and 1776. At the end of 1775, the British army in the North needed provisions and sent a fleet south to purchase Georgia rice. The fleet assembled off Tybee Island in early February 1776, however, some ships had arrived in January, which prompted the Georgia Committee of Safety to arrest Royal Governor James Wright. He was able to escape and made it on board a British ship.

As Georgia and South Carolina militia gathered, on March 2, the British landed on Hutchinson's Island in the Savannah River just above the town, with the goal of securing several rice boats. A few Americans got there before the British and were in the process of unrigging the boats when they were captured and held by the British. Whigs on the bank opened fire with their artillery. They also sent a fire boat downstream, which burned a few of the rice boats, but two of the boats were secured and carried off by the British. The action, called the Battle of the Rice Boats, and the escape of the royal governor, left Georgia largely in American hands. Many Loyalists left the colony for Florida, and some joined a Loyalist partisan leader by the name of Thomas Brown.[9] Except for some ill-fated attempts to raise an army to attack St. Augustine, Florida, Georgia would see little military activity until very late in 1778.

While British regular units would not be seen in South Carolina in 1776 after the attack on Fort Moultrie, the conflict heated up between Loyalists, Whigs, and Indians in the backcountry. Cherokees who favored England began raiding frontier homes from Georgia to Virginia in July 1776. Loyalists sometimes joined in these attacks. Other Loyalists joined the Whigs against the Indians. On July 15, partisan Loyalist David Fanning led 88 Cherokees and 102 Loyalists against Lindley's Fort on Rabun Creek, where some American settlers had taken refuge. The attack was unsuccessful, and as the Loyalists withdrew, they were pursued by the Americans who captured some of the Loyalists.[10]

On July 31, Colonel Andrew Williamson led a detachment of militia on an expedition to Cherokee country to thwart the Cherokee and Loyalists attacks. He was joined by Captain Andrew Pickens and some Catawba Indians. On August 1, Williamson arrived before the fortified Indian village of Seneca Old Town (now under Lake Hartwell) and met a severe fire that threatened to destroy his detachment. Pickens was able to gain the high ground and fire into the stockade, forcing the Cherokees to withdraw.

Around August 11, Pickens made a reconnaissance away from the main body and was surrounded by Cherokees. Forming a circle, he was able to hold off the Indians until his brother Joseph arrived with a relief force. The "Ring Fight," as it was called, cost Pickens 11 men, while the Cherokees lost 65 killed and 14 wounded.[11] The village was burned and Williamson's expedition continued on a path of destruction of Cherokee villages into North Carolina, burning their towns, destroying crops, and eventually killing an estimated 2,000 Indians while losing 99 men.[12] The Cherokees were forced to sue for peace at the Treaty of DeWitt's Corner on May 20, 1777 and would remain at peace until 1780.

News of the Declaration of Independence did not make it to South Carolina until August 2, 1776, but, when it did, it essentially ended any hope of a peaceful resolution of issues between England and America. Some 2,000 South Carolinians enlisted as Continentals or state troops over the next two years, however, there continued to be no threat from the British.

The year 1777 was peaceful throughout South Carolina with no major campaigning by either antagonist, although it is reasonable to assume small parties of Whigs and Loyalists continued to harass each other. The rebel government in South Carolina took advantage of the lack of activity to pass an act to banish Loyalists, and many fled the colony.[13] As enthusiasm for militia duty waned, the South Carolina General Assembly ordered undesirables into active duty and attempted to attract volunteers by offering cash and land. In 1778, they became desperate enough to allow slaves to occupy up to one third of the militia roles. In 1779, Lieutenant Colonel John Laurens, along with his father Henry Laurens, proposed raising a regiment of Black soldiers. John had proposed the idea at the very beginning of the war, but Henry, although sympathetic, warned him of the difficulties that would occur. Now Henry, along with William Drayton, supported the idea of proposing it to Congress to authorize South Carolina to proceed. Congress actually resolved that South Carolina and Georgia raise 3,000 Black soldiers but left the final decision to the individual states. The idea was thoroughly defeated in the South Carolina General Assembly.[14]

Despite manpower problems and no action, South Carolina Continentals remained at their stations in Charleston through 1778, during which time they were training and preparing.[15] North Carolina remained relatively quiet. In Georgia, American Major General Robert Howe led a failed expedition toward British-held St. Augustine early in 1778. The attempt was abandoned in July due to sickness.[16]

While 1778 was nearly dormant in terms of military activity, the year would prove critical for the Southern colonies. Far to the north in New York, British Major General John Burgoyne had surrendered his army to the Americans after the battle of Saratoga in October 1777. As a result, the North American rebellion became a global conflict. France, Spain, and later the Netherlands, entered the conflict against the British. For the British ministry, the North American colonies became a secondary priority to the protection of the homeland and its global empire. The protection of the West Indian colonies was especially important, as they provided Britain with cotton, sugar, coffee, and indigo. In turn, Georgia and South Carolina, where Loyalism supposedly thrived, gained greater importance than the Northern colonies, as they supplied the West Indian plantations with rice and meat to feed the slaves. Historian Stephen Conway asserts that as far as the British were concerned, "from that point on [the end of 1778], the war in North America was pursued for essentially Caribbean purposes."[17]

Britain Looks South

The British ministry persisted in the belief that the Southern colonies contained significant pockets of loyalism. Thus, it was that with the Northern campaign bogged down, British Lord George Germain, serving as secretary of state for the American Department, looked again to the South. He ordered General Clinton, now in command of all British forces in the colonies, to mount a campaign southward. In his letter to Clinton, Germain informed Clinton of his promotion and laid out the strategy he and King George III believed would win Britain the Southern colonies after operations in the North were concluded. It is worth quoting a long passage of this letter, which demonstrates that while the ministry may not have had a solid grasp of the political situation in the Southern colonies, they did have a surprising level of understanding of the Southern landscape:

> ... it is the King's intention that an attack should be made upon the southern colonies with a view to the conquest and possession of Georgia and South Carolina. The various accounts we receive from those provinces concur in representing the distress of the inhabitants and their general disposition to return their allegiance ...
>
> The ideas entertained here of the most effectual mode of making an attack upon the southern provinces lead to the taking possession of Georgia as soon as the reinforcements arrive or the conclusion of the expeditions against the northern provinces will admit of your making a detachment for that purpose. A corps of 2000 men it is supposed would be fully sufficient to take and keep possession of Savannah, and when the time of their departure is fixed it will be proper to send orders to General [Augustine] Prevost at St Augustine to march a detachment of that garrison with the Florida Rangers and a party of Indians to attack the southern frontiers, while Mr. [John] Stuart brings down a large body of Indians towards Augusta. The submission of that province cannot fail to be the immediate consequence of these movements, and as great numbers of the back inhabitants would probably avail themselves of the communication being opened with Georgia to join the King's troops there, such force might be collected as, when the troops destined for the attack on Charleston should arrive, would be capable of penetrating into South Carolina between Mount Pleasant and Parisburg [Purrysburg] to take possession of that tract of pinelands which separates the plantations on the seacoast from the back settlements, thereby dividing the province in the middle and opening an easy communication with the loyal inhabitants in North Carolina and, by cutting off all succor and retreat from the planters on the seacoast, reduce them to the necessity of abandoning or being abandoned by their slaves or submitting to the King's authority.

The letter continues to outline the plan of attack on Charleston:

> The number of troops that it is supposed would be sufficient to reduce Charleston is about five thousand, for although the entrance of the harbor and the line of the town which fronts to it is strongly fortified, yet it is imagined that by landing on James Island which is accessible to ships of a small draught of water by Stono Inlet, Fort Johnson might be reduced and a passage secured through Wappoo

> Creek for the flat-bottomed boats to get into Ashley River without danger, or that the harbor would be so far opened that the ships by taking advantage of a fair wind might pass the fort on Sullivan's Island and the batteries at White Point and land the troops behind the works, where the town is entirely open and no resistance is expected. Could a small corps be detached at the same time to land at Cape Fear and make an impression on North Carolina, it is not doubted that large numbers of the inhabitants would flock to the King's standard ...[18]

Clinton sent Lieutenant Colonel Archibald Campbell to Georgia with some 3,500 soldiers who arrived off Tybee Island around December 23, 1778. On December 29, a slave whose name may have been Quamino Dolly, led the British through a swamp allowing them to get to the rear of the American lines. Howe's army was taken front and rear, causing a rout and forcing the Americans to abandon the city. The Americans lost 83 killed and 453 made prisoner, as well as much armament including three ships, three brigs, 48 cannon, 23 mortars, and 817 muskets.[19]

The remnants of General Howe's army retreated to Purrysburg, South Carolina, along the Savannah River, and joined forces with Major General Benjamin Lincoln, who had been named commander of the Southern Continental Army back in September 1778 and had finally made it to Charleston on December 4. The British also had a change in command. Major General Augustine Prevost moved north from Florida and took command of the British forces in Georgia. He acted quickly, sending Campbell north to capture Augusta, Georgia, while he marched upriver to confront Lincoln at Purrysburg.

Augusta was quickly in British hands at the end of January 1779, however, they would not be there for long. Disappointed by the lack of Loyalist turn-out, Campbell realized he could not hold the village and abandoned it on February 13. The next day, American militia commander Colonel Andrew Pickens proved Campbell correct when Pickens surprised a Loyalist militia force at Kettle Creek, Georgia. The Loyalist spirit had not been completely dormant, as Colonel James Boyd had managed to raise a detachment of around 350 men from the Spartanburg, South Carolina region. On the march to Augusta, they gained an additional 250 men. Boyd crossed the Savannah and camped on the north side of Kettle Creek. Following Boyd was Pickens, who caught up with Boyd and attacked the camp on the morning of February 14 in a three-pronged assault. Boyd managed to organize a defense and withstood Pickens for an hour before Boyd fell and the Loyalists were broken, losing 40 killed and wounded, and 70 captured. The Americans lost nine, and 23 were wounded.[20] Like the defeat at Moore's Creek Bridge, North Carolina, this defeat did much to quell Loyalist ambitions in the Georgia backcountry until the fall of Charleston.

Prevost, meanwhile, had also suffered a reverse when he landed a force on Port Royal Island near Beaufort, South Carolina. William Moultrie, now a brigadier general, was sent to defend Fort Lyttleton but arrived too late. The American commander there had spiked the cannon and abandoned the fort. Crossing Port Royal ferry and entering Beaufort, Moultrie learned of the British presence on the island and marched out of town where he met them in a stand-up battle on February 3. The American militia performed well until their ammunition ran low, and Moultrie commenced a slow retreat, however, the British also withdrew at about the same time. Casualties were light on both sides, but still the British withdrew, having already accomplished what they were there for; the destruction of Fort Lyttleton. Both sides claimed victory.[21]

The British secured a major victory on March 3, 1779 at Briar's Creek, Georgia. A large reinforcement of mostly North Carolina militia under Brigadier General John Ashe had arrived at Purrysburg back on January 29. Ashe joined South Carolina Brigadier General Andrew Williamson who had been watching Campbell in Augusta. When Campbell retreated, Ashe followed him to Briar's Creek, where he found the Paris Mill bridge destroyed. While the Americans were camping there and repairing the bridge, a veteran British detachment marched around them and attacked from the rear. After heavy fighting, the American militia collapsed before a British bayonet charge. Georgia Continentals held firm but were surrounded and had to surrender. The Americans lost 377, while the British only lost 16.[22]

Now both Lincoln and Prevost decided to take risks, which put Charleston in great danger. At the end of April, Lincoln left Brigadier General William Moultrie in the low country and marched north to Augusta with nearly 4,000 men, hoping his presence would dampen any Loyalist uprisings. Prevost, with some 3,000 soldiers, decided to make a run for Charleston. Crossing the Savannah, Prevost quickly swept past the American guard at Purrysburg and another detachment at Coosawhatchie, South Carolina, commanded by Lieutenant Colonel John Laurens, and marched northward. Moultrie, with the remaining American forces, rushed ahead of the British and was in Charleston by May 7. Lieutenant Colonel Mark Prevost, Augustine's brother, arrived before Charleston on May 11 with the van of the British army. If Moultrie had not beaten the British to Charleston, the town might have been taken without a fight.

Despite Moultrie's protests, town authorities in Charleston wanted to negotiate a peace. Amazingly, Prevost turned down the town's offer, which included the colony's future neutrality, stating he was not there for legislative purposes, but in a military capacity. Moultrie then took charge, saying the American army would stand and fight, and began strengthening defenses. Meanwhile, Prevost learned that Lincoln, who had originally believed that Prevost's raid was simply a diversion, was racing back to Charleston. Recognizing the possibility of being caught between two American forces, Prevost fell back to James Island. He was, however, in no hurry to return to Savannah. As he withdrew, he raided plantations for food and forage, and left a detachment of 900 men at Stono Ferry, between Johns Island and the mainland. There he built three redoubts on the north or James Island side as a *tête-du-pont*, protecting the ferry.

Lincoln decided to attack these defenses on June 20. First, he ordered Moultrie with a detachment to cross onto James Island as a feint. Arriving in front of the Stono Ferry defenses, Lincoln gave orders to charge the British position with the bayonet. His men stopped short of the British defenses and instead exchanged fire, despite his pleas to press the attack. His right flank managed to penetrate the British leftward defenses momentarily but was then quickly thrown out. As British reinforcements appeared on the opposite bank, Lincoln decided to withdraw. A rally by the British was repulsed, bringing the engagement to a close. The Americans lost a total of 155 in killed, wounded, and missing, while the British lost 130.[23]

Through the hot summer of 1779, neither side made any significant moves. The main British forces remained in Savannah, with a small detachment at Port Royal, South Carolina. The Carolina backcountry was in relative peace and under the control of the Whig militias. Lincoln's army was in Charleston training, but also withering away as enlistments expired. The good news for the Americans was that help was on the way.

The Siege of Savannah

On September 1, 1779, a French fleet arrived off the coast of Georgia under the command of Admiral Charles Hector d'Estaing. The fleet had suffered greatly while at sea, and d'Estaing debated with his captains about how long they could remain off the coast. Indeed, D'Estaing would probably not have stayed, except his ships had been so damaged by storms, it was dangerous to return to the open sea without completing the repairs. He sent word of his arrival to General Lincoln by five French frigates, and a rendezvous date was set for September 11. The date passed without the arrival of Lincoln's command, the van of which finally arrived on September 13. By that time, the French had landed troops on Georgia soil 14 miles from Savannah. Lincoln's full army finally arrived three days later. Then he learned that d'Estaing already had given Prevost 24 hours to decide if he was going to surrender or fight. This unilateral move did not sit well with Lincoln and already strained relations between the allies got worse. The two commanders eventually agreed on a siege, which required French guns to be brought to the edge of town.

On the British side, Prevost had acted quickly to recall his detachments from the backcountry, and his numbers had reached 3,200 regulars plus an unknown number of Loyalists. He had used the 24 hours d'Estaing had offered to improve his defenses and made good progress while the French and Americans bickered.

The allied bombardment finally began on October 3. With continued pressure from his captains to withdraw, d'Estaing decided to assault the now-well-fortified British lines on October 9. Prevost's defenses were impressive, including redoubts, batteries, and a line of earthworks with ditches and abatis in front. The strongest position was the Spring Hill redoubt, on the western corner of the defenses, protecting open ground.

Here the main attack was planned, with feints along the front to confuse the British defenders.

The allied attack was a disaster. None of the feints made any impression. The main attack against the Spring Hill Redoubt, consisting of three French and two American columns, was thrown back. The French were torn apart by grapeshot. The Americans, with Francis Marion leading the attack, broke through the abatis, crossed the ditches, and planted their flag on the parapet in fierce hand-to-hand fighting, but were then checked and thrown back.

Some 1,500 Americans and 3,500 French troops fought in the battle against 4,800 British. The Americans lost 239 killed and wounded, the French 585, and the British 55.[24] One of the casualties was William Jasper, who repeated his Fort Sullivan heroics at the Spring Hill Redoubt. Jasper grabbed the 2nd Regiment's colors after two bearers had been cut down, but he too was wounded and was carried back to the American camp where he died.[25]

Lincoln wanted to continue the siege, but the French wanted out. By October 19, the Americans were back across the Savannah River in South Carolina, and the French were back on their ships. As Lincoln returned to Charleston, everyone knew that Charleston was the next target of British attention. While the main American army marched for the city, the 2nd South Carolina Regiment was left at Sheldon, South Carolina, to watch for the coming invasion.

The Fall of Charleston

As Lincoln struggled to fortify Charleston, the British reinforced their army in Georgia. At the end of January 1780, the first of 88 transports, 30 men of war, and 8,700 soldiers began to arrive off Tybee Island, Georgia, with Sir Henry Clinton in command. The fleet had met rough seas that scattered the ships, and those that survived trickled in throughout February. One ship, full of Hessians, had been blown across the Atlantic Ocean and found itself off the coast of England. Most of the cavalry horses were lost. Clinton did not wait though, and in consultation with his advisors, including Lieutenant General Lord Charles Cornwallis, he decided to send nearly 2,000 men north to recapture Augusta and then join the rest of the army before Charleston. On February 11, 2,000 British grenadiers and light infantry landed on Simmons (now Seabrook) Island to begin the campaign to take Charleston.[26]

Lincoln sent Moultrie, a detachment of light infantry under Francis Marion, and dragoons to skirmish and harass the invaders. Skirmishing continued through February and March as Lincoln improved defenses in Charleston and pleaded with the militia to turn-out, but the British noose gradually tightened around the city. Lincoln also pleaded with South Carolinians to let him raise a pioneer battalion of Black troops, which was rejected. By the first week of March, Clinton had constructed a supply depot on James Island. By March 11, the British had occupied the remains of Fort Johnson, across the harbor from Charleston. On March 30, they began the first parallel siege line, 800 yards from the American lines, north of Charleston.[27]

From this point on Charleston was under formal siege. Lincoln received some good news on April 7 when 700 Virginia Continentals arrived, however, the following day, the British navy anchored off Fort Johnson, having passed the bar and the channel and passed Fort Moultrie's defenses. There they were out of range of Fort Moultrie and could support the British land forces. This was a serious blow to Lincoln's defense of Charleston.

How had the Americans allowed the British fleet to enter the narrow channel into Charleston Harbor without much resistance? Early on, Lincoln had counted on the difficulty of crossing the bar and negotiating the narrow navigable channel into Charleston Harbor as being an important part of his defenses. Congress had sent four ships mounting 112 guns to assist in the defense of Charleston. South Carolina had added another four ships, and with two French ships, Lincoln's little fleet had a total of 260 guns under the command of Commodore Abraham Whipple.

At the end of January, Lincoln was told that stationing the fleet just inside the bar to defend the harbor was unfeasible due to a combination of tides, depths, and winds, and the need to remain anchored such that the broadside of the defending ship faced any vessel attempting to pass. Not believing it, he ordered a study of the channel, but the result was the same. Eventually, when asked where the American fleet might anchor safely and defend the city, Whipple answered that they would operate in conjunction with the guns of Fort Moultrie, even though Whipple had earlier mentioned that they might anchor off the North Breaker head and defend the bar there. Lincoln in the end did not order Whipple to defend the bar but left it to Whipple to determine the best location for his fleet. Whipple did remove channel marker buoys and recommend that the Patriots destroy the lighthouse and blacken the white steeple of St. Michael's Church, all to hinder the British. Nevertheless, the British managed to survey and mark the channel themselves. Meanwhile, Whipple stationed his ships adjacent to Fort Moultrie and began the construction of a series of sunken ships, cable, and chains to block the harbor inside the channel. He also ordered fire ships to make ready, but they were never completed.

On March 20, six British ships and accompanying smaller vessels crossed the bar into Five Fathom Hole. The Americans were now outgunned 286 to 248, and it was Whipple and his fellow captains' opinion that they could not hold position and that the obstructions would not stop the British fleet. Lincoln and his officers were furious at the fleet's unwillingness to fight and ordered them to fall back closer to Charleston. Whipple moved the fleet to the Cooper River where it was now useless as a naval defense of Charleston, and the British held the harbor.[28]

Charleston was now effectively surrounded, and the British offered terms, which Lincoln refused. While the main British forces harassed Lincoln's defenses, light troops were sent into the countryside surrounding Charleston to prevent any possibility of Charleston being reinforced. On April 14, British Lieutenant Colonel Banastre Tarleton surprised a Patriot force at Monck's Corner, capturing many excellent dragoon horses.[29]

By April 17, a second British parallel had been completed, and the town was under constant bombardment. Life along the front lines of both sides was dangerous and horrendous. A Hessian officer, Captain Johann Ewald, reported:

> The dangers and difficult work were the least of the annoyance: the intolerable heat, the lack of good water, and the billions of sandflies and mosquitoes made up the worse nuisance. Moreover, since all our approaches were built in white, sandy soil, one could hardly open his eyes during the south wind because of the thick dust, and could not put a bite of bread into his mouth which was not covered with sand.[30]

Lincoln sought the advice of his council who had mixed feelings on continuing. Some wanted to offer terms, while others urged that the Continentals be evacuated. It was, however, the Privy Council who insisted that the Continentals stay, threatening to open the gates and assist the British in capturing the fleeing Continentals if they left.[31] Lincoln decided to offer terms on April 21. He included a provision allowing the Patriot troops to withdraw. The offer was refused. By this time a third parallel was under construction. Finally, on April 24, the Americans, for the first time, attempted a sortie, which was thrown back by fire from the second parallel.[32] The following evening, nervous British troops along the third parallel panicked and ran, only to be fired upon by their fellow soldiers on the second line, thinking they were another American sortie.

Time was against the Americans, however, and when Tarleton surprised an American detachment at Lenud's Ferry on May 6, and Fort Moultrie fell on May 7, Patriot morale was devastated. Negotiations began on May 8, and on May 12, Lincoln surrendered. American losses were catastrophic. Some 89 were killed and 140 wounded, but over 5,600 Continentals and militia surrendered. Three hundred cannon were lost. Huge amounts of gunpowder, food, and stores were lost, along with three frigates. Among the victims were thousands of slaves whom the British gathered and sent off to the Caribbean Islands. The British lost 76 killed, 189 wounded, of nearly 13,000 men involved in the campaign. Shortly after the surrender, a British soldier tossed a loaded musket onto a pile of arms, causing 4,000 pounds of captured gunpowder to explode, killing as many as 300 soldiers and civilians, and destroying some 3,000 captured muskets.[33] Still, there were many more cartridges and muskets that survived and would be used to arm Loyalist units for the rest of the war.

The Patriot defense of Charleston had been a debacle. Historian David B. Mattern concludes that:

> It was a military disaster—much greater than the loss of the town alone would have been. Lincoln, a general known for his "prudence," had jeopardized the entire Southern Department by his unwise decision to defend Charleston to the bitter end. However understandable his reasoning, however unrelenting the pressures place upon him, the fact remained that Lincoln had sacrificed his better judgement to the threats and entreaties of South Carolina's civil authorities.[34]

Battle of the Waxhaws, May 29th, 1780. (Print Makers H. B. Hall, J. B. Longacre, A. H. Richie, Max Rosenthal, Wikimedia Commons/the New York Public Library)

An otherwise good man, Lincoln was clearly not up to the task he had been assigned.[35]

The British wasted no time in subduing the backcountry villages after the capture of Charleston. By May 15, Cornwallis was on his way to Camden with Lieutenant Colonel Banastre Tarleton, whose Legion ranged across the northern part of the colony to block American reinforcements still heading for Charleston. Tarleton was an aggressive and confident officer. On May 29, he caught up with Colonel Abraham Buford with a detachment of Virginia Continentals that had marched from Virginia to Camden but had fallen back upon learning of the fall of Charleston. Buford's troops were slaughtered by Tarleton at the Waxhaws. The Americans lost 316 men killed and wounded, nearly a 70 percent casualty rate, in comparison to Tarleton's 17.[36]

Two other British columns marched for Ninety Six and Augusta that June, securing the two most important villages in the northwestern part of the backcountry. Throughout South Carolina, Loyalists and Provincial troops assisted the British regulars in subduing the countryside. Many in rebellion turned themselves in. Notable Whigs such as Isaac Hayne, Isaac Huger, Andrew Pickens, and Andrew Williamson all convinced their militia to accept British parole and go home. Hayne, Huger, and Pickens would later take up arms again, while Williamson retired to his home at Whitehall Plantation.[37] Lieutenant Colonel Alexander Innes of the Provincial South Carolina Royalists wrote Cornwallis from the middle of the colony on June 8 that:

> As to the general disposition of the country, I have found it as favorable as your Lordship can wish. Several of our friends from the different districts have been with me and are returned to assure the loyal of every protection. They [Loyalists] are assembling in many places, and the most violent rebels are candid enough to allow that the game is up and are coming in to make their submission in great numbers.[38]

Clinton then put Lieutenant General Cornwallis, his second in command, in charge of the Southern Theater with over 6,000 rank and file and left for New York. An experienced combat leader, Cornwallis had participated in many Northern campaign battles like Long Island, Brandywine, Germantown, and Monmouth. He and Clinton would soon differ on Southern campaign strategy, and Cornwallis would eventually surrender his command at Yorktown, Virginia. It would be Clinton, however, who would be blamed for the loss.[39]

In at least one area, history would be correct in blaming Clinton. Before leaving for New York, Clinton most assuredly made a mistake that would help lead to the loss of the Southern colonies. Prior to the fall of Charleston, he had restrained Loyalists from activities which might place them in danger of Whig response. With Charleston taken, he now urged them to join British forces in "re-establishing peace and good government," since the Southern colonies were all but secure and "nothing appeared to be wanting toward the entire suppression of the rebellion but the occupying a few strong posts in the upper country, and the putting arms into the hands of the King's friends for their defense against the straggling parties of rebels who might be still lurking amongst them."[40]

With such confidence, Clinton issued a proclamation on June 3, 1780, declaring that no person could remain neutral in the present crisis. All had to proclaim loyalty and assist in subduing the rebellion.[41]

This demand did not sit well with those South Carolinians who simply wished to return to their farms, while emboldening those who were still in rebellion. Lieutenant Colonel Lord Francis Rawdon, who along with Cornwallis, would be left behind in South Carolina, lamented:

> That unfortunate proclamation of the 3rd has had very unfavorable consequences. The majority of the inhabitants in the frontier districts, tho' ill disposed to us, from circumstances were not actually in arms against us. They were therefore freed from the paroles imposed by Lt Colonel Turnbull and myself, and nine out of ten of them are now embodied on the part of the rebels. I must own that several likewise who were excepted from the indulgence have, notwithstanding their paroles, taken the same active part against us.... Perhaps I ought not to question the expediency of that proclamation, but I do so immediately feel the effects of it that I may fairly be excused.[42]

In Georgia, the summer was tense but mostly quiet. Georgians captured in Charleston returned home, many passing by British-held Augusta, and the British governor there did not press them to give up their arms. The British were so confident of their conquest of Georgia that they sent their Georgia troops to St. Augustine, Florida. Only in Wilkes and Richmond Counties were there any American strongholds. Georgian Lieutenant Colonel Elijah Clarke led a gang of Whigs into South Carolina in August, and in mid-September they would attempt an attack against Augusta, which was thwarted by the arrival of reinforcements from Ninety Six.[43]

In North Carolina, Lord Cornwallis pleaded with Loyalists to restrain from any uprising until after the summer harvest, which would allow him to move regulars into the colony. After years of Whig control, however, Loyalists could not resist gathering to take revenge. As many as 1,300 assembled at Ramsours Mill, North Carolina, under Lieutenant Colonel John Moore. They were attacked by Patriot militia commander Lieutenant Colonel Francis Locke on June 20. Both sides lost around 150 men, and both sides quickly dispersed. This action, like Moore's Creek Bridge, dampened any major Loyalist factions from organizing in North Carolina for the time being.[44]

While some Whigs decided the rebellion was all over, especially in Georgia and North Carolina, in South Carolina, most thought otherwise. Although Pickens and Williamson were gone, the South Carolina backcountry erupted. Between June 1 and August 1, there were 16 small engagements in modern-day Spartanburg, York, Chester, Fairfield, Kershaw, Marlboro, and Lancaster counties.[45] Whig militias formed under elected leaders including William Hill, Edward Lacy, William Bratton, Richard Winn, and Andrew Neel. These leaders often shared command; with Lacy, Bratton and Winn joining together to defeat Loyalists at Mobley's Meeting House on June 8.

Meanwhile, British Legion captain Christian Huck destroyed William Hill's Iron Works on June 18. Huck soon met his fate when he was surprised at Williamson's Plantation where Lacey, Neel, Bratton, and Hill joined forces on July 12. Huck and his provincials, consisting of 35 British Legion dragoons, 20 New York Volunteer Infantry, and 50 Loyalist militia, had set out to capture William Bratton and arrived at Bratton's plantation home located along the South Fork of Fishing Creek in modern day York County, South Carolina. Bratton was not home, and Huck threatened his wife to tell him where Bratton was. She refused and eventually Huck moved his detachment to James Williamson's house, only a few hundred yards away. The combined command of Whig militia learned of Huck's whereabouts and rode all night to Williamson's. Prior to the dawn, they split their forces into three groups, and attacked Huck's camp from three sides, killing Huck and 30 British soldiers and wounding 35, to their loss of only one man. The victory, although small, was an important boost to American morale coming only two months after the fall of Charleston.[46]

These backcountry militia leaders often acted on their own while being loosely organized under the overall authority of Thomas Sumter, whose plantation had been burned by Tarleton. Sumter was elected "general" on June 15, but there was no standing Whig government, and it was largely a ceremonial position. Two of Sumter's early battles were at Rocky Mount on July 30 and Hanging Rock, South Carolina, on August 6.

At Rocky Mount, Sumter, with around 600 men, attacked a British outpost consisting of 150 New York Volunteers and 150 South Carolina Loyalists commanded by Lieutenant Colonel George Turnbull who were secure behind fortified log houses, surrounded by abatis. Sumter called for their surrender and was told to come and take the position. He sent several assault waves against the post and was able to breach the abatis but could not take the houses. He then resorted to pushing burning wagons against the houses, but a sudden rain squall put out the fires. After nearly eight hours of shooting, Sumter called off the siege.[47]

The Battle of Hanging Rock was a fierce fight that is often overlooked in narratives of the Southern campaign, perhaps because it was so close to the disaster at Camden 10 days later. It was actually two battles, the first being a raid by American Major William R. Davie, who with 80 mounted men attacked Colonel Morgan Bryan's North Carolina Provincials encamped at a plantation on August 1. Davie caught several Loyalists against a fence and slaughtered them and captured 60 horses. Sumter followed on August 6. He divided his forces into three detachments and attacked the British who were encamped in three different unfortified locations. Among the British forces were the Prince of Wales American Volunteers, British Legion Infantry, and Colonel Samuel Bryan's North Carolina Provincials under the overall command of Major John Carden.

The attack was uncoordinated, with Bryan's troops taking the brunt of the attacks. Fighting was close up with bayonet charges, and while the British were forced to fall back, they did not flee and instead formed a square. Carden led the Prince of Wales unit in a flank counterattack, but the attack was thwarted. The battle became confused, with Davie also flanking some of the Loyalists, but Sumter's men began to plunder the British camp and found alcohol among the camp supplies. Running out of ammunition and dealing with intoxicated soldiers, Sumter decided to withdraw. Casualty reports in these battles are rarely accurate, but Sumter's biographer lists 20 men killed, 40 wounded, and 10 missing of Sumter's forces, while the British combined regulars, provincials and Loyalists lost 130 killed and an equal number wounded, and 75 made prisoner. They also lost valuable horses and stores.[48]

The Battle of Camden

These victories improved Whig morale, and their hopes rose higher with the news that help in the form of American Continental forces were on their way south. While Charleston was under siege in the spring, General George Washington sent reinforcements of Maryland and Delaware

Continentals under Major General Baron Johann de Kalb south to assist Benjamin Lincoln. En route, de Kalb learned of Charleston's capture. He stopped his march and encamped near Buffalo Ford, North Carolina, on July 19, to await further orders. Congress, against Washington's advice, decided to send the hero of Saratoga, Major General Horatio Gates, to command the second Continental Army. Gates arrived at de Kalb's camp on July 24 and took command. Gates reported that a large detachment of Virginia militia under Brigadier General Edward Stevens was on its way, and that he also expected the arrival of North Carolina militia under Major General Richard Caswell. Thus, Gates was under the impression that nearly 4,000 men would be under his command. Much to the surprise of de Kalb and other officers, Gates put the army on the move only a few days later and marched into South Carolina with the goal of taking the British stronghold at Camden.

The march was difficult. Gates had chosen the most desolate part of the backcountry as his route toward Camden. It was a hot August, and men became ill eating green corn and peaches, the only food available. Lieutenant Colonel Lord Francis Rawdon in Camden marched out to delay Gates, but fell back toward Camden, avoiding a showdown along Lynches River. Eventually, Gates reached Rugeley's Mill, 13 miles north of Camden. The Virginia militia finally caught up with Gates on August 14 after a hard march.

Gates looked at the situation and decided that Rugeley's was indefensible. He wanted to increase the pressure against the British and decided to move closer to Camden. A hillside with a creek in front seven miles from Camden appeared to be a better location, and on the night of August 15, at 10pm, Gates's army began a march southward along a narrow road through a deep pine forest.

Lord Cornwallis, who had only recently arrived in Camden and taken over command of the British forces there, also saw the disadvantages of Gates's camp, having been informed of its location by a deserter. Ironically, he began a march north at the same hour as Gates, along that same road, with the intent to surprise Gates the following morning. Cornwallis had a formidable army consisting of the 23rd and 33rd Regiments of Foot, 71st Highlanders, Tarleton's Legion, North Carolina Royalists, Samuel

Bryan's North Carolina Volunteers, and the Volunteers of Ireland. The two forces met at 2:00am in a deep but open pine forest with high grass all around.

Tarleton's dragoons immediately charged into Gates's leading cavalry. Gates had placed light infantry along both flanks about 300 yards into the woods, and they moved forward to flank the cavalry who fell back, but then Legion infantry advanced, and a sharp but brief fight ensued. After the skirmish, both sides fell back. Gates, with his army stretched along the road all the way back to Rugeley's, could not retreat, while Cornwallis was happy not to have to march all the way to Rugeley's. His troops had just crossed a small creek only a few minutes before and had taken time to reform before proceeding up a gradual slope where the two forces met. Now, both sides prepared for what was inevitably going to be a major battle when dawn came.

Gates aligned his forces in the conventional manner with his Continentals, consisting of the 2nd Maryland Brigade and Delaware Regiment on his right of the road. On the left, he stretched his North Carolina Militia and on the far left, the Virginia Militia. His 1st Maryland Brigade had become disorganized in the night skirmish and were placed behind the front line in reserve. This deployment covered the wide plateau at the battle site, with flanks bordered by swampy morasses on either side. Cornwallis decided to let his men rest along the road, and then when morning light came, he followed Gates's deployment, placing his regulars on the right and his Provincials on the left. This configuration placed Cornwallis's best units opposite of Gates's worst units. Cornwallis put his 71st Highlanders and Tarleton's Legion dragoons in his rear as a reserve.

With dawn breaking around 4:00am, Cornwallis's regulars deployed to the right and were spotted by the Americans, and the battle began with an artillery barrage firing canister against the British regulars. Although taking casualties, the British regulars charged Gates's militia with bayonets, and the militia immediately fled, most without firing a shot. As the militia ran, the 1st Maryland opened ranks and let them through, then reformed to meet Cornwallis's regulars. On the opposite side of the road, Cornwallis's left flank, under the command of Lord

Rawdon, deployed and charged. That battle was hotly contested and quickly became clouded by musket and artillery smoke in the humid August air.

In effect, two battles on the opposite wings were being fought, with a gap in between them, and Cornwallis saw his opportunity as the gap grew wider. He sent Tarleton and the 71st into that gap. Gates's army was crushed; the 1st Marylanders were overwhelmed. Meanwhile Gates's right flank fought heroically until they discovered Tarleton's cavalry in their rear. Then they began a fighting retreat, falling back in small groups, making their way off the battlefield. Tarleton's dragoons were let loose and chased the retreating American army 22 miles up the road to Hanging Rock. Perhaps as many as 800 Americans were killed and wounded, and 700 prisoners taken. The British lost 68 killed, 245 wounded, and 11 missing.[49] Among those who received mortal wounds was the respected Major General Johann de Kalb who commanded the right flank of the American front lines. Cornwallis is reported to have found de Kalb dying on the battlefield, and remarked "I am sorry, sir,

Battle of Camden, Death of De Kalb, August 1780. (Engraving after Alonzo Chappel, c. 1931–1932, Wikimedia Commons/National Archives and Records Administration)

to see you, not sorry that you are vanquished, but sorry to see you so badly wounded." De Kalb was carried to Camden where he later died.[50]

For the British, the victory seemed, at least for the moment, to have subdued the Southern Colonies. Within four summer months, the Americans had lost two large Continental armies. Joyful Loyalists in the North were entertained by an advertisement, facetiously attributed to Gates, in James Rivington's New York *Royal Gazette* that announced:

> REWARD,
> STRAYED, DESERTED, OR STOLEN, from the Subscriber, on the 16th of August last, near Camden, in the State of South Carolina, a whole ARMY, consisting of Horse, Foot, and Dragoons, to the amount of near TEN THOUSAND (as has been said) with all their baggage, artillery, wagons, and camp equipage. The subscriber has very strong suspicions, from the information received from this Aide de Camp, that a certain CHARLES, Earl CORNWALLIS, was principally concerned in carrying off the said ARMY with the baggage &c.[51]

Partisan Warfare Fall of 1780

Despite two major British victories against the rebellion within four months, the backcountry Whigs seemed oblivious to the defeats or the lack of support of a functioning continental force. Without that regular force, through the fall of 1780 the American cause in the Southern Colonies was held together by partisans, who achieved victory after victory in small but significant battles and skirmishes. Francis Marion, for instance, had joined Gates on his march into South Carolina, and was dispatched by Gates to take charge of the Williamsburg District militia the evening before the battle of Camden.

Arriving August 17 at Witherspoon's Ferry, Marion took command and began his career in the eastern part of South Carolina as the "Swamp Fox." He gathered and destroyed boats along the Santee River as ordered by Gates, and surprised a detachment of British at Great Savannah, releasing 150 Continental soldiers captured at Camden on August 24. From that point on, Marion was on the move, using the region around Snow's Island on the Pee Dee River as a base of operation and sallying forth from there to harass the British throughout the fall of 1780. He defeated Loyalist detachments at Blue Savannah (September 4), Black Mingo (September 29), and Tearcoat Swamp (October 25).

At Blue Savannah along the Little Pee Dee River, Marion dispersed Loyalist cavalry then ambushed the accompanying infantry. At Black Mingo he divided his small forces into three detachments and successfully performed a night attack against Loyalists camped at Dollard's Tavern adjacent to Shepherd's Ferry on Black Mingo Creek. At Tearcoat Swamp he again made a night attack against a Loyalist camp, capturing much-needed supplies and 80 horses. Marion made two unsuccessful raids of the British post at Georgetown and eluded Tarleton when the British cavalryman chased him through the low country. Marion's continual guerilla war thwarted the British efforts to subdue the rebellion in the eastern part of the colony.[52]

Meanwhile, Thomas Sumter, the "Gamecock," continued his operations in the upper backcountry and, like Marion, gave the British fits. Although not intentional, Sumter's raids and attacks often drew the British toward him and away from catching up to Marion. Sumter had attacked and captured a small redoubt called Carey's Fort just prior to the battle of Camden, and afterward marched north with the captured supplies. He was surprised by Tarleton while encamped at Fishing Creek, two days after the battle of Camden, losing 150 killed and wounded, and 310 captured. Sumter also lost the stores he had obtained from Carey's. Sumter recovered, however, and on October 6, Whig Governor John Rutledge made him a brigadier general and placed him in command of the South Carolina militia.

Two battles in particular checked British ambitions in the backcountry and revived Whig morale even more that the actions of Marion and Sumter. The first was at Musgrove's Mill on August 19, 1780. There, in another example of combined commands, Colonel Elijah Clarke, Colonel Isaac Shelby, and Colonel James Williams, with 200 Georgia, North Carolina, and South Carolina militia, rode some 40 miles to intercept a British detachment camped at Musgrove's Mill along the Enoree River. Once there, the Patriots learned that the British had been reinforced and that they now faced as many as 500 Loyalists, consisting of the South Carolina Royalists, New Jersey Volunteers, 1st Battalion of Colonel James DeLancey's brigade, the Dutch Fork Militia, and a few of Loyalist David Fanning's militia, all under the command of Colonel Alexander Innes.

With their horses exhausted, the Whigs realized they could not retreat and decided to go on the defense, forming a line across a ridge above the river. Then they sent some skirmishers ahead to meet the oncoming Loyalists and then fall back slowly, drawing them into their trap.

The Loyalists marched up the hill and when within 150 yards of the American lines, they started firing—too far away to do much damage. The Americans waited until they were close in and then let loose a devastating first volley. A second volley destroyed the Loyalists who were trying to reform. That broke them, and they fell back down the hill in terror as the Americans charged into their lines. In the battle, the British lost some 60 killed and wounded, with 70 prisoners, while the Americans lost only 4 killed and 7 wounded. The victory at Musgrove's Mill helped blunt the effect that the defeats at Camden and Fishing Creek had had on backcountry morale.[53]

The second significant victory that fall was the defeat and death of Major Patrick Ferguson at Kings Mountain on October 7, 1780. Ferguson was an intelligent British officer and inspector of the Loyalist militia. In September he marched into North Carolina and camped at Gilbert Town. There he issued a proclamation to the "Overmountain Men" of the Watauga Settlements that if they did not surrender to the British, he would "march over the mountains, hang their leaders, and lay the country waste with fire and sword."[54] Militia colonels Isaac Shelby and John Sevier took exception to Ferguson's announcement, and, along with Virginia militia leader William Campbell, they agreed to rendezvous at Sycamore Shoals, Tennessee, on September 25. With various other militia streaming in, the Patriots eventually numbered over 1,000 men.

By September 30, Ferguson had left Gilbert Town, with the goal of engaging Elijah Clarke who had made that unsuccessful attack against British-held Augusta earlier in the year. Then Ferguson learned of the Overmountain Men and began a surprisingly slow retreat toward Cornwallis who was near Charlotte, North Carolina. On October 5, the Americans recognized they might not catch up to Ferguson and selected 700 men to continue forward on horseback in a forced march.

At Cowpens, South Carolina, the Overmountain Men rendezvoused with South Carolina militia under Colonels Hill and Lacey. The combined force of around 900 pressed on and finally caught Ferguson, who had camped atop Kings Mountain, on October 7. The Americans divided into various commands and surrounded the Loyalists. Then the Americans attacked up the mountain, using the trees and rocks for cover, and whenever the Loyalists charged them with the bayonet, the Americans ran back down, only to start back up the mountain again when the Loyalists withdrew. As losses added up, Ferguson's circle of men constricted into an open area along the top of the hill where the Whigs were firing point blank at them from all sides. Ferguson mounted his horse and attempted to break out, but he was hit and mortally wounded by several Whig balls. With their leader gone, the Loyalists attempted to surrender, but it took some time to get the Americans to stop firing, and many more Loyalists fell. The Loyalists lost 157 killed, with another 163 too wounded to be moved. Some 698 prisoners were taken. The Patriots lost 28 killed and 62 wounded.[55]

Some historians consider Kings Mountain the turning point of the war in the South. It certainly caused Cornwallis to withdraw from North Carolina back to Winnsboro, South Carolina, as he feared that the American backwoodsmen might continue southwest and take both Camden and Ninety Six. Furthermore, Loyalists in the backcountry were nowhere to be seen, and any further attempt to rally Loyalist support in the backcountry was becoming hopeless. Henry Clinton, reminiscing upon the effect of Kings Mountain, noted that "though in itself confessedly trifling, [it] overset in a moment all the happy effects of our successes at Charleston and His Lordship's glorious victory at Camden, and so encouraged that spirit of rebellion in both Carolinas that it never could be afterward humbled."[56]

Cornwallis, who with the rest of his army was camped in Charlotte, left the village on October 12. On the retreat, the weather turned stormy, and the roads became soft, muddy, and nearly impassable. He had to abandon 20 wagons of supplies, while his army struggled to find food and forage. Cornwallis fell ill, but the army finally made it to Winnsboro on October 29, where they could rest, refit, and wait for reinforcements.[57]

Sumter, meanwhile, was struggling to find men; many having gone home after the victory at Kings Mountain. He was camped at Fishdam

OVERVIEW OF THE AMERICAN REVOLUTION • 29

Major Engagements in South Carolina

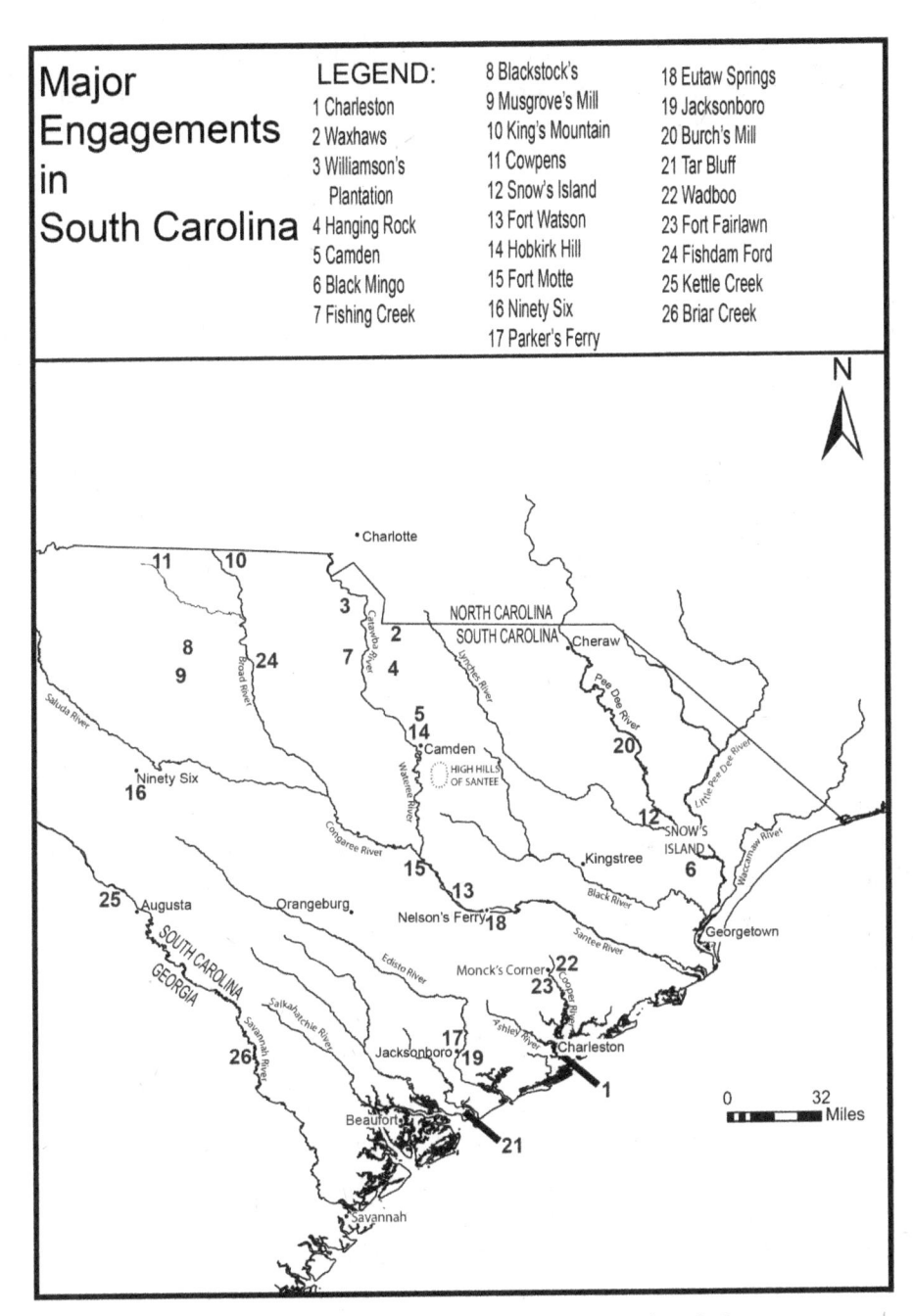

LEGEND:
1 Charleston
2 Waxhaws
3 Williamson's Plantation
4 Hanging Rock
5 Camden
6 Black Mingo
7 Fishing Creek
8 Blackstock's
9 Musgrove's Mill
10 King's Mountain
11 Cowpens
12 Snow's Island
13 Fort Watson
14 Hobkirk Hill
15 Fort Motte
16 Ninety Six
17 Parker's Ferry
18 Eutaw Springs
19 Jacksonboro
20 Burch's Mill
21 Tar Bluff
22 Wadboo
23 Fort Fairlawn
24 Fishdam Ford
25 Kettle Creek
26 Briar Creek

Major Engagements in South Carolina. (Noah Safari)

Ford on November 9, when he was surprised by Major James Wemyss with some of Tarleton's dragoons and the 63rd Regiment of Foot in a night attack on the camp. The Americans, however, quickly rallied and stood firm, thwarting the British attack in a confusing battle. Sumter was nearly captured in his tent, but escaped out the back as two dragoons entered the front. Both sides retreated, the Whigs dispersing, while the British left their wounded in a nearby farmhouse. Among them was Wemyss. The British lost 8 men and 25 prisoners; the Americans 4 killed and 10 wounded.[58]

Then on November 20, Sumter defeated his old adversary Banastre Tarleton at Blackstock's Plantation, a battle whose intensity would seem to warrant more attention than it receives. Sumter was on the run from Tarleton in the upcountry. A British deserter had informed him that Tarleton was closing in. Likewise, Tarleton, with his Legion and the 63rd Regiment of Foot, had heard from a prisoner that Sumter had been warned of his coming. The chase was on. Sumter stopped at Blackstock's along the Tyger River, where a woman who had seen the British warned him that Tarleton had mounted his men and left his artillery behind in order to catch up with Sumter. Blackstock's Plantation, consisting of a log house and outbuildings, was on a hill, with the Tyger River behind the hill and a small stream in front. With Sumter were a host of backcountry leaders like William Bratton, William Hill, Edward Lacey, and Elijah Clarke. There Sumter decided to make a stand, leaving a rear guard to watch the road approach. As his men prepared dinner on November 20, the alarm was given. Tarleton had arrived.

When Tarleton saw how well the Americans were deployed, he paused and decided to wait for his artillery to arrive. Sumter, however, decided to prod Tarleton into action and sent out skirmishers, while Lacey worked to flank Tarleton. Sumter's skirmishers raked the dismounted 63rd but were forced back to the plantation buildings where riflemen began picking off the approaching British regulars. Lacey was able to close in on the British cavalry unseen and dropped several with rifle fire before being forced back. Tarleton charged the Americans violently but was never able to force them out of their log buildings. The British possibly lost as many as 92 dead, including Major John Money, and 100 wounded.

The Americans lost only three killed and two wounded, including Sumter, who took a ball which passed through his shoulder, taking away some of the bone and inflicting great damage.[59]

Greene Takes Command

At Camden back in August, General Horatio Gates and his command had fled the battlefield in utter defeat. As Tarleton's cavalry slashed its way north, Gates proceeded ahead of them and arrived at Salisbury, North Carolina. From there he continued on to Hillsborough, North Carolina, where he attempted to reconstitute his continental command. The defeat was humiliating, and Congress lost confidence in his leadership.

On October 5, Congress opened a court of inquiry into the events of August 16. At the same time, they turned to General George Washington to appoint a new commander in the Southern Theater, and without any hesitation, Washington chose Major General Nathanael Greene. Greene did not take formal command of the Southern army until December 3, the day after he arrived at its camp near Charlotte, North Carolina. There he found an army of at most 2,307 poorly equipped men, with only 1,482 fit for duty. To make matters worse, the veteran Maryland and Delaware units were down to just 949.[60]

Greene was an experienced combat leader who had learned his trade in major battles in the North, including Trenton, Princeton, and Brandywine. Furthermore, he had gained experience in managing the logistics of warfare when he was appointed quartermaster general. He reorganized that branch into an effective and essential unit, a job necessary but without the glory of combat command.

Greene was a planner with tremendous foresight. As he made his way southward to his new command, he took time to examine the Virginia and North Carolina topography and ordered surveys of the rivers and streams. Indeed, on December 1, 1780, he wrote Virginia Brigadier General Edward Stevens that Lieutenant Colonel Edward Carrington was exploring the Dan River, and that Stevens should appoint an intelligent officer to explore up the Yadkin to gather information (like the depth of water, obstructions, and current). The officer was to then continue and:

> ride across the Country ... and report the Distance and Conditions of the Roads. At the upper Saura I expect the officer will meet the Party exploring the Dan River. I wish him to get the Report of that party also, and forward with his, as that is the Foundation of the whole. I also wish the officer to make enquiry respecting the Transportation that may be had from the Yadkin to the Catawba River, and whether the Transportation cannot be performed with Batteaus down that River."[61]

This planning would be essential to the success of Greene's later retreat across North Carolina ahead of Lord Cornwallis in the spring of 1781.

Upon arrival at camp, one of the first things Greene did was write Francis Marion a letter of introduction, asking Marion for intelligence and to continue his partisan war. Greene had to ride to see Thomas Sumter, who was still recovering from his Blackstock's wound, and together they plotted strategy for the backcountry. Then, with great courage, Greene divided his army, sending a large detachment west of the Catawba River under Brigadier General Daniel Morgan to support the militia forces in the upcountry and press toward British-held Ninety Six. On December 20, Greene marched with the remaining command southward into South Carolina and camped along the upper Pee Dee.

With winter beginning, many of the partisan forces in South Carolina went into camp. Marion fought a skirmish at Halfway Swamp at the end of December and then camped on Snow's Island along the Pee Dee River. There were skirmishes by other partisans at Rutledge's Ford, North Carolina, Rugeley's Plantation, Long Cane, Sampit road, and Hammond's Store throughout December and early January.[62] Two of those battles were fought by Lieutenant Colonel William Washington and his dragoons, operating under the overall command of Daniel Morgan.

At Rugeley's Plantation, Washington caught up with a detachment of Loyalists in a fortified barn on December 1. He surrounded the fort and had his men cut down a pine tree which they mounted on a carriage so as to appear as if it were a cannon. He summoned the defenders to surrender and seeing the "Quaker" cannon, the Loyalists gave up.[63] The second, at Hammond's Store, might have been a massacre reminiscent of the Waxhaws, but this time against the Loyalists. Washington was chasing a detachment of Georgia militia under the command of Lieutenant Colonel Thomas Waters who was ransacking Whig homesteads in the Ninety Six region. Waters encamped on top of a hill near Fair Forest, South Carolina. Washington attacked Water's detachment on December 27, and the Loyalists fled down the hill and were slaughtered, with around 150 Loyalists killed or wounded and 40 captured, while the Americans had no losses. One American officer wrote that they had Waxhaws on their minds.[64]

In the northern backcountry, Daniel Morgan arrived at Grindal's Shoals on December 25.[65] Near Winnsboro, South Carolina, Cornwallis now found himself between the two American forces with a decision to be made. If Cornwallis moved toward Greene, the British posts at Ninety Six and Augusta would be open to Morgan's advance. If he went after Morgan, the low country and the British supply line to Charleston would be exposed to any movement south by Greene.

There was, however, a more promising way to look at Cornwallis's situation. Sandwiched between the two American forces and with superior numbers of regulars, could the British possibly move quickly to destroy Morgan before Greene was able to reinforce Morgan? With such a plan in mind, Cornwallis decided to send his most aggressive officer, Banastre Tarleton, west to find Morgan and push him northeast. Cornwallis at the same time would march north and block Greene from reinforcing Morgan.

With his usual vigor, Tarleton launched a forced march, crossing flooded streams and rivers swollen from winter storms to catch Morgan. Morgan, however, was not running. Instead, he arranged a rendezvous of his regulars and militia at the Cowpens, a road intersection northeast of modern-day Spartanburg. Tarleton eventually caught up with Morgan on January 17, 1781, but Morgan was prepared, having chosen the best location to make use of his forces. The exact numbers Morgan had at his disposal are not known, but his aide, Major Edward Giles, reported 290 Maryland and Delaware Continental light infantry, 350 South Carolina and Georgia militia under Andrew Pickens, 170 Virginia militia under a Major Francis Triplett, and William Washington's cavalry estimated to be around 82, totaling 892. It is quite possible that Morgan's force was much larger, as militia continued to arrive in camp the evening before the battle. Archaeologist Lawrence Babits estimates the number to be between 1,800 to 2,400 men. Tarleton arrived at the battle with as many as 1,150.[66]

Morgan's tactical deployment has become a standard case study in 18th-century battlefield tactics, and Greene would make use of it later, with modifications, at the battles of Guilford Court House and Eutaw Springs. Morgan deployed his command in three successively stronger lines. His first line were skirmishers, consisting of South Carolina and Georgia riflemen. In the second line, Morgan placed his South Carolina militia under Andrew Pickens, and the third line consisted of Maryland, Delaware, and Virginia Continentals, and Virginia militia and State Troops. The final line was supported by Lieutenant Colonel William Washington's Continental Light Dragoons and mounted militia. These second and third lines were higher up a gradual slope than the first line and were out of sight when Tarleton arrived.

Tarleton charged forward without concern, pressing a frontal attack against the American skirmishers. The skirmishers fired and fell back as ordered in good form through the second line. Tarleton's regulars continued forward at a trot with fixed bayonets to meet the second line. Waiting until the British were close, the militia then let loose a volley of aimed fire. The British line was stunned, reformed, came forward again, and were hit again.

Undaunted, the British pushed forward, and this time the militia line fell back in good order. Seeing the second line retreat, the British believed they were winning, only to advance and find a third line of regulars. Despite taking heavy casualties, the disciplined British regulars halted and reformed with those that remained.

At this point, the battle became hot, with both sides firing at close range. Tarleton committed his cavalry and 71st Regiment in reserve, attempting a double envelopment. The 71st pressured the American right flank, and the line began to fall back. Strong leadership by Morgan and his subordinates, however, kept the men in order and although the line fell back, it suddenly faced about and gave the shocked British a well-aimed volley. This was followed by a charge and the arrival of Washington's cavalry to thwart the British dragoons, at the same time the Patriot militia returned to the fight. It was too much for the British who broke and ran. Babits places the American losses between 127 to 148 killed and wounded. The British lost 100 killed, 200 wounded, 29 officers and 500 privates taken prisoner, 2 artillery pieces, 35 baggage wagons, 800 muskets, and 100 dragoon horses.[67]

In addition to derailing Cornwallis's plans, Tarleton's defeat was equally a boost to American morale, not only in South Carolina but also in the North where Congress voted Morgan a gold medal. Tarleton's loss reduced Cornwallis's army by one-quarter, mostly in the form of light troops who had served as scouts, foragers, and screeners for the main army.

Race to the Dan

Although Cornwallis wrote to Henry Clinton that "It is impossible to foresee all the consequences that this unexpected and extraordinary event may produce but your Excellency may be assured that nothing but the most absolute necessity shall indue me to give up the important object of the winter's campaign," Cornwallis was furious and nearly brokenhearted when he learned of Tarleton's defeat. Yet, hope returned with the arrival of Major General Alexander Leslie and a reinforcement of Hessians, regulars, and Loyalist militia.[68] Cornwallis's goal now was to find and destroy Morgan. Leaving Lord Francis Rawdon in charge of British field forces in South Carolina, Cornwallis marched northward to Ramsour's Mill, North Carolina, to cut off any chance of Morgan rendezvousing with Greene. Once there, Cornwallis learned that Morgan had made it across the Catawba River, after first retreating to Gilbert Town, North Carolina. Nevertheless, Cornwallis decided to press on, reasoning "I see definite danger in proceeding, but certain ruin in retreating."[69] At the mill, Cornwallis burned his baggage and most of his wagons, intending to travel fast and light.

Thus, began what historians refer to as the "Race to the Dan." It was a chase across North Carolina to the Dan River in Virginia, with Cornwallis and his army one step behind Greene and Morgan all the way.

It would be a desperate race, yet, Greene's correspondence at this time hints that he had a unique understanding of his strategic advantage in the overall Southern campaign. He wrote:

> I am here in my camp of repose [camp along the Pee Dee River], improving the discipline and spirits of my men, and the opportunity for looking about me. I am well satisfied with the movement, for it has answered thus far all the purposes for which I intended it. It makes the most of my inferior force, for it compels my adversary to divide his, and holds him in doubt as to his own line of conduct. He cannot leave Morgan behind him to come at me, or his posts of Ninety-Six and Augusta would be exposed. And he cannot chase Morgan far, or prosecute his views upon Virginia, while I am here with the whole country open before me. I am as near to Charleston as he is, and as near to Hillsborough as I was at Charlotte; so that I am in no danger of being cut off from my reinforcements, while an uncertainty as to my future designs has made it necessary to leave a large detachment of the enemy's late reinforcements in Charleston, and move the rest up on this side of the Wateree .... At present, my operations must be in the country where the rivers are fordable, and to guard against the chance of not being able to choose my ground.[70]

Along the Catawba, Morgan prepared defenses of the fords, including Beattie's and Cowan's to block Cornwallis's progress. Greene joined

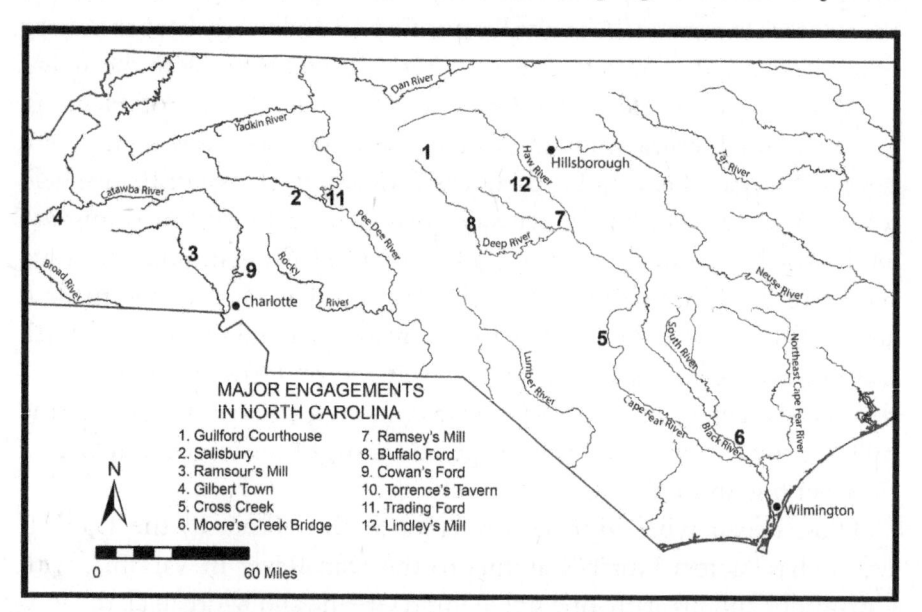

Major Engagements in North Carolina. (Noah Safari)

Morgan on January 31 at Beattie's Ford to discuss strategy, and that same day, the British appeared on the opposite bank. Morgan and Greene left Brigadier General William Lee Davidson with militia to defend the fords. Cornwallis attacked at dawn. Using a diversionary attack at Beattie's, the main attack was across Cowan's Ford; the British wading across with bayonets fixed. The militia put up a short fight, but once Davidson was killed, they fled the battle, and Cornwallis was across the Catawba. Tarleton quickly followed up by defeating another militia detachment at Torrence's Tavern.[71]

Meanwhile, Morgan had moved to the Yadkin River, crossing at Trading Ford. Brigadier General Isaac Huger, who commanded Greene's half of the army, had been enroute to Salisbury, but with Cornwallis across the Catawba, he was ordered to Guilford Court House. Cornwallis pressed ahead and found Morgan on the opposite bank of the Yadkin. With the river too high to cross, Cornwallis looked upstream for another way.

On February 7, 1781, Morgan and Greene arrived at Guilford Court House, joining Huger. The army was in no shape to fight. Neither was Morgan. He had joined the American cause early in the war, playing a major role in the failed invasion of Canada where he was captured at Quebec. Exchanged in 1777, he fought in the Saratoga campaign, retired but returned, and was promoted to brigadier general in 1780. The hard fighting had taken a toll on his health. His piles and sciatica were too painful to continue, and he was granted a leave of absence.[72]

With Morgan gone, Greene placed 700 light infantry and cavalry under the command of Adjutant General Otho Williams. His orders were to act as a screen between Cornwallis, now at Salem, North Carolina, and Greene at Guilford Court House. Cornwallis knew Greene would make for the safety of Dan River in Virginia and believed that Greene would have to cross somewhere at the upper or western fords. Greene knew better; that there were boats to ferry his army across the Dan lower downstream, and he marched for the lower ferries on February 10. For the next four days, Williams skirmished with Cornwallis's van, keeping the British from Greene's main body of troops as they marched for the lower ferries. On the evening of the February 14, Greene was across the Dan.[73]

Having stripped his army bare to catch Greene, Cornwallis was now in a desperate situation, some 240 miles from his supply base in Charleston and 150 miles from Camden. Greene was safely on the north side of the Dan River, and Cornwallis had no boats to make a crossing. Instead, he decided to march to Hillsborough, North Carolina, where he arrived on February 22. There he issued a proclamation inviting Loyalists to join him.[74]

There was little response from the Loyalists, and Cornwallis found few supplies at Hillsborough. Greene, meanwhile, refitted and rested his troops, and sent his cavalry back across the Dan to harass the British. Virginia militia poured into his camp and, across the river, Andrew Pickens awaited with a detachment of South Carolina militia. For the next couple weeks, tensions would be high as British and American cavalry met in several skirmishes. In one event, Lieutenant Colonel Henry Lee's dragoons trotted into Colonel John Pyle's Loyalist detachment. The Loyalists thought Lee's green-jacketed soldiers were members of Tarleton's Legion. Even as the Loyalists were hacked to death, they pleaded that they were loyal to the king, still thinking that they were being attacked by their allies. Nearly 90 of them were killed at what became known as Pyle's massacre.[75] Other skirmishes occurred at Clapp's Mill and Wetzel's Mill. Both sides trended westward, Cornwallis seeking food and forage, while Greene grew stronger seeking an advantage.

Guilford Court House

Cornwallis needed to engage Greene, both to eliminate the threat but also to keep those few Loyalists who had rallied to his proclamation in the field. He camped at New Garden Meeting House, a largely Quaker settlement, and Greene arrived at Guilford Court House about 12 miles away. Now both sides wanted a battle. Cornwallis, with over 1,900 men, was desperate, and Greene, having been reinforced and now numbering some 4,300, was looking for an opportunity.

Cornwallis began his march toward Greene early on the March 15. Greene received intelligence that Cornwallis was on his way and made use of Morgan's deployment at Cowpens, placing his army in three lines. The first line consisted of two brigades of North Carolina militia in the center, with Continentals on the flanks in forward echelon and cavalry on the extreme flanks. Three hundred yards behind them was the second line of Virginia militia. Like Morgan at Cowpens, Greene placed his Virginia and Maryland Continentals on the third line and on higher ground. Unlike Morgan, Greene had no reserve, and the lines were farther apart. The distance between the lines and the forest environment meant that, unlike Morgan's deployment, the lines could not fully support each other.[76]

After morning cavalry skirmishing, Cornwallis arrived around 1:30pm and began deploying his men. On his left he placed his veteran 33rd and 23rd Regiments of Foot. On the right were the 71st, guards, and Hessians. A second line of Grenadiers and guards were behind, with jagers, light infantry, and Tarleton's cavalry in reserve. The battle opened with artillery fire on both sides, and then the British moved forward.

The North Carolina militia in the center stood briefly, but after some had fired, they ran away. Meanwhile, veterans on the flanks stood. In facing these flanks, the center of the British line opened, and Cornwallis was forced to bring forward part of the reserve to fill in the front line. The British drove on, hitting the second line. Here a fierce battle broke out; the Virginia militia holding and then slowly falling back, bolstered by Washington's cavalry in support on the right. The American left and British right had pushed off away from the main line, and a separate battle emerged from the main line.

As the Virginia militia gave way, the British pushed forward only to meet the Patriot third line. On the British left, ferocious fighting broke out between the two veteran enemies, and the British 33rd was stunned by a counterattack. Likewise, on the right, the British forced the 2nd Maryland back but was counterattacked by the 1st Maryland and Washington's dragoons. Point-blank volleys rang out; bayonet and swordplay ensued. Cornwallis, in a desperate move to stop Washington's cavalry, ordered his artillery to fire into the melee, causing casualties on both sides. Tarleton came forward to reinforce Cornwallis, but the thick woods blunted his efforts.

By this time, Greene decided it was best to withdraw, and Lee was left to screen an orderly retreat. The British were too exhausted to push farther, although Tarleton did some hacking at retreating militia. Greene counted 22 militia killed, 73 wounded, and 885 missing, while the Continentals lost 57 killed, 111 wounded, and 161 missing. He also lost four cannon. Cornwallis may have held the field; however, his losses were catastrophic. They totaled 532 officers and men who would never be replaced. Before Cowpens, Cornwallis had some 3,300 men. Now after Cowpens, the Race to the Dan, and Guilford Court House, he was down to some 1,400.[77]

Cornwallis was left to bury the dead and care for the wounded while Greene retreated north to Speedwell's Iron Works to await the enemy's next move. Cornwallis fell back to New Garden Meeting House, regrouped, and on March 18 slowly began a march eastward, leaving most of the wounded in the care of the Quakers. Greene followed behind. Cornwallis camped briefly at Ramsey's Mill and then continued his eastward trek for Cross Creek. Wiliam Dickson, living along Cornwallis's retreat route, wrote his cousin in Ireland:

> The whole country was struck with terror; almost every man quit his habitation and fled, leaving his family and property to the mercy of merciless enemies. Horses, cattle, and sheep, and every kind of stock were driven off from every plantation, corn and forage taken for the supply of the army and no compensation given,... The outrages were committed mostly by a train of loyal refugees, as they termed themselves, whose business it was to follow the camps and under the protection of the army enrich themselves on the plunder they took from the distressed inhabitants who were not able to defend it.[78]

Meanwhile, Greene, with his militia melting away as usual after a battle, decided to halt to rest his diminishing army once Cornwallis left Ramsey's Mill.[79]

Greene Returns to South Carolina

Back at the end of January 1781, the British under Major James Craig had captured Wilmington, North Carolina, as a supply depot with access to the sea and as a place to rally the North Carolina Loyalists. At Cross Creek, Cornwallis thought he would find supplies from Wilmington and Loyalists. He found neither, so on April 1 he marched for Wilmington and was camped outside there by April 7. Although Greene wanted to do battle with Cornwallis, many of the militia had served their time and left the army. Further pursuit of Cornwallis was dangerous. Instead, Greene boldly turned his back on Cornwallis and returned to South Carolina, crossing the state line around April 16, 1781.

Greene's decision to enter South Carolina was a brave move. He was leaving Cornwallis in his rear to face the British in South Carolina. Farther north, Benedict Arnold was in Virginia with another British army, blocking the possibility of American reinforcements from the Northern colonies. Greene reasoned that his march into South Carolina would create a dilemma for Cornwallis. He explained:

> I am determined to carry the War immediately into South Carolina. The enemy will be obliged to follow us or give up their posts in that State. If the former takes place it will draw the War out of this State and give it an opportunity to raise its proportion of Men. If they leave their posts to fall [in South Carolina], they must lose more than they can gain here [in North Carolina]. If we continue in this state, the enemy will hold their possessions in both.[80]

Greene's strategic goal was to move against British-held Camden, the keystone of the British occupation of the backcountry. In support of this move, he wanted Pickens and his militia to keep the British and Loyalists busy in the upcountry, especially around Ninety Six. Greene also wanted Sumter to join him in the fight against Rawdon at Camden. Meanwhile, Greene's plan called for Henry Lee and Francis Marion to slip between Camden and Charleston and attack the British supply line.[81] They were also to keep an eye on Lieutenant Colonel John Watson in Georgetown and intercept him if he attempted to join Rawdon at Camden.

Thus, before moving south, Greene detached Lee and his Legion to watch Cornwallis's movements and make sure he continued eastward. Then Lee turned south to find Marion. Lee and Marion were already acquainted. Greene had detached Lee to join Marion in January 1781, and the pair had attacked the British at Georgetown. The effort had been a failure because it was planned as a two-pronged attack, and the two prongs failed to coordinate their attack. After the battle, Lee was recalled, to assist Greene in the Race to the Dan campaign.

A lot had happened in South Carolina since Cornwallis burned his wagons and chased after Greene in the early months of 1781. With no

Continental army in the colony, the British had battled with partisans like Pickens, Sumter, and Marion. Some 25 battles and skirmishes had occurred between the battle of Cowpens and Greene's return to South Carolina.[82] Marion was left unsupported when Lee returned to Greene's army, and Rawdon chased Marion across the eastern part of the colony until being recalled to Camden because Sumter was harassing British outposts west of the Santee. Rawdon then refocused on Marion, and at the beginning of March, John Watson was ordered to find and destroy Marion. Watson marched from Fort Watson along the north bank of the Santee River. Marion, however, was nearby.

Marion and Watson met first at Wiboo Swamp, and Marion was forced to break off when Watson brought up his artillery. They met again at Mount Hope Swamp, and again Marion withdrew. Then Watson turned north to cross the Black River at Lower Bridge, just south of Kingstree, South Carolina. Marion's riflemen raced ahead and blocked Watson at the bridge until Marion could bring up the rest of his command. Watson attempted to cross downstream at a ford, but Marion's riflemen picked off his artillerymen. Watson was forced to break off his campaign and recuperate. He settled in at nearby Witherspoon's Plantation.

Watson then decided he had had enough and needed to get to the safety of Georgetown. Marion harassed him all the way, engaging in yet another skirmish at the Sampit River bridge around March 20. There, Marion again placed his riflemen across the bridge from where Watson was situated, while the rest of Marion's militia attacked Watson's rear. Watson was forced to use his artillery to push Marion back, while he sent some infantry across the river with bayonets fixed to break through the riflemen. The tactic worked, as Marion's riflemen were no match for British bayonets.

Meanwhile, probably unknown to Marion at the time, a second British detachment out of Camden under Lieutenant Colonel Welbore Ellis Doyle found Marion's camp on Snow's Island and destroyed it. Marion attempted to catch up to Doyle and found him across Witherspoon's Ferry along Lynches River, but Doyle fell back up the river road along the west bank of the Pee Dee. With Lynches in flood stage, Marion had to find a crossing upstream of the ferry, and Doyle got away. By the time

Marion halted the chase, he was some 20 miles north of Snow's Island and contemplating retreating into North Carolina when he learned of Greene's return and the pending arrival of Lee.[83]

Elsewhere in South Carolina, Sumter, having recovered enough from his Blackstock's wound to get back on a horse, had in February engaged in a series of largely unsuccessful attacks against the British outposts at Fort Granby across the river from modern-day Columbia, Belleville, or Thomson's Plantation along the Congaree, and Fort Watson along the Santee. While unsuccessful, the attacks did temporarily draw the British away from Marion. Sumter attacked Fort Granby first on February 19, but when it became a siege and the British under Lieutenant Colonel Welbore Ellis Doyle arrived to come to the fort's rescue, Sumter withdrew.

Instead of retreating north, however, or perhaps because Doyle forced him, Sumter marched south and downstream to the McCord's ferry, crossed the river, and attacked Thomson's Plantation on February 22. There, once again frustrated at the delay, Sumter attempted an attack across an open field, and his men suffered greatly. Falling back again to Manigault's Ferry along the Santee, he was successful in capturing a British supply train that was coming up the river road. Unfortunately for him, he put the supplies on a barge with the idea of using them to attack Fort Watson downstream on the opposite bank. The barge was guided by a man sympathetic to the British cause, and he returned the supplies to the British at Fort Watson. Sumter still continued with his plan and attempted an attack on a British detachment near the fort but was once again defeated. He was then forced to retreat back up the river and was able to escape the British and make his way to the backcountry.[84]

In the upper backcountry, Elijah Clarke and Andrew Pickens threatened the British in the Ninety Six District. At Beattie's Mill, Clarke defeated a Loyalist detachment commanded by Major James Dunlap on March 23. The prisoners, including Dunlap, were marched to Gilbert Town, North Carolina, and along the way, Dunlap was murdered. Pickens reported the murder to Greene and British Lieutenant Colonel John Cruger who commanded the British at Ninety Six.[85] In Georgia, Loyalists and Whigs skirmished in raids and ambushes, while the British regulars in Savannah and Augusta strengthened their defenses.

With Greene arriving near Camden, Marion and Lee rendezvoused and marched for their first target, Fort Watson. It was a stockaded post sitting 23 feet above the surrounding landscape atop an Indian mound along the Santee River. Watson's men had flattened the top, shaved the sides of the mound, and added three rows of abatis, creating a strong defensive position. The Americans arrived on the afternoon of April 15 and would continue to besiege the occupants through the week. The British remained snug in the fort throughout, as the Americans were without artillery. The defenders' only real difficulty was a lack of water, having been cut off from Scott's Lake, an old oxbow of the Santee River and their normal source. The British solved that problem by digging a well at the base of the mound. The frustrated Americans were unable to get too close to the fort, although they managed to drag off many of the supplies that the British had recaptured from Sumter that were outside the fort. Marion and Lee begged Greene for a cannon and waited, while many of Marion's troops left due to an outbreak of smallpox.

Eventually American Major Hezekiah Maham suggested that they build a tower to fire down into the fort. Logs for the tower were cut and rolled down next to the Indian mound in the dark and by morning were ready to fire. The British inside built a traverse to hide behind, but on the final day, April 23, while riflemen in the tower fired into the fort, a detachment attacked the abatis, broke it down, and made for the main gate. While the British officers were still full of fight, the men in the fort grounded arms, compelling the officers to surrender.[86]

During the siege of Fort Watson, Greene and his Continental army arrived near Camden on April 19. After a skirmish and reconnaissance, he decided that laying siege to the fortified village was not possible with his army. Instead, he encamped on Hobkirk's Hill, a wooded ridge, a mile and a half north of Camden's fortified village. Greene hoped that his presence there would draw out Rawdon beyond his walls. It did.

On the morning of April 25, Rawdon armed all men fit for duty and marched for Greene. Although his objective had been to get Rawdon into the open, the timing of Rawdon's attack was not optimal for Greene. A supply train had arrived shortly before the battle, and the hungry American soldiers were cooking, eating breakfast, or washing up.

Rawdon appeared before Greene's left flank and attacked. Greene quickly formed his army and stretched it along the ridge, attempting to flank Rawdon on both sides, but Rawdon threw in his reserves and lengthened his lines, and a furious fight broke out.

Rawdon was surprised to hear Greene's cannon roar. He had gained intelligence before the battle that Greene was without his artillery, which had been true at the time Rawdon heard it. However, the artillery had returned the day before, and now, aligned along the ridge, the artillerymen began to fire canister against the British line. At the same time, Greene ordered a bayonet charge and ordered William Washington's cavalry to charge the British rear. At this critical point, the 1st Maryland line became disordered as Colonel John Gunby, the regiment's commander, ordered his unit to fall back to re-form.

Samuel Mathis explained the confusion that resulted as the British advanced:

> Colonel Gunby suffered them [the British] to come up within a few paces and then ordered his men to charge without firing. Those near him, hearing the word first, rushed forward, whereby the regiment was moving forward in the form of a bow.
> Colonel Gunby ordered a "halt" until the wings should become straight. This turned the fate of the day. Previously being ordered not to fire and now ordered to "halt," while the British were coming up with charged bayonets, before the colonel could be understood and repeat the charge, the enemy were in among them and made them give way.[87]

This miscommunication caused confusion all along Greene's line, despite the flanking units on either side of Gunby's Marylanders pushing forward. Greene, seeing the emerging chaos and ever cautious, ordered a withdrawal, which was done in good order. He fell back a couple miles to the north.

During the heat of the engagement, Washington's cavalry had attempted to get behind the British line, but because of heavy woods and brush, ended up far to the British rear. There Washington found several civilians and wounded soldiers, whom he captured. Losses on either side were approximately even. Greene's army of around 1,550 lost 266, of whom 18 were killed. Rawdon's 900 lost 258, of whom 38 were killed.[88]

Greene reported to Samuel Huntington, president of the Continental Congress, that, "Our Army is in good spirits, and this little repulse will make no alteration in our general plan of operation."[89] On the day of battle, unbeknownst to Greene and Rawdon, Lord Cornwallis abandoned Wilmington and began his march to Virginia. Except for the British at Ninety Six, Rawdon was on his own in the backcountry, and his supply line to Charleston was about to be completely cut.

After the capture of Fort Watson, Lee and Marion had moved closer to Camden with orders from Greene to keep an eye out for John Watson in Georgetown and block him if he attempted to rendezvous with Rawdon in Camden. They were free to cross the Santee if necessary, and a six-pounder cannon finally arrived to increase their firepower. They were also to continue with their efforts to capture the British western posts of Fort Motte, Fort Granby, and Orangeburg.

Crossing the Santee near Fort Watson, Lee and Marion just missed Colonel Watson's detachment that had marched from Georgetown to Monck's Corner to pick up reinforcements and then proceeded along the western bank of the Santee, looking to avoid the Patriot forces. Watson got across the Santee just below the confluence of the Congaree and Wateree Rivers at Buckingham's Ferry and made his way to Camden. Now across the river on the west side, Marion and Lee decided to march north to the newly constructed Fort Motte. They arrived on May 6, surrounded the fort, and began another siege. Greene had by this time retreated all the way to Rugeley's Plantation some 13 miles north of Camden, where Gates had camped before the disastrous battle of Camden. Then Greene crossed the Wateree River.

Rawdon, meanwhile, was contemplating his own situation. He was cut off from Charleston, and there seemed no other option than to abandon Camden and fall back toward Monck's Corner. Yet, he determined to at least make one last attempt to push Greene away before that happened.

On the evening of May 7, Rawdon crossed the Wateree, looking to engage Greene once again. He found Greene on a well-protected ridge along Sawney's Creek. An attack would be suicidal against Greene in that position, so Rawdon did an about-face and returned to Camden on the afternoon of the May 8. The next day, he posted orders for the evacuation of Camden.

Since the return of Greene to South Carolina, Thomas Sumter had been keeping the cause alive in the upcountry. Greene had wanted Sumter to support him on the western flank of Camden, however, Sumter acted on his own, making a campaign southward first to block the British at Friday's Ferry and then make another attack on Fort Granby. With Marion and Lee at Fort Motte, Sumter moved farther south and captured the British post at Orangeburg on May 12.[90]

Fort Motte fell the same day. The fort consisted of a ditch and palisade surrounding the house of Mrs. Rebecca Motte. It was a strong position, much stronger than Fort Watson had been. Marion and Lee's plan was to dig a sap toward the fort and, once the trench was up close along the fort's protective abatis, make a desperate charge. They placed the six-pounder cannon on a mound of dirt east of the fort and would use it to keep the British from defending themselves along the fort's walls.

Some 150 yards north of the fort was a deep depression where slaves began to dig the sap toward the British. As they proceeded towards the fort, Marion's riflemen kept the British heads down. About 40 yards north of the fort, the sap split to the east and west, and once these parallels were near enough for an attack, the Americans decided to shoot flaming arrows onto the top of the house. If the British attempted to put out the fire, the cannon would fire canister at them and drive them off. The plan worked. Muskets were used to shoot the arrows onto the roof, and when the roof caught fire, the British were driven off by canister. The British 184-man detachment was forced to surrender.[91]

Shortly after the siege, Greene arrived under escort and met Marion face to face for the first time. Greene's orders were for Lee and Marion to split up and pursue separate objectives. Marion moved southward and encamped along the Santee. Then he was given permission to achieve a goal long sought: the capture of Georgetown. He took it without firing a shot on May 28.

For his part, Lee was ordered north to take Fort Granby. Arriving there, he found a detachment of Whigs under Colonel Thomas Taylor continuing the siege that Sumter had begun on May 2. Together they took the fort on May 15. Greene brought his army to Granby afterward, and they split up the hoard of supplies the Patriots had captured from both Motte and Granby. Then Greene detached Lee to the west to capture Augusta, Georgia, while Greene marched for the British at Ninety Six.

During the siege of Fort Motte, Rawdon had destroyed the defenses surrounding Camden, burned supplies, gathered up his army, and began his retreat down country. He left his seriously wounded and sick behind, with an equal number of American prisoners. The retreat train included slaves and Loyalists seeking escape and refuge from the Americans. Both the besiegers and the besieged at Fort Motte were aware that Camden had been abandoned, and both thought that Rawdon was coming to rescue the fort. Some sources claim that they could see Rawdon's fires across the river from the high bluff where Fort Motte was located.

Rawdon, however, continued south and crossed the Santee at Nelson's Ferry and learned of Fort Motte's fate. Gaining intelligence that Greene was at Fort Motte, Rawdon marched up the west side of the river to seek revenge, but getting word that Greene was there in force, a false rumor as it turned out, decided to destroy the redoubt at Nelson's Ferry and fall back to Monck's Corner.

Siege of Ninety Six

Ninety Six was much like Camden, a heavily fortified village. It had redoubts and a palisade around the village and a star-shaped fort east of the village. Greene felt more confident about taking Ninety Six than he did Camden, and he decided to lay siege. The effort turned out to be the longest of the Southern campaign, lasting 29 days, 8 days longer than the siege of Yorktown that was to come. In spite of the effort, the siege of Ninety Six would prove to be unsuccessful.

It can be argued that poor decisions by the Americans, combined with strong leadership by the British commander, Lieutenant Colonel John Cruger, contributed to the failure to capture the village. Greene's army initially consisted of 908 Maryland, Delaware, Virginia, and North Carolina Continental soldiers, plus 66 North Carolina militia, and 3 six-pounder cannon. Beyond the siege trenches, an unknown number of militia patrolled the surrounding area, attempting to block any Loyalist reinforcement. Inside the fortifications, Cruger commanded Provincials, New Jersey Volunteers and New York Loyalists, and an unknown number of South Carolina Loyalist militia, perhaps totaling between 550 and 850 defenders. They had only 3 three-pounder cannon, but had numerous small swivel guns.[92]

Greene began his siege with a tour around the town seeking weaknesses. Then he dispersed his men in small camps, surrounding the village, and then opened formal siege operations which he turned over to Colonel Thaddeus Kosciuszko. The colonel was an experienced engineer, having been successful in the fortification of American defenses at Saratoga. For some reason though, at Ninety Six, he aimed his siege operations against the strongest part of the British defense, which was the star fort. Later he would be criticized for this move, especially since he had made no attempt to cut the village off from its water source along Spring Branch north of the village. Perhaps Greene could also be blamed for the oversight, especially since he had earlier suggested to Marion and Lee that they cut off the British water supply at the siege of Fort Watson. Kosciuszko later defended his decision, arguing that he believed Cruger surely had dug wells in the village. In fact, the British had not.

Kosciuszko began the siege with a poorly placed 3-gun battery; some critics claiming it was only 70 yards from the star fort. The British sallied forth from their fort across the short distance and captured entrenching tools and slaves. Learning his lesson, Kosciuszko restarted, constructing the next battery at a considerably greater distance from the fort, probably anywhere from 300 to 400 yards out. He also opened formal trenches that zigzagged toward the fort. As the siege trench pushed forward toward the star fort, Greene's cannon bombarded the fort and town. Greene's artillery bombardments began on May 24 and continued throughout. The British, for their part, did not remain passively in their fort. They made near-daily sorties against the Americans.

By June 3, Greene felt he had put enough pressure on Cruger to demand the British surrender. He was wrong. Cruger's troops were comfortable behind their defenses, and his only weakness was getting water from the creek. Cruger rejected Greene's offer. Greene responded with a bombardment from his batteries firing enfilade. On June 4, the Americans attempted to set the town and the star fort afire by firing flaming arrows onto the roofs of various buildings, but Cruger countered by putting out the fires and that evening removing all roofs. He also countered with yet another sortie against the American line.[93]

Over 50 miles south of the siege, Henry Lee was making progress against British-held Augusta. The town had two forts, Fort Grierson (a fortified house), and Fort Cornwallis, which defended the town, but they were too far apart to support each other. Lee arrived before Augusta on May 18, to find a host of veteran backcountry leaders blockading the forts, including Andrew Pickens, Elijah Clarke, and Isaac Shelby. Lee and Pickens decided the first order of business was to take another British post on the South Carolina side called Fort Galphin or Dreadnought. This was quickly accomplished by Captain John Rudulph (some sources say Major John Rudolph or Captain Micheal Rudulph), and resulted in capturing much-needed lead and powder. At Augusta, the Americans attacked Fort Grierson first, and the battle was quickly over. The Loyalists saw them coming and fled the fort, some scattering toward the river while others ran for Fort Cornwallis. Thirty of them were killed in the rout.

Taking Fort Cornwallis was more difficult. The Whigs began by digging trenches toward the fort from the riverbank. The formidable Loyalist Lieutenant Colonel Thomas Brown commanded the defenses and made two sallies against the trenches. In heavy fighting, his men were repulsed both times. Meanwhile, Lee resorted to the construction of another Maham Tower to fire down into the fort as had worked at Fort Watson, but this time with a cannon in the tower. Brown made a two-pronged attack against both the tower and the trenches on May 29. For the next couple days, the two sides fired their cannon at each other, which ended up with Brown losing his artillery. Lee and Pickens planned an all-out assault, but Brown decided that he had done enough and surrendered on June 5.[94] Lee marched for Ninety Six the next day, leaving Pickens to collect supplies and follow on.

When Lee arrived on June 8, he set up camp on the west side of the village. Greene was glad to have Lee's help with the siege, and Lee began formal trenching toward the western redoubt, called Holmes Fort.

Back on the other side of the village, the American siege works had reached the outer defenses of the star fort at the abatis, and Kosciuszko began digging a mine with the goal of setting off a bomb under the fort. The British attempted yet another sortie on June 9, discovered the mine, captured some American soldiers, and wounded Kosciuszko, bayonetting him in the buttocks.

On June 14, Kosciuszko completed construction of a 30-foot Maham tower, to get above the walls of the star fort so that sharpshooters could fire into the fort. The British countered by adding sandbags along the top of the star-fort parapet and digging a traverse, as they had done at Fort Watson. The American fire was effective enough, though, to suppress British artillery fire during the day. A British attempt to fire hot shot at the tower failed.

Across the way to the west, Lee sent a sergeant and a small detachment of six men across an open field in broad daylight to set fire to the abatis around the Holmes Fort redoubt. The results were not surprising; the detachment was gunned down.

On June 17, the British abandoned Holmes Fort, exposing their safe access to Spring Branch. Now they could only attempt to get water at night, sending slaves out to gather the water. Inside the star fort, the British began to dig a well, but after digging 25 feet below the surface and finding no sign of water, the effort was abandoned.[95]

As the British situation at Ninety Six became more desperate, the strategic situation was changing. A force of 3,000 British soldiers arrived in Charleston. Part of that force under the command of Lord Rawdon was assembled to relieve Ninety Six. With Rawdon's Camden detachment, his army numbered around 2,000.

On June 10, Rawdon left Monck's Corner with the goal of rescuing Ninety Six. Greene soon learned of Rawdon's march and ordered his militia leaders, Sumter and Marion, to stop or at least delay Rawdon, and Pickens to assemble his militia and join Greene. The march northwest in the June heat was devastating to the unacclimated British, and many were lost along the way.

However, the American militia failed to show. Sumter was willing, but poor intelligence of Rawdon's objective caused Sumter to march and counter march, and he was essentially outmaneuvered. Marion, for his part, was along the Santee and was reluctant to leave the lower Santee open to possible British excursions and foraging. As Rawdon moved farther inland, the chances of getting help from Marion diminished. Thus, Greene's siege was increasingly threatened as Rawdon grew closer to Ninety Six.

Greene decided he had to act before Rawdon arrived. Remarkably, according to Henry Lee, Greene decided to make an all-out assault based on the desire of his men, who had labored hard and long to dig the trenches, and urged him to try.[96] On June 18, Greene ordered the attack from both the east and west sides of Ninety Six, with the main effort being against the star fort. The attack began with pioneers, under the cover of a bombardment, charging forward with axes to chop through abatis. Behind them were a select group of Continentals from the Maryland and Virginia regiments, some carrying long poles with hooks to pull down the sandbags on the top of the star-fort parapet. Overhead, riflemen from the tower fired at the defenders, while more Continental soldiers, who were to be the main assault party, fired "by platoons" from the closest parallel.[97]

The initial rush, called the "forlorn hope," became confused and crowded once it reached the bottom of the ditch at the base of the fort walls, and British soldiers fired down on them and used locally forged spears to repel any Americans who made it close to the top of the fort's wall. Then, two detachments of British sallied out of the back of the fort, one going right, the other left, flanking the forlorn hope on both sides and using their bayonets against the attackers. Meanwhile the main American attack was pinned down by British fire and never materialized. Greene, seeing a disaster unfold, decided to withdraw rather than push more men into the maul. On the other side of the village, Lee's men gained the redoubt and found it abandoned.

There was not much else to do at that point other than lift the siege. Greene knew Rawdon would arrive soon, so he gave the order to prepare to leave. Total American casualties for the siege were 58 killed, 76 wounded, and 20 missing. The British lost 27 killed and 58 wounded.

Greene left Ninety Six on June 20, and Rawdon arrived the next day. Rawdon immediately pushed on to catch Greene, however, it was soon clear that Greene had made his escape, and Rawdon turned back to Ninety Six. While Greene retreated across the Tyger and Broad Rivers, Rawdon began what Greene had failed to do; destroy Ninety Six. Rawdon left 1,400 men for Cruger to do the job, and then headed back to the low country. Cruger destroyed the fortifications, broke up materiel he could not transport, and burned the town to the ground. Loyalist families followed Cruger's command as they retreated to Orangeburg. Ironically, for the Americans, the costly battle of Ninety Six was unnecessary. When Rawdon abandoned Camden back in May, he had written Cruger, ordering him to destroy and abandon Ninety Six. However, neither of the two riders sent made it to Ninety Six to deliver the message.

The British Confined

By the end of June 1781, the British no longer controlled the backcountry. Camden, Augusta, Ninety Six, and Georgetown were all free of the British. Fort Watson, Fort Motte, Orangeburg, and Fort Granby, the forts along their lifeline to the backcountry, had been captured. Only Charleston and Savannah remained in British control, while the regions surrounding them became the new war zone. Nonetheless, the Americans were too weak to keep the British within either town's walls or even lay siege. Therefore, the war would continue for another year and a half.

Through the early part of the hot month of July, Rawdon and Cruger retreated southward toward Orangeburg, harassed by American detachments. Rawdon's route took him toward the Congarees, and he lost a sizable portion of his cavalry to Colonel Lee's dragoons. The detachment had ventured beyond the main body to forage, and around 50 officers and men were surprised and captured. Cruger's march was hounded by Pickens, however, Pickens withdrew when he heard of Indian attacks in the upcountry. Marion attempted to intercept a detachment of British reinforcements under Lieutenant Colonel Alexander Stewart marching out of Charleston for Orangeburg, however, he took the wrong road and the two forces passed each other along parallel roads. Both British and Patriots horses suffered immensely due to the heat. Nevertheless, Greene followed behind the British main force and by July 12 was within 4 miles of Orangeburg. There he found Rawdon in too strong a position to attempt an attack. Rawdon, for his part, prepared for battle. Greene knew that an attack against Rawdon would not be successful, and instead deployed and hoped Rawdon would come out beyond his strong position, but Rawdon did not take the bait. Then Greene decided to retire to the High Hills of the Santee to rest and refit his army.[98]

Besides the heat, during this time food and forage became extremely hard to find. The campaign had always been difficult, but Henry Lee noted that "never did we suffer so severely as during the few days' halt here." Lee continued:

> Rice furnished our substitute for bread, which, although tolerably relished by those familiarized to it from infancy, was very disagreeable to Marylanders and Virginians, who had grown up in the use of corn and wheat bread. Of meat we literally had none; for the few meagre cattle brought to our camp as beef would not afford more than one or two ounces per man. Frogs abounded in some neighboring ponds, and on them chiefly did the light troops subsist. They became in great demand from their nutritiousness; and, after conquering the existing prejudice, were diligently sought after. Even the alligator was used by a few; and, very probably, had the army been much longer detained upon that ground, might have rivalled the frog in the estimation of our epicures.[99]

July and August of 1781 in the low country were especially brutal, and the 19th-century writer William Gilmore Simms proclaimed them the "dog days" for their heat and humidity. Yet, the heat did not stop the fighting.[100] Thomas Sumter asked Greene for permission to attack the British posts at Monck's Corner and Dorchester and wanted Marion's and Lee's regiments to join him. Greene and his army were cooling off in camp in the High Hills of the Santee, but he allowed Sumter to proceed and encouraged Marion and Lee to cooperate under Sumter's command. Altogether, Sumter, Marion, and Lee had as many as 1,000 to 1,100 men.

Taking the post at Dorchester was left to Lee, and that was quickly accomplished because the British had abandoned the post. Marion, with Sumter behind him, advanced toward Monck's Corner, where British Lieutenant Colonel James Coates commanded around the same number of troops as the Americans had. Coates got wind of the Patriots and moved to Biggin Church, a strong brick structure five miles away.

Early in the morning twilight, the Americans saw that the church was burning. Coates was making his break for Charleston, and the chase was soon on. Lee's and Colonel Wade Hampton's cavalry were in the American lead, Marion followed with mounted infantry, and behind him Sumter brought up the rear.

Coates destroyed the bridge across Wadboo Creek, forcing the Americans to find a ford upstream. On July 17, he camped at Shubrick's Plantation and placed a detachment and howitzer at Quinby Bridge immediately east of the plantation. Lee came up first and charged the British at the bridge. Not all his men made it across, because the British had loosened the bridge timbers, which fell off as the lead horses galloped across. The horses behind them refused to jump the gaps.

The outnumbered men who made it across were met by furious fire from British skirmishers. The British troops then fell back, taking their howitzer, and settled into the plantation house, barns, and slave quarters to await the Americans. Marion and Lee consolidated their forces and decided the British were too strongly positioned to be attacked without their own artillery and infantry support.

Sumter arrived with the infantry but without artillery, late in the afternoon, and, against Marion and Lee's advice, ordered an attack. Marion's detachment was ordered across an open field under fire. They then returned to support Colonel Thomas Taylor's men who were taking heavy fire and facing a bayonet charge. Although Marion's reinforcement forced back the British attack against Taylor, they took heavy casualties. Sumter finally called off the attack. Taylor was furious with Sumter, and although Marion never officially complained, he and Lee left Sumter that evening and marched 15 miles away without saying goodbye. That was the last time either officer would serve with Sumter.

Sumter resigned soon thereafter because South Carolina Governor John Rutledge issued a proclamation against the looting of Loyalists the following month, which effectively nullified Sumter's Law. This "law" was actually an edict to draw more men into the militia as it allowed new recruits, both officers and men, to be paid in horses, clothing, and slaves for enlisting. Sumter would get these commodities and slaves from the Loyalist plantations that he raided. Greene reluctantly agreed to Sumter's plan, while Marion would have nothing to do with it. Rutledge's proclamation ended the controversy.[101]

Toward the end of August, Greene asked Marion to aid Colonel William Harden in the low country southwest of Charleston. British foraging parties had been operating in the area, and Harden was in no health to do much about it. Marion circled around the enemy forces north of Charleston, crossed the Edisto River, and found Harden's troops scattered with Harden unable to organize them. Over the next several days, Marion rallied Harden's militia while looking for an opportunity to confront the enemy.

On the afternoon of the August 30, Marion set up an ambush along an oft-used road leading northeast toward Dorchester about a mile southwest of Parker's Ferry. He had some 445 men that included about 80 saber men. The British foraging party was stronger than he was, consisting of about 500 Hessians, British regulars, and mounted Loyalists, and two artillery pieces. Still, Marion hoped they would pass the ambush site on their way back to Charleston.

While setting the ambush, Marion learned that there were 100 additional Loyalists camped at the ferry up the road. Nevertheless, Marion placed his front line about 40 yards off the road in a thick swampy woods just north of a road intersection. To his rear he placed more men, and still farther back, he placed his cavalry. The plan was for the British to pass along the road and when their van got to the north end of the front line, to open fire. That would be the signal for Marion's second line to come up and his cavalry to charge down the road.

Unfortunately for Marion, just before sunset, a few of the Loyalists from the ferry came down the path and saw Marion's men in the woods. A few of the Patriots could not resist the urge to shoot, which sent the Loyalists back up the road to the ferry, chased by some of Marion's swordsmen. The noise of those shots attracted the British commander who ordered his infantry off the road so that his cavalry could come to the rescue. The Loyalist dragoons galloped ahead, ran into the ambush, and were decimated. In the confusion, they were unable to turn back and had to run through the entire ambush toward the ferry.

By that time, the British infantry came up and a full-scale exchange was brewing when someone in Marion's line panicked, yelling they were being flanked. They were not, but still they fell back and Marion was unable to rally them. His second line had failed to move up to support the ambushers. Meanwhile, the British also fell back, especially after their all their artillerymen had fallen. The British lost some 20 killed and 80 wounded. The Americans only lost one killed and three wounded. Marion left battlefield, with most of his ammunition gone.[102]

Eutaw Springs

Meanwhile, Greene, who had been resting his army in the cool High Hills through most of August, broke camp on August 23, looking for a fight. Lieutenant Colonel Alexander Stewart had taken over as field commander of the British forces after Lord Rawdon had asked to be relieved of command because of his failing health. Unfortunately for Rawdon, he did not have a direct route back to Britain. He was captured on the high seas, but was soon exchanged.

Greene marched slowly toward Charleston, requesting Pickens and Marion to join him. Greene soon learned that Stewart was camped at Eutaw Springs, along the south bank of the Santee, not far from Nelson's Ferry. Stewart, however, did not know exactly where Greene was.

Moving downstream along the south Santee road, Greene and Pickens arrived at Burdell's Tavern, around seven miles north of Eutaw Springs. Marion joined them on September 7. With Greene were some 2,276 regulars and militia, while Stewart's command was 1,793.[103]

Once again, Greene chose a version of the tactical deployment used at Guilford Court House and Cowpens, but this time he would attack rather than defend. Marion commanded the American front line, consisting of a battalion of South Carolina militia, two battalions of North Carolina militia in the center, and another South Carolina battalion on the left under Pickens. Behind them were three brigades of Continentals under Otho Williams. Both lines had artillery. Lee's Legion protected the right flank, and South Carolina state troops were on the left. William Washington's cavalry and Captain Robert Kirkwood's Delaware Continentals formed a reserve.

The British were warned of the American approach that morning by two deserters, and Stewart sent out 190 men to gain more information.

Battle of Eutaw Springs. (Artist, Alonzo Chappel, c. 1858, from the New York Public Library)

They met Greene's van, and a short fight broke out before the British withdrew, with the loss of some 40 prisoners. This action drew in a detachment of unarmed British foragers who had been sent out earlier looking for food. Between the reconnaissance detachment's losses and the capture of the foragers, perhaps as many as 400 British were made prisoner before the main battle started.

The skirmish and collecting prisoners took time, however, and Greene caused further delay by deploying his line of battle early in the belief that the main British line was near. In fact, it was still three miles away. He also issued each man a ration of rum. Greene's troops had difficulty marching in line through the woods, and Stewart's skirmishers increased their struggle to maintain their lines.

At around 9:00am, the two front lines finally met. Stewart's men were all veterans, and most were regulars like the 3rd, 63rd, and 64th Regiments of Foot and Provincials. Colonel John Cruger, the excellent British officer who defended Ninety Six, was also there. They formed up in front of their camp in one line, with the Santee River on their right, and anchored by veteran light infantry under Major John Majoribanks, slightly behind the main line in a thicket next to the river. Stewart had a few cavalrymen and infantry in reserve. Behind them was a brick house, which would prove to be a stout defensive position for the British in the battle.

Unlike Camden, the American militia did not flee, opening a fierce fire against the British line. After several volleys, the North Carolina militia began to give way, but North Carolina Continentals replaced the militia, and the battle raged on. Then the American left began to fall back, and the British charged, only to be met by the second American line. At this point, the British line stopped and began to withdraw.

As the Americans advanced on their left, they were checked by the British light infantry in the thicket. William Washington's cavalry was ordered forward to push them out of the thicket, but he charged without infantry support, and they suffered greatly as they attempted to navigate the thicket. Washington's horse was killed and fell on him, pinning him to the ground while a British soldier bayonetted him. Washington was captured and survived his wounds.

By this time, the center British line was nearly destroyed. As the British fell back through their tents, the Americans followed and became entangled in the camp, and some men began looting. A British detachment of New York Volunteers had made it into the brick house and began picking off the Americans. Greene brought his artillery forward to pound down the house, but British fire killed or wounded all his artillerymen. Then, Major Majoribanks's men emerged from the thicket and captured the Americans' guns.

At this point. Greene had seen enough and ordered a withdrawal. His men had performed well, but were tired, without water, and low on ammunition. He left a reserve and returned to Burdell's Plantation.

The casualties were high on both sides. The British lost 84 killed, 351 wounded, and 257 missing. The Americans lost 139 killed, 373 wounded, and 8 missing.[104] The American officers suffered greatly, including Andrew Pickens who was wounded, and as mentioned William Washington who was wounded and captured. On the British side, Majoribanks suffered a mortal wound. Though the British held the field, both sides declared victory. In hindsight, Greene had lost the battle but had once again bloodied the British field forces and won a strategic victory. The battle of Eutaw Springs was the last large-scale engagement in South Carolina during the American Revolution.

Marion and Lee were ordered to keep an eye on Stewart's movements. General Paston Gould had been made overall commander of British forces in the South back in June. Up to this point, he had chosen to remain in Charleston because of rumors of a French fleet off the coast. Now he moved out to reinforce Stewart.

As Stewart fell back down the road nearer to Monck's Corner, Greene advanced, still open to battle. He halted about 12 miles from Stewart and then fell back and decided to march back to the High Hills of the Santee to rest and refit. Greene was encamped there by September 16.[105]

As Greene rested his army, he must have contemplated what he had accomplished since his return to South Carolina. With the help of Lee and Marion primarily, he had pushed the British regulars out of the backcountry. At this point, south of Virginia, the British only held the urban pockets along the southern coast of Savannah, Charleston, and Wilmington. Soon the major fighting would move to Virginia.

Yorktown

When Lord Cornwallis arrived at Wilmington, North Carolina, back in April 1781, he was in desperate straits. Since the turn of the year, he had lost half his army of 3,224. He needed reinforcements, and he was undecided as to what to do. Through much of April he debated, mostly with himself, about whether to return to South Carolina or go north to Virginia. On April 10, he wrote Major General William Phillips, commanding British forces in Virginia, that he was contemplating a rendezvous where he had something to fight for. Even as late as April 22, though, Cornwallis was still thinking of a return to South Carolina. Eventually, in May he had decided that his best opportunity for a victory lay to the north.[106]

This outcome was contrary to the wishes of General Henry Clinton, who was Cornwallis's superior but who Cornwallis had largely ignored since Guilford Court House. Cornwallis's decision to march north to

Virginia, in hindsight, was the first in a series of mistakes he would make, which would eventually end in his surrender at Yorktown, Virginia, that fall.

While Clinton can certainly be held accountable for the strategic errors he made, he wisely summed up the results of Cornwallis's decision in going north. Writing to Lord George Germain in May of 1781, Clinton still wished Cornwallis would return to South Carolina instead of marching to Virginia, noting, "And I even have my doubts whether his lordship's march to the northward will draw after him (as he expects) the rebel General Greene, who I fear will endeavor either to invest Camden or by placing himself between that place and Charleston render Lord Rawdon's situation very hazardous."[107] In fact, because of Cornwallis's move to Virginia, Greene was able to invest Camden and allow Marion and Lee to get between Camden and Charleston.

Cornwallis joined Phillips's army at Petersburg, Virginia, on May 20 to find Phillips had died. There Cornwallis once again dithered, worried about the American forces under Marquis de Lafayette and rumors of a French fleet in the vicinity. Cornwallis sought out Lafayette but failed to draw him into a battle. By June, Lafayette had been reinforced by Brigadier General Anthony Wayne and Major General Friedrich von Stueben, and Cornwallis moved to Williamsburg. Still depressed, Cornwallis began thinking of returning to South Carolina.

Events, however, conspired to keep him in Virginia. First Clinton, whom Cornwallis had been arguing with since his arrival in Virginia, requested some 2,000 of his men for operations in New York. Second, in order to fulfill Clinton's request, Cornwallis abandoned Williamsburg and was in the process of crossing the James River when he discovered Wayne and Lafayette close behind. Cornwallis drew them into a trap and gained an encouraging victory. Third, he learned that General Alexander Leslie was being sent as reinforcement to South Carolina. Then Clinton countermanded the order for Cornwallis to reinforce him and instead ordered Cornwallis to hold Old Point Comfort as a British fleet was in need of a safe winter anchorage. Point Comfort proved unsuitable, and Cornwallis decided to substitute Yorktown for the fleet's safety.[108]

Cornwallis began constructing works across the York River from Yorktown at Gloucester Point in early August. Progress was slow, as was his troops' evacuation of his former encampment at Portsmouth. It wasn't until August 22 that Cornwallis was able to report to Clinton that the evacuation was complete and that Cornwallis was ready to fortify Yorktown itself.[109]

The Americans, meanwhile, were closing in. General George Washington and French Lieutenant General Jean-Baptiste Donatien De Vimeur comte de Rochambeau established communication with French Admiral François Joseph Paul Comte de Grasse, who was sailing for North America. Rochambeau suggested the Chesapeake as a possibility for joint operations, and on August 19, Washington and Rochambeau began the 400-mile march south.[110] At the end of August, the French appeared off the coast and began landing troops on Jamestown Island on September 2. A brief naval battle on September 5 between de Grasse and British Admiral Thomas Graves resulted in the British returning to New York for repairs. Cornwallis was now without hope of support, but he still had some 8,400 soldiers under his command.[111]

While Cornwallis was full of vigor, his tactics were unhelpful. As the Americans and French surrounded him, he pulled in most of his outer defenses, concentrating his men in the village while allowing Washington and Rochambeau to open siege operations close to his position. Events on October 9 and 10 were the beginning of the end. On October 9, the combined French and American army opened an artillery barrage, and the following day Cornwallis received word that Clinton's reinforcements would be delayed. On October 14 and 15, the Americans and French captured Cornwallis's redoubts near the river. Finally, in desperation, Cornwallis took the offensive. On the morning October 16, he attempted a sally against a French artillery emplacement and then attempted to cross over to Gloucester Point, but the weather prevented the crossing. Both efforts failed miserably. The next day, he asked for a 24-hour cessation for negotiations. On October 19, he surrendered his command of over 8,000 soldiers and sailors.

Residual Operations

The news of Cornwallis's surrender did not reach Lord Germain in London until November 25, 1781. Germain immediately went to the

Prime Minister Frederick Lord North, who "opened his arms, exclaiming wildly, as he paced up and down the apartment during a few minutes, 'Oh, God! It is all over!' Words which he repeated many times, under emotions of the deepest consternation and distress."[112] North was correct. Yorktown was the climax of the American Revolution, but the British still occupied land in the Northern colonies, and in the Southern campaign, held the large coastal towns of Savannah, Charleston, and Wilmington. There would be two years of negotiations before a treaty was agreed to and signed, and in the meantime, more men would die.

One hot spot in the fall of 1781 was in eastern North Carolina. Cornwallis had left Major Craig in command of the British detachment at Wilmington with orders to abandon the town upon Cornwallis's entry into Virginia. Craig, however, decided to stay and in August attacked and dispersed Patriot militia, burned and looted plantations, and raided New Bern. He then continued westward, looting more plantations.

Perhaps Cornwallis's march through the country and Craig's raids finally inspired the local Loyalists. Although Loyalists like David Fanning had been active during the summer months of 1781 and cooperated with Craig in raids and skirmishes, many North Carolina Loyalists, who had remained intimidated by American Whigs through most of the war, now rallied to Fanning's flag. Some 950 Loyalists joined him and marched to Hillsborough, where on September 12, they surprised the Rebel government and captured Governor Thomas Burke. According to Burke, 15 soldiers were killed and 20 wounded. Some 200 were captured, including 71 Continentals. Unfortunately for the Loyalists, some of the men raided the town's stores and found liquor, which they quickly sampled. Fanning was able to get control of the men and marched them out of town, but they were only able to march for a few miles before they were too exhausted to go farther.

The next day, the Loyalists walked into an ambush at Lindley's Mill, set up by a detachment of Whig militia under the command of Brigadier General John Butler. The head of the column took a heavy volley before a tense battle broke out. The Loyalists fell back to regroup and found a building called Spring Friends Meeting House to protect their prisoners. Then Fanning decided to try to flank the Whigs who were dug in on higher ground. He surprised the Americans, and General Butler ordered a retreat, but Colonel Robert Mebane convinced the men to hold and about that time Fanning took a ball in the arm. This halted Fanning's attack, and both sides fell back. Eventually the Whigs withdrew without resistance. In the four-hour battle, both sides suffered many casualties, and Governor Burke remained a prisoner.[113]

To the west, Brigadier General Griffith Rutherford rallied the Patriot militia and marched east to avenge the atrocities of Major Craig and in doing so, probably committed a few atrocities himself. In mid-October, Rutherford defeated a detachment of Loyalists at Raft Swamp and then marched for Wilmington. Rutherford did not have artillery and was not strong enough to capture the fortified town, and Craig was not strong enough to march out and fight in the open. Thus, Rutherford and Craig became locked in a stalemate until November 18, when Craig, this time, obeyed orders to abandon Wilmington. Large numbers of Loyalists left with him, and North Carolina was now under the control of the Americans.[114]

South Carolina was also dealing with a resurgence of Loyalism. William Cunningham, or "Bloody Bill," and other detachments engaged in a long circular raid from Charleston, northwestward to Ninety Six, and then to the Congarees and back. Cunningham himself engaged in 22 separate actions.[115] Among the larger engagements was Cloud's Creek, where Patriot militia were essentially massacred after they ran out of ammunition, and another was at Hayes Station on November 19. There Cunningham executed 12 Patriots after they had surrendered. Cunningham then turned south and made for Charleston with Andrew Pickens on his tail. Passing Orangeburg, Cunningham decided to hide in the swamps of the Edisto River. Pickens found one of his camps and killed some 20 Loyalists on December 20. Cunningham, however, made it back into Charleston.[116]

Since Eutaw Springs, General Nathanael Greene had rested his army in camp in the High Hills of the Santee. It was not until October 27 that news of Yorktown reached him. There was much celebrating, however the army was experiencing outbreaks of malaria and dysentery. Those wounded at Eutaw Springs suffered the most, as there was no ability to care for them. Supplies and ammunition were also in short supply, as was clothing and shoes. The army was for all purposes paralyzed. It was not until November 19 that Greene was able to get the army back on the move. His goal was to confine the British in Charleston while avoiding another major battle.[117]

On December 1, Greene arrived in front of the reoccupied British post at Dorchester with an advanced detachment, and, after a skirmish, the British abandoned the post for good this time.[118] Greene continued his march southward, and on December 9, his army arrived at Round O, across the Edisto River southwest of Charleston, placing himself between the two British armies at Charleston and Savannah. Welcomed reinforcements from Virginia under Major General Arthur St. Clair arrived from on January 4, 1782.[119] Greene had been desperate for reinforcements and had even proposed to South Carolina Governor Rutledge to enlist African Americans. John Laurens followed by introducing a bill in the South Carolina Legislature to enlist 2,500 slaves. The bill was rejected.[120] The British, meanwhile, were actually no better off. By Henry Clinton's understanding from the Adjutant General, they only had 4,576 men fit for duty in South Carolina, 691 in Georgia, and 456 in East Florida, along with 2,283 sick and wounded, and 1,341 prisoners at the beginning of 1782.[121]

At this point, the British in the South were only holding onto Charleston and Savannah. On the North American strategic front, British aims were merely to hold onto those port towns with the troops already deployed, while encouraging the Loyalists to more offensive actions where possible. Yorktown, it appears, had taken the wind completely out of the British sails. As Lord Germain wrote to Clinton on January 2:

> The fatal issue of the Virginia expedition and the loss of so fine a body of men as were made prisoners at York Town must of necessity occasion an alteration in the mode of prosecuting the war in North America, for no more regiments or corps can be sent from this country, it being only proposed to keep up those which are already in America as near as possible to their establishments by recruits.

Their purpose, as Germain noted, was to maintain those ports still under British control and act where possible with the Navy against any seaports held by the Americans to obstruct their trade and keep them from acting against the British. The British forces were to refrain from offensive action with the object to subdue the colonies, but to assist any Loyalists who would. Germain explains:

> It is nevertheless his [the King's] purpose that you should give all possible encouragement to the loyalists in every province to preserve in their attachment to this country; and if any number of them shall think themselves sufficiently strong to effect a restoration of the constitution with the assistance of a small force, it is His Majesty's pleasure that you do furnish them with arms and ammunition and send them such a force ...[122]

In January, Wayne was sent south with a little over 500 men, mostly militia, to take control of Georgia. Like Laurens, Wayne had also sought to enlist African Americans but was turned down. Consequently, Wayne had nowhere near enough men to capture Savannah, but he harassed British posts until they fell back into the city. Wayne also defeated an attempt by Creek Indians to surprise him at the end of January 1782. From then until July, Wayne kept the British bottled up in Savannah. The British proposed a truce but were turned down, and the city remained under a siege until the British finally abandoned it on July 11, 1782.[123]

In South Carolina, Greene remained with his main army at Round O to the west of Charleston, with Sumter to the northwest, Marion operating to the northeast, and Lee in command of the American cavalry. Greene again found himself in a situation in which victory was just out of reach. He had the British loosely confined to the strong post at Charleston, however, he lacked the necessary numbers to tightly bottle-up the enemy or conduct an actual siege. Meanwhile, many veterans of his officer corps, including Lieutenant Colonel Henry Lee, Brigadier General Thomas Sumter, Lieutenant Colonel John Eager Howard, and Colonel Otho Williams all retired through the winter and spring of 1782. Marion and Sumter were appointed as Senators as the state legislature reformed in nearby Jacksonborough, and Andrew Pickens was appointed to the House of Representatives. Greene was also losing many enlisted men, who, like the officers, were getting tired of war and inaction. Rumors spread that the war was ending. Desertions were up, as were incidents of mutiny in the ranks. This problem would plague Greene throughout the year.

The British were no stronger. They had to find food and forage and thus continued to break out, raiding and foraging around Charleston. In one major foray in late February, Lieutenant Colonel Benjamin Thompson learned of Marion's men camped at Durant's plantation on

Wambaw Creek and surprised them. Marion left the legislature, rallied his troops, and went in search of Thompson.

At Tidyman's plantation, along the lower Santee River, Marion was resting, when Thompson suddenly appeared. Marion deployed and attacked, but his cavalry became confused maneuvering around a pond, which caused them to fall back, and Thompson countercharged. Although Marion was able to rally the men, many retreated into the swamp. Thompson killed several of Marion's men and captured many horses. In Charleston, there was some exuberance among the Loyalists as a false rumor spread that Marion had drowned in the battle.[124]

Skirmishing continued through the spring and summer among Loyalist and Whig militias, including small engagements called John Town (May 24), Dawkin's Defeat (May 28), Sharp's Skirmish (June 1), and Capers's Scout (July), but no large-scale battles occurred until late August.[125] On August 27, 1782, the Americans lost John Laurens in a battle at Tar Bluff, South Carolina, along the Combahee River. As noted, the British were conducting raids in the low country south of Charleston, and Greene sent Brigadier General Mordecai Gist to intercept any British parties coming up the river. Gist arrived at Combahee Ferry and ordered fortifications to be built 12 miles south of the ferry at Tar Bluff. Laurens, eager for action, asked to command the work and was given permission. When a number of British boats came downriver, Laurens fired upon them, and the British deployed a detachment of soldiers upstream to disperse Laurens and destroy the battery. Although Gist was marching in relief, Laurens chose to attack before reinforcements could arrive and was killed along with several other men. When Gist got there, a battle ensued, and the British were forced to retreat, but not before they captured the howitzer at the fort.[126]

The second engagement was on August 30 and turned out to be Francis Marion's last battle. Marion was camped at Wadboo Plantation southeast of Monck's Corner across the Cooper River. Among his militia were "new-made men," former Loyalists, who had signed a treaty with Marion earlier and were now soldiering on under the Swamp Fox's command. Wadboo was ideal for keeping an eye on British movements to the north and east of Charleston.

A detachment of British Provincial cavalry and African American dragoons under the command of Major Thomas Fraser were in the area foraging. Each side learned of the other's presence around the same time. Marion prepared his camp for an expected battle, placing his men along an avenue of cedars in front of the plantation house and in various outbuildings. Then he sent some dragoons as bait to find and lure Fraser to the plantation. Fraser fell for the scheme and chased Marion's cavalry into the trap. Fraser's dragoons took the brunt of furious volleys from the Americans secure in the cedars, and lost some 20 men, including 4 killed. Fraser was able to salvage the battle a bit by capturing an ammunition wagon, causing Marion to disperse. However, Marion was soon back at the plantation after Fraser left.[127]

Greene's army remained restless. The rumors that the war was ending were in fact, true. Overseas, rumblings to abandon the colonies had begun in the British government when the news arrived of Cornwallis's surrender back in the fall of 1781. The debate continued until the House of Commons voted to abandon the war in February 1782. When the current commander of British forces, General Alexander Leslie, learned of the vote, he sent a proposal for a ceasefire to Greene in May. Greene was skeptical but passed it on to Congress. Meanwhile, malaria plagued the army, and Greene moved it to Ashley Hill Plantation in July, 15 miles from Charleston. In spite of this effort, the malaria problem persisted.

Although Greene did not know it, Leslie received orders to abandon Charleston on August 1, but it would take until December to gather enough ships to evacuate soldiers, Loyalists, and slaves. The British navy remained strong but had suffered severely since 1775, losing some 2,000 merchant ships. As they planned the evacuation, besides 4,127 British officers and troops, 4,230 Loyalists signed up to leave the colony forever, along with 7,163 African Americans, the latter overwhelmingly slaves.[128] Also unknown to the South Carolina armies, in November, America and Britain signed a preliminary treaty in Paris.

The Final Acts

The final crossing of swords in South Carolina occurred on James Island in a short but hot skirmish called Dill's Bluff on November 14, 1782.

Thaddeus Kosciuszko had learned of British woodcutters emerging from Fort Johnson to gather wood and aimed to ambush them. The British were prepared, however, and after a heavy exchange of fire Kosciuszko soon realized he was well outnumbered. He quickly fell back.[129]

On December 14, 1782, the British army left Charleston. It took two days. Civilians staying behind were restricted to their homes. As Greene's army, with Major General Anthony Wayne at the head, entered the town, the last of the British army was at Gadsden's Wharf, still embarking. Some British and Hessian soldiers took the opportunity in the chaos to desert.

The British were gone from South Carolina, but there was still an army to keep in the field for Nathanael Greene. Supply and morale problems continued to plague him, and Charleston was unprotected.

On February 4, 1783, the British declared hostilities with the colonies over. On April 11, Congress followed up. Now Greene could dismiss his army. He did so on June 21, 1783, embarking the Northern soldiers on ships homeward. Greene personally did not leave Charleston until August 11.[130]

Amazingly, peace negotiations had begun as far back as September 27, 1779, when Congress elected John Adams to begin the discussion with England. It was not until April 1782 that England sent Richard Oswald to begin talks with the American committee in Paris, and the ministry gave permission to Oswald to treat with the commissioners of the United States, on September 19, 1782. The treaty was formally signed on September 3, 1783. The Americans got independence, a great deal of the land from the sea to the Mississippi, and freedom to fish off Newfoundland.[131]

It was a remarkable victory of a loose collection of colonies over an established global superpower. How could the seemingly weak defeat the obviously strong? One explanation, certainly in South Carolina, lay in the superior Patriot leadership.

Profiles in Leadership

Henry Laurens and Creating Change

Henry Laurens was born in Charleston in 1724. His family had arrived there in 1715, after immigrating from England as part of the mass exodus of Calvinist Protestants or Huguenots brought on by the revocation of the Edict of Nantes in 1685. The family quickly prospered, and Laurens was sent back to England to complete a three-year clerkship in the London countinghouse of James Crokatt.[1] Upon his return to South Carolina in 1747, Laurens learned his father had died just days before.[2] As the eldest son in the family, Laurens inherited considerable wealth.

Shortly thereafter, Laurens joined with George Austin to open an import-export business. The firm capitalized on the system of triangular trade between America, Europe, and Africa, exporting such products as rice, indigo, and naval stores and importing rum, sugar, and slaves. Austin & Laurens expanded to include George Appleby in 1759 and continued to operate until 1762 when the partnership dissolved by mutual consent.[3] That same year, Laurens purchased a 3,000-acre plantation known as "Mepkin" on the western branch of the Cooper River in the St. James Goose Creek Parish.[4]

As was common among South Carolina's elite gentry, Laurens was active politically and as a member of the militia. He was elected to the Commons House of Assembly of South Carolina in September of 1757.[5] In this capacity, Laurens was among those charged with first dealing with the rising Cherokee threat in the backcountry and then with responding to the oppressive efforts of the British to recoup expenses from the French and Indian War through new taxes on the colonies.

In spite of a fragile Anglo-Cherokee alliance, violations and atrocities by both sides escalated in the late 1750s. In 1759, South Carolina Royal Governor William Henry Lyttelton declared what proved to be an ill-advised war on the Cherokees and launched a punitive expedition against them. After a costly and bloody campaign, a humiliating treaty was imposed on the Cherokees that virtually ensured that fighting would later be renewed.[6]

In the midst of this turmoil, Laurens was appointed as a lieutenant colonel in the militia on September 6, 1760 and subsequently raised a unit of 1,200 men.[7] That same year he was re-elected to the Commons but was unable to serve because of his military obligations. Chief among these duties was to lead the provincial regiment that was part of Lieutenant Colonel James Grant's expedition against the Cherokees in 1761. Like so many of his command, Laurens was struck by the brutality of the campaign. "This work tho necessary," he wrote, "often makes my heart bleed. The Cherokees has totally abandoned these Towns & fled with their wretched Women & Children across the Mountains.... They have already suffer'd greatly & will be reduced to extreme misery as the Winter advances." It was through such ruthless but effective measures that the Cherokees were defeated.[8]

With that threat subsided, Laurens turned his attention to the political work of the Commons. Laurens's personal preference for order, as well as the interwoven nature of British economic interests and his own, caused him to chafe at the riotous aspects of Charleston's response to the Stamp Act of 1765. He urged peaceful compliance until the law could be repealed.

The death of Laurens's wife in 1770 served as the impetus for Laurens to relocate to England the next year so that his two sons could continue their education. While there, Laurens remained attuned to events unfolding in the colonies. For example, in 1774 he was 1 of 38 Americans who signed the Boston Port Bill petition, which opposed the Tea Act, a measure that closed the port of Boston and demanded that the colonists make reparations for the tea destroyed during the Boston Tea Party.

By the time Laurens returned to Charleston in November of 1774, tensions had intensified. After British soldiers and Patriot militia clashed at Lexington and Concord, Massachusetts, on April 19, 1775, the

Provincial Congress of South Carolina met in June and elected a 13-member "Council of Safety" to act as the supreme executive authority in the province until a permanent government could be established. The Council members were Henry Laurens, Charles Cotesworth Pinckney, Rawlins Lowndes, Thomas Ferguson, Arthur Middleton, Thomas Heyward, Thomas Bee, John Huger, Miles Brewton, James Pearson, Willian Henry Drayton, Benjamin Elliott, and William Williamson. Laurens was elected President of the Council, a role in practical terms equivalent to governor.

Henry Laurens. (Artist, Lemuel Francis Abbott, 1781 or 1784, Wikimedia Commons)

The work ahead of Laurens was monumental. Troops had to be raised and deployed. Supplies had to be requisitioned. Funds had to be dispersed. Correspondence had to be initiated and answered. Committees and commissions had to be formed and their work monitored.

Leading Change

Effecting such transformative organizational change is perhaps the greatest challenge a leader can face. John Kotter argues that it can best be navigated by an eight-step process of: Establishing a sense of urgency; Creating the guiding coalition; Developing a vision and strategy; Communicating the change vision; Empowering broad-based action; Generating short-term wins; Consolidating gains and producing more change; and Anchoring new approaches in the culture.[9] The course followed by Laurens and the Council of Safety is illustrative of Kotter's approach.

Effecting change is very difficult, because Kotter notes, in the midst of change, "pain is ever present."[10] A strong reverence for the status quo, complacency, and preference for "the devil we know versus the one we don't" plague the effort to create change. Thus, Kotter's first step of "establishing a sense of urgency" is as difficult as it is essential.

Unfortunately, it often takes a crisis to rouse people to change, leading Kotter to note that "visible crises can be enormously helpful in catching people's attention and pushing up urgency levels."[11]

The crises that established the sense of urgency that led to the creation of the Council of Safety are fairly obvious: the specific Cherokee threat and the general breakdown in law and order in the backcountry, increasing British oppression such as the "taxation without representation" embodied by the Stamp Act, and the armed clashes between British and Patriots at Lexington and Concord. Amid such a crisis environment, the Provincial Congress had the sense of urgency needed to create the Council of Safety, and the Council itself responded in kind. Understanding what was at stake, the Council held its first meeting just two days after its establishment. Although he does not often get credit for it, it was economist Paul Romer who in 2004 first declared that "a crisis is a terrible thing to waste."[12] The Provincial Congress and the Council of Safety did not waste the crisis unfolding before them in South Carolina in 1775.

Kotter's second step is "creating a guiding coalition." Such was the Council of Safety. Always intended as an interim measure, the Council was designed to deal with the immediate situation while preparing for a permanent government to be established. Kotter notes that the guiding coalition must represent "the combination of trust and common goal shared by people with the right characteristics."[13] The Council of Safety boasted such a combination. Like Laurens, its members were drawn from the "leading men" of South Carolina society. Consider what futures lay in store for them: Laurens was destined to succeed John Hancock as the President of the Continental Congress. Thomas Heyward and Arthur Middleton would be two of the four South Carolinians to sign the Declaration of Independence. William Henry Drayton would become the chief justice of South Carolina's Supreme Court. John Huger would serve two terms as the intendent or mayor of Charleston. James Pearson served as vice president of South Carolina and was followed by Thomas Bee, who held the office under the new title of lieutenant governor. Rawlins Lowndes would serve as president or governor of South Carolina. Charles Pinckney was perhaps the principal author of the United States Constitution. In addition to these impressive capacities, the Council's members had the trust of each other and the community based on their status as being among the class of merchants, planters, lawyers, and other elites that comprised the era's public leadership. This public trust was facilitated by the fact that the Council was almost evenly divided between conservatives and progressives.[14]

Next in Kotter's model comes "developing a vision and strategy." While Kotter declares vision to be "essential," he also notes that it is but one element of a larger system that also includes strategies, plans, and budgets.[15] The work of the Provincial Congress and the Council of Safety represents all four elements.

Kotter describes vision as "a sensible and appealing picture of the future."[16] Although the tension between the British Crown and the American colonies ultimately erupted in an open war for independence, that outcome was not considered inevitable in 1775. There were many moderate colonists, including Laurens, who hoped war could be avoided and political reconciliation achieved. Thus, the vision articulated by the Provincial Congress was of "strengthening[,] securing[,] & defending the Colony," rather than taking aggressive and offensive action.[17]

Kotter describes strategy as "a logic for how the vision can be achieved."[18] As an interim measure, the Council of Safety was that logic. The Provincial Congress charged "that the Council of Safety shall have the supreme direction[,] regulation[,] maintenance[,] & ordering of the Army & of all Military establishment & arrangements." In order to do so, the Council was granted the "power & authority" to fulfill the vision by doing "all such matters & things … as shall by them be judged & deemed expedient & necessary."[19] Through the Council of Safety, the Provincial Congress created a logic of granting executive powers of an emergency nature.[20]

Kotter describes plans as "specific steps and timetables to implement the strategies."[21] Illustrative of this element of the system would be the Provincial Congress's provision to raise three regiments of regular troops. Two regiments were to be provided by Andrew Williamson, a prominent and relatively well-to-do planter in the Ninety Six District.[22] The Council of Safety's agreement to pay Williamson three shillings per man per day[23] is an example of budgets, which Kotter describes as "plans converted into financial projections and goals."[24]

Kotter's fourth step is "communicating the change vision." As part of this process, the Provincial Congress adopted on June 3 an "Association for Public Defense" that explained how, as the result of developments at Lexington and Concord, change was required and what that change entailed. Now, the inhabitants of South Carolina would have to bind together to secure "Freedom and Safety" from the oppressor. Such measures would require obedience to whatever the "Continental or Provincial Councils shall decree is necessary." While vowing to "resist force with force," the declaration also described reconciliation as "an Event which we most ardently desire."

Copies of the Association for Public Defense were printed, distributed throughout the colony, and signed by all supporters of the cause. The document declared that:

> The actual commencement of Hostilities against this Continent by the British Troops in the bloody Scene on the 19th of April Last, near Boston, and the Increase of arbitrary Impositions from a wicked and despotic Ministry—and the Dread of Insurrections in the Colonies, are Causes sufficient to drive an oppressed People to the use of Arms. We therefore Subscribers, Inhabitants of South Carolina, holding ourselves bound by that most Sacred of all Obligations, the Duty of good Citizens toward an injured Country and thoroughly convinced that under our present distressed Circumstances, we shall be Justified before God and Man, in resisting Force by Force, Do unite ourselves under every Tie of religion and of Honour and associate as a Band in her Defence, against every Foe; Hereby solemnly engaging that, whenever our Continental or Provincial Councils shall decree is necessary, we will go forth and be ready to sacrifice our Lives and Fortunes to secure her Freedom and Safety. This obligation to Continue in full Force until a Reconciliation shall take place between Great Britain and America, upon constitutional principles—an Event which we most ardently desire. And we will hold all those Persons inimical to the Liberty of the Colonies, who shall refuse to subscribe this Association.[25]

Modern best practices for this step of Kotter's process emphasize a more nuanced approach to communication[26] than that modelled in the Association, but the document nonetheless stands as an exemplar of clarity and alignment.

Kotter's next step is "empowering broad-based action." The idea here is to tap into the enormous potential the organization's members represent to create positive change and improve performance.[27] One example of this step employed by the Council of Safety was to send a three-person commission into the backcountry to help generate support for the Patriot cause. William Henry Drayton, a planter and lawyer; Reverend William Tennent of the Independent or Congregational Church in Charleston; and Pastor Oliver Hart of the Baptist Church in Charleston were selected for this important mission.

The commission faced a difficult task and enjoyed mixed success at best. At an August 17 meeting at Tory Thomas Fletchall's plantation on Fairforest Creek, Fletchall told the Patriots that he "would never take up arms against his King, or his countrymen; and, that the proceedings of the Congress at Philadelphia, were impolitk, disrespectful, and irritating to the King." Yet, four days later at a barbecue at Captain William Wofford's Iron Works on Lawson's Fork Creek, the commission found enough Patriot support to form the "Spartan Regiment," from which the modern city of Spartanburg traces its name, to be commanded by Colonel John Thomas. Terry Lipscomb sums up the ambiguity of the situation, noting that "many settlers of the interior were to remain loyalists throughout the Revolution, but when British troops finally invaded South Carolina, the most stubborn resistance they encountered came from the back country patriots."[28]

The backcountry also provides an example of Kotter's sixth step, which is "generating short-term wins." Because the work of transformational change is long and arduous, Kotter argues that short-term performance improvements are important in at least six ways. First, they give the effort reinforcement by showing those people involved that their sacrifices are paying off. Second, they serve as causes of celebration and positive feedback that build morale and motivation. Third, they provide concrete data that can be used to help fine-tune vision and strategies. Fourth, they undermine naysayers and resisters. Fifth, they help provide those higher in the hierarchy with evidence that the transformation is working. Sixth, they build momentum.[29]

The fact that short-term wins are needed is illustrated by the interpersonal dynamics of the First Provincial Congress, where for the first time both backcountry and lowcountry delegates sat side-by-side to work together in a formal legislative assembly. The backcountry delegates had little patience with the slow pace of parliamentary procedure and the "fine speeches" they considered to be a ploy by the low-country contingent "to weary them OUT in order to thin the House and transact business their own way." At one point, Henry William Harrington, a spokesman from the Welsh Neck settlement of upper Pee Dee, rose and threatened to lead a walkout of his fellow frontiersmen unless the assembly concluded its business that very day. Laurens lamented the backcountry delegates' unrealistic expectations, noting that "according to their Ideas everything might have been completed with extreme facility and no more words than are necessary in the bargain and sale of a Cow."[30]

Amid such an environment, it was important for the Patriots to score a short-term win in the backcountry. After the siege at Ninety Six ended in a stalemate between Williamson and Loyalists commanded by Patrick Cunningham and Lieutenant Colonel Joseph Robinson, the Council of Safety dispatched a second force into the backcountry. These were 2,500 men commanded by Colonel Richard Richardson. In the ensuing "snow campaign," Richardson's men captured Fletchall and launched a devastating attack on Cunningham's camp. The campaign demonstrated that the Provincial Congress had the power, with numbers and force, to subdue the Loyalists in the backcountry. John Gordon concludes that "by these early actions ... the side arrayed against the British had won a considerable prize: the control, however tenuous, of the South Carolina backcountry, and quiet along the frontier." However, like all short-term wins, Richardson's victory did not settle matters in the backcountry. If anything, Cherokee support for the British had only strengthened and would not be crushed until August of 1776 with a brutal expedition led by Williamson.[31]

Such short-term wins are precursors for Kotter's seventh step of "consolidating gains and producing more change." The success in the backcountry combined with the repulse of the British attack on Charleston at the battle of Sullivan's Island on June 28 to create very favorable conditions for the Patriots. From that point forward, Gordon notes that "South Carolina was free to do as it chose in the work of building a unified policy by joining in purpose and goals the powerful men of the lowcountry with the new men of the backcountry."[32]

The final step in Kotter's model is "anchoring new approaches in the culture." As new institutions were formed, the Council of Safety had served its purpose and became no longer necessary. On the morning of March 26, 1776, the Second Provincial Congress convened. When it reassembled in the afternoon, it did so as the "First Assembly of the State of South Carolina" and approved the new State Constitution. South Carolina now had declared itself to be a state, rather than a colony. John Rutledge was elected to be its first president, and Henry Laurens, his work with the Council of Safety complete, became the vice president.

Peter Northouse considers that "the primary function of leadership is to produce change and movement." "Leadership," he explains, "is about seeking adaptive and constructive change."[33] In leading the Council of Safety, Laurens fulfilled Northouse's mandate and illustrated Kotter's eight-step model of change.

Richard Furman and Charismatic Leadership

Richard Furman was born on October 9, 1755, in Esopus, New York, but within a year moved with his family to South Carolina. Raised in the Anglican tradition, Furman converted to the Baptist faith in 1771. He was ordained in the Baptist ministry in 1774 and quickly became the pastor of the recently constituted church at High Hills. During the "big meeting" held at High Hills that began in December 1773 and continued into 1774, Furman met Oliver Hart, pastor of the Baptist church in Charleston.[1] Hart was 51 and Furman 18, but in spite of their age difference, the pair embarked on an enduring friendship and fellowship, and both proved to be zealous promoters of the Patriot cause.

As tensions mounted between Britain and the American colonies, the populations of Hart's Charleston and Furman's High Hills communities viewed the developments differently. In the mid-1770s—indeed until much later—John Gordon describes South Carolina as being "in many respects two separate and distinct entities." The first was the seaboard "lowcountry" with its rich network of plantations. The majority of the planter-merchant oligarchy there was of English heritage, but an elite of French Huguenots played the dominant role. This area controlled the colony's courts, commerce, and government.[2]

The "backcountry" was basically everything else. It included the farthest reaches of the frontier as well as settlements dotting the best lands along the rivers that stretched from the coast to the interior. The northwestern reaches of the backcountry bordered the mountains that belonged to the

Cherokees. There, the inhabitants were a hodgepodge of Scotch-Irish, English, Welsh, Germans, and others, many of whom had moved south from Pennsylvania and Virginia. They resented the low country's control over the economy and the government, and, as a crime wave swept over the region in the summer of 1766, they particularly lamented the lack of law and order. Largely Baptist, Presbyterian, and Lutheran, they also cringed that their tax dollars went to support the established, but minority, Anglican Church. Feeling ignored and neglected, many saw the British Crown as a surer safeguard to their interests than a low country they felt was focused on its own aggrandizement.[3]

Thus, on the eve of the Revolution, events were unfolding differently in the two regions of South Carolina. In the thriving commercial center of Charleston, economic developments did much to shape public opinion. There, the colonists increasingly felt the pressures of British efforts to recover the costs incurred during the recently concluded French and Indian War. A series of regulatory measures and taxes was passed that culminated in the Stamp Act of 1765. Riotous crowds took to the streets of Charleston to protest the legislation and broke into houses suspected of harboring stamps. When the act was repealed in 1766, the city enjoyed a "great and prolonged celebration."[4]

The Stamp Act merely gave way, however, to further measures that many colonists found oppressive. One was the Tea Act of 1773. This act allowed the struggling British East India Company to export tea duty-free from Britain while the earlier Townshend Acts continued to impose taxes in the colonies. While not as dramatic as the Boston Tea Party, trade ships arriving in Charleston in late 1773 and 1774 were met by open hostility, and their tea was seized and placed in a warehouse and left unused for years.[5] An accompanying mass meeting held at Charleston's Exchange Building on January 3, 1774, adopted a resolution against importing or buying tea taxed to raise revenue in America.[6]

In the backcountry, isolation protected the region from so profoundly feeling the effects of the British regulatory encroachment that plagued the coastal population. Instead, the defining issue was the quest for law and order; a concern that gave rise first to vigilantism and then, more formally, to the "Regulators," a group sworn to support each other and "to execute the Laws against all Villains and Harbourers of Villains."[7] The backcountry also petitioned the provincial government for assistance, demanding more schools, jails, courts, and courthouses; stricter regulations of taverns; restrictions on "hunters"; and the creation of parishes that would provide backcountry representation in the assembly. While some in Charleston came to recognize "a kind of desperation" that was leading the backcountry to take matters in its own hands, many on the frontier saw little tangible action being taken.[8]

Richard Furman. (Artist unknown, before 1825, Wikimedia Commons)

Feeling left to their own devices, the Regulators stepped up their campaign against the outlaws, but as the Regulators gained ascendancy, they too became part of the problem. Having largely defeated the outlaws by the winter of 1767–1768, the Regulators turned their attention to the vagrants, gamblers, "infamous women," low-level pilferers, and delinquent husbands and fathers deemed as undesirable elements of backcountry society. In the process, they often usurped the authority of justices and constables, and imposed their own extra-legal punishments. In the ensuing backlash against the excesses of the Regulators, a new organization of self-proclaimed "Moderators" was formed, but Rod Andrew describes the new group as "perhaps less principled and more opportunistic" than the Regulators. Only the intervention of colonial authorities and a few backcountry leaders avoided a pitched battle between the Regulators and Moderators in March 1769. Finally, in November the King's approval of the assembly's Circuit Court Act satisfied most of the backcountry's grievances, but many blamed the coastal planters and merchants more than the King for the slow pace of change.[9] As a result and under the leadership of influential men like Robert Cunningham and his brother Patrick, a strong Tory sentiment took root in the backcountry.[10] With some three-fourths of the colony's white population residing there, the situation in the backcountry could not be ignored by those advocating separation from Britain.[11]

Thus when South Carolina set up a provincial government in 1774, the backcountry was a major concern. When the First Provincial Congress convened in its second session in June 1775, it established a Council of Safety, headed by Henry Laurens. Authorized to exercise broad executive powers in matters of defense and finance, the Council dispatched planter and lawyer William Henry Drayton, Reverend William Tennent III of the Independent or Congregational Church in Charleston, and Pastor Oliver Hart of the Baptist Church in Charleston to go to the frontier to help rally backwoodsman to the Patriot cause. The commission was of limited success, and various militia bodies began to form in the backcountry; some Whig and some Tory.[12]

Among the leaders of the Loyalist militias were the Cunningham brothers. The Whigs were anxious to keep the Cherokees on their side or at least neutral, and in an effort to appease the Cherokees, the Council of Safety sent them a shipment of powder and lead in the fall of 1775. Already feeling alienated, many Loyalists felt the Council of Safety was supplying the Cherokees so they could attack Loyalists. With tensions already high because of the earlier arrest of Robert, Patrick Cunningham ambushed the convoy on November 3 and seized the ammunition. Whig militia led by Colonel Richard Richardson responded by attacking Cunningham in his camp at the Great Cane Brake on December 22.[13] Cunningham barely escaped, but his force was shattered. With the principal Tory resistance broken, the Whigs launched a devastating campaign against the Cherokees in 1776. At this point, some Tories were so alienated that they committed what would earlier have been the unthinkable act of joining the Cherokees in fighting against white South Carolinians.[14] Under such circumstances, the backcountry was far from secure.

Richard Furman was active amid these developments. Although not a member of the Drayton–Tennent–Hart commission, Furman was conducting his own efforts in the backcountry. One example is a lengthy letter he wrote in November of 1775 "to the Residents Between the Broad and Saluda Rivers Concerning the American War for Independence," who were then believed to be readying themselves for resistance against the South Carolina Provincial Congress. After describing himself as having made "an impartial inquiry concerning the transactions of both parties," Furman proceeded to deliver a detailed and well-reasoned defense of the Congress and appeal to his "Friends, Brethren, and Fellow-Subjects" to "join in with the Great body of America; and as friend with friend, endeavor to promote the good of the whole."[15]

Around the time Furman wrote his letter, a three-day battle was occurring at Ninety Six between Whig forces commanded by Major Andrew Williamson (later promoted to Colonel then Brigadier General) sent to regain the powder captured by Cunningham and a Loyalist force led by Cunningham and Joseph Robinson. Colonel Richardson was dispatched to reinforce Williamson, and en route he was given a copy of Furman's letter. Richardson was so impressed by its eloquence that he had copies made and delivered in advance of his army to help sway public opinion.[16]

Soon after the Continental Congress adopted the Declaration of Independence on July 4, 1776, Furman marched off to Charleston with a volunteer company commanded by his brother Captain Josiah Furman and prepared for military service. By then, however, Furman's value as a spokesman for the Patriot cause was well-known, and Governor John Rutledge instead persuaded Furman to return to the backcountry where Rutledge argued that Furman's influence as a minister and supporter of independence would excel his contribution as a soldier in uniform.[17] Even the enemy seemed to agree, with Lord Charles Cornwallis reportedly stating that he "feared the prayers of the Godly youth more than the armies of Sumter and Marion." Although the declaration may well be archetypical, the fact that Cornwallis later placed a bounty of a thousand pounds on the capture of Furman certainly is indicative of the threat Cornwallis felt that Furman posed.[18]

Furman lived up to Rutledge's expectations, making effective and often-times dangerous visits to Tory settlements to champion the Patriot cause and its quest for civil and religious liberty.[19] He also used his position at the High Hills church to wield influence. The Charleston Association had been organized in 1751 at the inspiration of Furman's friend Oliver Hart to cultivate relationships among the Ashley River, Euhaw, and Welsh Neck churches. Although Furman's church at the High Hills was not a member of the Association, the body convened there in 1776 rather than in Charleston "on account of the troubles there." This conference of "dissenting churches," that is non-Anglican ones, prepared for submission to the Assembly a petition that read in part:

> That there never shall be any establishment of any one denomination or sect of Protestants by way of preference to another in this state. That no Protestant inhabitant of this state, shall by law, be obliged to pay towards the maintenance and support of a religious worship that he does not freely join in or has not voluntarily engaged to support, nor to be denied the enjoyment of any civil right merely on account of his religious principles, but that all Protestants demeaning themselves peaceably under the government established under the constitution shall enjoy free and equal privileges, both religious and civil.

When the Assembly adopted the Association's petition on January 11, 1777, the Anglican establishment that had been in existence since 1706 was eliminated.[20]

Oliver Hart reported the work of the conference to Furman in a letter of February 12. Recognizing the importance of Furman to the cause, Hart wrote:

> I hope we shall have your Voice and influence for the junction there proposed. We have now no Prospect of association with the churches on the Frontier. If you and the Congarees will come into the Plan it will be strengthening of us all.

Furman and the High Hills church promptly accepted this invitation and united with the Charleston Association.[21]

When Charleston fell in May of 1780, Furman's position became untenable. Fearing for the safety of himself and his family, he moved to North Carolina near the Virginia line on the Mayo River.[22] A refugee for the duration of the war, Furman only returned to the High Hills in the autumn of 1782. Years later, Alexander Garden would pay tribute to Furman's contribution to the Patriot cause writing, "strenuous in opposition to the invaders, he fought and he preached with energy and effect, and the recollection of his zeal to promote unanimity and steady resistance to the encroachments of the enemy ... demonstrated that ... patriot fire that warmed his youthful bosom."[23]

Charismatic Leadership

Furman's contribution to the Patriot cause serves as an example of charismatic leadership; a leadership theory built largely on the work of R. J. House and bearing many similarities to transformational leadership. Charismatic leaders not only have special personality characteristics that facilitate their leadership, but their charisma is also validated by their followers. Furman's actions and his relationship with the backcountry are very consistent with the five specific types of behaviors that Peter Northouse writes are demonstrated by charismatic leaders.[24]

First, Northouse states that charismatic leaders "are strong role models for the beliefs and values they want their followers to adopt."[25] Jay Conger adds that such leaders "build exceptional trust by demonstrating a total dedication to the cause they share with followers."[26] Furman's willingness to risk his own safety in travelling throughout Tory territory is an example.

Second, charismatic leaders "appear competent to followers."[27] They instill confidence in their subordinates by their own abilities and make extensive use of personal example and role modeling.[28] In support of this characteristic, Furman's biographer James Rogers writes that it was "as a frontiersman himself, and a young minister of dissenting faith who had traveled and preached among them, [that] Furman could address dissidents as 'Friends, Brethren, and Fellow-Subjects'" in his November 1775 letter.[29]

Third, charismatic leaders "articulate ideological goals that have moral overtones."[30] In his November letter, while acknowledging that there may be grievances born by the backcountry against the low country, Furman admonishes "that taking up arms is not the most likely way to get redress." If his letter "may be a means to convince any to stop the effusion of blood," he continues, "I shall have gained my end. Which that it may be, is my sincere and hearty prayer to Almighty God."[31]

Fourth, "charismatic leaders communicate high expectations for followers, and they exhibit confidence in their followers' abilities to meet these expectations."[32] To this end, Furman implores his backcountry readers to "join in with the Great body of America; and as friend with friend, endeavor to promote the good of the whole."[33] Charismatic leaders also employ "empowerment practices to demonstrate how their vision can be achieved."[34] Furman challenges his fellows that if they "appoint some sensible and honest men, that you should confide in, to inquire into the truth of those things I have asserted, you may be assured you will find them true."[35]

Fifth, charismatic leaders "arouse task-relevant motives in followers that may include affiliation, power, and esteem."[36] Furman's encouragement of his church at High Hills to join the Charleston Association in the pursuit of religious liberty and, in the words of Hart, to "render us more conspicuous to the State," is an example.[37]

Lastly, Loizos Heracleous and Laura Alexa Klaering note that "powerful rhetoric, the ability to capture an audience through outstanding oratorical skills, is thus tightly intertwined with charismatic leadership."[38] Furman was an accomplished orator who Rogers declares was able to "use language with exalted and persuasive eloquence."[39] Even more specifically, recognizing that "an important aspect of charisma is the relationship among leader, audience, and context," Heracleous and Klaering identify the criticality of a "leader's ability to customize their rhetoric."[40] It was perhaps in this ability to connect so intimately with the residents of the South Carolina backcountry that Furman's charismatic leadership was most apparent.

William Jasper and Heroic Leadership

Little is known for certain of William Jasper's pre-Revolutionary War history. By most accounts, he was of Irish origins, and the city of Savannah, Georgia, where he was killed in battle on October 9, 1779, has certainly accepted this assumption.[1] In 1888, the city erected a monument to Jasper in its Madison Square, and on the eve of each St. Patrick's Day, a wreath is laid there. The Savannah St. Patrick's Day Parade Committee credits Jasper with having "served as an inspiration to the Irish immigrants of Savannah during the period before the Civil War," to include their formation of the Irish Jasper Greens militia in 1842 which served in both the Mexican War and the Civil War.[2]

Charleston also has great reason to be proud of Jasper; in this case because of the heroism that he displayed on June 28, 1776, during the battle of Sullivan's Island. Sullivan's Island is one of the several narrow, low-lying barrier islands that protect Charleston's harbor. On it, Patriots under the command of Colonel William Moultrie had built a fort made out of palmetto logs on its channel end and positioned dug-in infantry and artillery on its other end. Jasper was a sergeant, serving with the Second South Carolina Regiment at this site known then as Fort Sullivan.

British Commodore Sir Peter Parker was confident that his fleet that included two ships, four frigates, and one sloop—a total of 270 guns—could easily pound the Patriots on Sullivan's Island into submission. As the British battered Fort Sullivan with their broadsides, one cannonball struck the fort's mast, and the "Moultrie" or "Liberty" flag fell to the ground outside the fort where it lay in the midst of the continued bombardment. This flag, with a crescent-shaped *gorget* emblazoned with the inscription "Liberty" in the upper-left corner of a field of blue, was an especially powerful symbol as it had been commissioned by Moultrie himself in 1775 in anticipation of the war with Britain. Moultrie described the significance of the flag in his memoirs, noting that "This was the first American flag which was displayed in South Carolina: On its being first hoisted, it gave some uneasiness to our timid friends, who were looking forward to a reconciliation: They said it had the appearance of a declaration of war ..."[3]

Realizing what was at stake, Jasper yelled something to Moultrie and then leaped down from the embrasure and grabbed the flag. As his comrades cheered, he brought the flag back safely inside the fort where he and Moultrie attached it to a makeshift staff and raised it again as a show of Patriot will and defiance.[4] Charleston County Public Library archivist and historian Dr. Nic Butler, surmises that "Jasper's dramatic act of bravery rallied the spirits of his weary comrades and may have turned the tide of the battle."[5]

Parker continued his bombardment, but the fort's spongy palmetto logs absorbed the blows, and the Patriot defense held. In turn, Moultrie's gunners concentrated their fire on Parker's two largest ships, inflicting nearly two hundred casualties on those two targets alone. As darkness fell, Parker broke off the action, retrieved the force landed earlier on the other side of the island, and sailed off to New York.[6]

Beyond the tactical considerations of the immediate battle, the successful defense of Fort Sullivan was a great strategic victory for the Patriot cause. South Carolina had long enjoyed close ties with Britain, especially in terms of mutual economic benefit. There was a strong Loyalist sentiment in the colony, and many in Britain thought that given the opportunity, many South Carolinians would rally around the Crown and take up arms against the rebels. Lieutenant General Sir Henry Clinton's later observation that "with [our taking of Charleston] I think we conquer the southern provinces and perhaps much more" reflects the strategic importance of Charleston in the eyes of the British. For the moment, however, the repulse of the British at Sullivan's Island served to thwart any Loyalist initiative and give the Patriot cause time to solidify and grow. It is for good reason that on June 28, 1777, South Carolinians began the tradition of celebrating "Palmetto Day" (eventually becoming more commonly referred to as "Carolina Day") in honor of this first clear Patriot victory in the Revolution.

Of the many American heroes on Sullivan's Island that day, it was Jasper who captured the popular imagination. The always exuberant Parson Mason Locke Weems described Jasper's heroics thusly:

> A ball from the enemy's ships carried away our flag-staff. Scarcely had the stars of liberty touched the sand, before Jasper flew and snatched them up and kissed them with great enthusiasm. Then having fixed them to the point of his spontoon, he leaped up on the breast-work amidst the storm and fury of the battle, and restored them to their daring station—waving his hat at the same time and huzzaing, "God save liberty and my country forever!"[7]

Weems was a clergyman and bookseller, who after the war took a manuscript written by Lieutenant Colonel Peter Horry about his service under Francis Marion and turned it into a romantic biography; a work which one recent scholar describes as "a hagiography full of dramatic scenes, many with obvious embellishment and some of dubious veracity."[8] Weems also invented the myth of George Washington and the cherry tree which he added to his fifth edition of his *Life of Washington*, published in 1806. In response to Weems's exaggerations, *Appletons' Cyclopaedia of American Biography* notes that a "charge of a want of veracity is brought against all Weems's writings, for it is probable he would have accounted it excusable to tell any good story to the credit of his heroes."[9] Indeed, Weems was in the business of creating larger-than-life heroes, but for whatever historical liberties he took in his works, they were rapidly devoured by a young republic yearning to establish a national identity. Through his romanticized biographies, Weems helped champion American values and shape the image of a model American citizen.[10] In Sergeant Jasper, Weems and America found such a hero.

In addition to Weems's portrayal, Jasper received many other honors. On July 4, Governor John Rutledge visited the fort and removed his own sword from his side and presented it to Jasper "as a reward for his bravery and an excitement to farther deeds of valor."[11] Rutledge also offered Jasper a commission which the modest soldier declined, explaining "were I made an officer, my comrades would be constantly blushing my ignorance, and I should be unhappy feeling my own inferiority. I have no ambition for higher rank than that of Sergeant."[12]

Like Savannah, Charleston enshrined Jasper in a monument. In the midst of the celebration of the Revolutionary War's Centennial, the city dedicated in 1877 a statue formally called "The Defenders of Fort Moultrie" (which was the name given Fort Sullivan after the battle), but commonly known as the "Jasper Monument." Located in the hallowed White Point Garden in the area of the Battery, the monument depicts a bronze sculpture of Jasper with his right arm outstretched, pointing towards Fort Moultrie, with the Moultrie Flag in his left hand. A bronze plate attached to the pedestal depicts Jasper's rescue of the flag. These and other treatments all capture Jasper as the heroic leader.

Heroic Leadership

Before the rise of the modern state, Alexander the Great served as the primary exemplar of heroic leadership. In that era, society worked "to accentuate and exaggerate the characteristics of those to whom it conceded leadership for war and conquest." Heroic leaders of Alexander's pattern were "champions of display, of skill-at-arms, of bold speech but, above all, of exemplary risk-taking." John Keegan notes that such a leader had to make for himself a mask; "a mask made in such form as will mark him to men of his time and place as the leader they want and need."[13]

In today's "time and place," Keegan notes that it is no longer sufficient for the leader to merely lead by "passing brave." Nor can the leader authenticate himself as a hero to his followers by merely confronting the specter of risk. Indeed, Keegan argues that today's reality demands the leader "must find the conviction to play the hero no more." In the place of such an active, personal role, Keegan points to the need for leaders to distinguish themselves from followers through "modesty, prudence and rationality."[14]

Keegan explains that in modern society, the leader cannot deflect risk from his followers by the singular role he takes for himself. In the post-heroic era, "the whole arena of struggle threatens everyone equally, if not indeed the led more directly than their leader."[15] While Keegan correctly describes the diffusing societal effects that have impacted leadership in the broad sense, there still remain the moments of crisis that demand the qualities of action, example, and risk-taking that marked Alexander—and Jasper—as a heroic leader.

The idea of Jasper as heroic leader aligns well with Chris Lowney's description of *magis* leadership. Summarizing a leader's duties, Lowney writes that "the leader figures out where we need to go, points us in the right direction, gets us to agree that we need to get there, and rallies us through the inevitable obstacles that separate us from the promised land."[16] Lowney calls this type of leadership *magis*, after the Latin word for "more." In braving enemy fire to rescue the highly symbolic Moultrie Flag, Jasper provided such inspiration. Lowney argues that "*magis*-driven leadership inevitably leads to heroism," which begins with each person considering, internalizing, and shaping his mission until it becomes personal."[17]

Although certainly romanticized, an 1876 version of the Jasper story epitomizes this trajectory from observation to heroic action. It begins with Jasper pleading to Moultrie, "Colonel, don't let us fight without a flag." "What can you do," Moultrie replies, "the staff is broken off?" In a crescendo of personal ownership, Jasper vows, "Then I'll fix it to a halberd and place it on the merlon of the bastion next to the enemy." With that Jasper leaped into the fray, secured the flag, and, "as he had promised," planted it in its position of prominence.[18] Even allowing for the poetic license of the day, it is easy to trace Jasper's rise to the *magis* level of leadership.

Before that pivotal day of June 28, 1776, there was little to earmark Jasper as such a hero. In his centennial address to the Georgia Historical Society, Charles Jones describes Jasper as "unknown to fame, of humble origin and slender means, without the advantage of education."[19] Francis Marion had noticed something in Jasper's character, however, and made him a sergeant. In that capacity, Jasper was "continuously with his company, faithfully discharging all duties devolved upon him and confirming himself in the confidence and esteem of his men."[20] Then, in the wink of an eye, this predictable regimen was gone, and Jasper's world was transformed. Lowney explains that leaders devote themselves to a routine of service, but when the opportunity arises, they must be able to surge to the *magis* level to meet the challenge. Indeed, Jones describes Jasper as "ever ready to encounter danger and always meeting it with entire self-possession," adding that Jasper's very name was "synonymous for all that was quick in conception and fearless in execution."[21]

Lowney also argues that heroic leadership of the sort Jasper demonstrated at Fort Sullivan comes "not just as a response to crisis but a consciously chosen *approach to life*."[22]

The case of Arland Williams is another such example. On January 13, 1983, Williams, like Jasper, found himself in a situation that completely changed his circumstances. Shortly after take-off from Washington National Airport, the Air Florida Flight 90 on which Williams was a passenger struck the 14th Street Bridge and plunged into the icy waters of the Potomac River. One of just six people to initially survive the crash, Williams repeatedly handed rescue ropes being dropped by a hovering helicopter to other survivors rather than saving himself. When the plane's tail section shifted and sank farther into the water, Williams was dragged under the water with it. He was posthumously awarded the United States Coast Guard's Gold Lifesaving Medal.

On May 19, 1993, President Ronald Reagan came to Williams's alma mater, The Citadel, to deliver the commencement address. By chance, The Citadel is located in Charleston, the scene of the epic struggle in which Jasper fought over two hundred years before. President Reagan described how Williams rose from ordinary passenger to hero. "When the challenge came," Reagan noted, Williams "was ready." Then Reagan went on to explain how men such as Jasper and Williams are able to reach such *magis* levels of leadership:

> For you see, the character that takes command in moments of crucial choices has already been determined. It has been determined by a thousand other choices made earlier in seemingly unimportant moments. It has been determined by all the little choices of years past—by all those times when the voice of conscience was at war with the voice of temptation—whispering the lie that it really doesn't matter. It has been determined by all the day-to-day decisions made when life seemed easy and crises seemed far away—the decisions that, piece by piece, bit by bit, developed habits of discipline or of laziness, habits of self-sacrifice or of self-indulgence, habits of duty and honor and integrity—or dishonor and shame.[23]

The capacity for *magis* leadership rests silently within men and women like Williams and Jasper, waiting only for the opportunity when it is needed. The reason, as novelist James Lane Allen explains, is that "adversity does not build character; it reveals it."

John Rutledge and Crisis Leadership

John Rutledge was born in Charleston in 1739, four years after his father had immigrated to South Carolina from Ireland. Sent to England to be educated, Rutledge was admitted to Middle Temple to study law and was called to the English bar in 1760. Later that year, he returned home and was admitted to the South Carolina bar in 1761.[1]

When he was just 22 years old, Rutledge represented Mary Cooke in her suit against William Lennox for repeatedly breaking promises to marry her. Cooke was awarded 2,500 pounds in damages, and Rutledge's "eloquence astonished all who heard him." David Ramsay, a contemporary of Rutledge's, declared that with his spectacular performance, Rutledge "burst forth at once the able lawyer and accomplished orator," and a large volume of business, involving "the most difficult cases" and "the largest fees," was soon his.[2]

In addition to his success as a lawyer, Rutledge was an active politician. He served in the Commons House of Assembly from 1761 to 1775 and was one of South Carolina's delegates to the Stamp Act Congress in New York City in 1765. Still, Rutledge was not an early advocate of independence.[3]

On March 26, 1775, Rutledge was elected president (or governor) of South Carolina. When a British fleet appeared off of Charleston Harbor in June 1776, Rutledge displayed the fortitude and determination that would characterize his role as a crisis leader in the Revolution. Major General Charles Lee, the commander of the Southern Department, urged abandoning the Patriot defenses at Sullivan's Island, but a resolute

Rutledge told Colonel William Moultrie "You will not [evacuate the fort] without an order from me. I would sooner cut off my right hand than write one."[4]

Although repulsed in their 1776 attack, the British returned to Charleston with a more determined force in 1780 and soon commenced siege operations. They broke ground on their first parallel on the night of April 1, and during the first week, they completed a line of six connected redoubts. The Patriot artillery fire did not appreciably slow progress, and by April 10, the British had cannon in place in two of the six batteries. At this point, the British commanders Major General Sir Henry Clinton and Admiral Marriott Arbuthnot were confident enough in their advantage to issue their first surrender demand. "Regretting the effusion of Blood and distress which much now commence," the pair felt compelled "conformant to humanity to warn the Town and Garrison of Charlestown of the havoc and devastation with which they are threatened from the formidable force surrounding them by Sea and Land."[5]

Major General Benjamin Lincoln, who had replaced Lee as commander of the Southern Department, summarily refused this initial British overture but obviously was gravely concerned. On April 12, he assembled his generals to sign a joint letter urging Rutledge to leave Charleston. Rutledge had previously rejected such recommendations from Lincoln, Moultrie, and others, arguing that he could not abandon his post in time of danger. This time, the fact that Lincoln's entire war council signed the request gave Rutledge the reassurance his conscience demanded.

Rutledge departed the next day, using the only remaining escape route across the Cooper River, and headed for the backcountry to begin his season as governor-in-exile. Before he left, he appointed Brigadier General Christopher Gadsden to the office of lieutenant governor in place of Thomas Bee who was then attending the Continental Congress in Philadelphia. Rutledge took John Lewis Gervais, Daniel Huger, and Charles Pinckney with him, leaving the civil government of Charleston in the hands of Gadsden and the more radical members of the Privy Council.[6] Before departing, Rutledge dismissed the South Carolina militia from active duty lest "they should be found in arms."[7]

Rutledge had made his escape not a moment too soon. The very next day, the British routed the American garrison guarding Monck's Corner and Charleston's vital corridor to communications with the interior. By April 19, the British had closed to within two hundred yards of the Patriot positions defending Charleston. While Rutledge was unsuccessfully attempting to stir backcountry militia to come to Charleston's aid, reinforcements from New York and Savannah had raised Clinton's force to ten thousand men. The end seemed but a matter of time. Indeed, on May 12, after some six weeks of siege, Charleston surrendered.

John Rutledge. (Artist, John Trumbull, c. 1791, National Portrait Gallery, Smithsonian Institution)

Rutledge arrived at Salisbury, North Carolina, on June 2 and soon decided that "the most effectual service which I could render to my Country was, to repair immediately to Congress, lay before them the Situation ... in the Southern States, and endeavour to obtain an Exchange of the Troops who are now Prisoners in Chas. Town, a Supply of Men, Arms, and military Stores, and an able and experienced General for the Command in the Southern department."[8]

When Rutledge reached Philadelphia on July 3, he learned that Horatio Gates had been appointed to that command position three weeks earlier. Rutledge then turned his attention to obtaining the necessary funds for South Carolina's defense and was able to secure authorization to draw on the Continental treasury to support his state troops. Maryland also advanced 14,000 pounds directly to Rutledge.[9]

Rutledge also had the opportunity to relay his strategic advice to General George Washington, urging him to dispatch a large joint and combined force to drive the British from South Carolina and Georgia as soon as the summer campaign season in New York had ended. A sympathetic Washington replied that he could not then send such a force, but asked Rutledge to send him information about supplies, possible landing sites, and enemy troop dispositions.[10]

In late August, Rutledge concluded that he had accomplished all that he could in Philadelphia and set out to join Gates's army. He had cause for some optimism based on his partial successes with Congress and news that partisan forces led by Thomas Sumter, Francis Marion, and Andrew Pickens had risen up to stem the British advances. Such hopes were dashed when Rutledge learned while at Susquehanna Falls in late August or early September of Gates's defeat at Camden. "At present, our prospect is truly gloomy," Rutledge confessed. Nonetheless, he continued "we must not, however, despair, tho' at present, I do not see how We are to retrieve our affairs."[11]

Rutledge set out for Hillsborough, North Carolina, where he met Gates and the remnants of his shattered command. He spent the next year with or near the main army as it traveled from Hillsborough to Salisbury to Charlotte to Cheraw. Rutledge's biographer James Haw records that "seemingly everything needed attention, and the governor set about doing what he could with his usual energy."[12]

Seeing Gates's depleted Continentals convinced Rutledge that "if any Thing material is done for our poor State in any reasonable Time it will probably be by our despised shabby Militia."[13] He therefore set out to legitimize organizational and logistical support to the South Carolinians in the field. One important step occurred on October 6 when Rutledge appointed Sumter as brigadier general in command of the state's militia, telling him the immediate task was "that all the enemy's outposts be broke up, and the several parties whom they have throughout the country cut off: In short, that they be harassed and attacked, in every quarter of So. Carolina and Georgia, where they can be to advantage."[14] Sumter's appointment was followed in December with appointments of Marion and Pickens.

Rutledge began a regular correspondence with Sumter and other partisan leaders, and in November he traveled some twenty miles from the Continental Army's camp at Charlotte to New Acquisition, South Carolina, to confer with Sumter. Seeing the impoverished condition of Sumter's men, Rutledge began advocating for help from North Carolina, and in January 1781, that state agreed to lend South Carolina 100,000 pounds to supply its militia.[15]

The greatest assistance to South Carolina occurred, however, the previous December when Nathanael Greene arrived in Charlotte as the new commander of the Southern Department. John Matthews had told Greene to expect to find in Rutledge a man of high character. "The more you know of him," Matthews explained, "the greater reasons you will have, for admiring his many amiable qualities, and extensive abilities. Both his heart, and his head are sound, and you will find him one of those characters, who improve on acquaintance."[16] Indeed, Rutledge and Greene would form an effective partnership and a deep mutual respect, and often shared hardships and dangers as they moved across North Carolina. On one occasion, which John Buchanan speculates was after the battle of Guilford Court House, the pair shared the same bed in a building "little better than a hovel." Each accused the other of being a restless bedfellow until they realized a hog had joined them in their humble accommodations. Such shared experiences seemed to create a bond between the men.[17]

Greene and Rutledge proved to be highly deferential to each other. On one occasion when Lieutenant Colonel Henry Lee purchased "a quantity of indigo for the purpose of procuring clothing" for his Legion, Greene admonished Lee that it would be "derogatory to Government for individuals to take a measure of that sort without the order of the Governor." Although Rutledge was "a man of great liberality," Greene counseled Lee to treat the Governor "with every degree of respect and attention." Lee promptly apologized and assured Greene that "it is impossible for me even to think of any act which can disturb the mind of the governor."[18]

Likewise, Rutledge was also very trusting of Greene and willing to accommodate him. Even when Greene and Rutledge were together, Greene felt the need that Marion and Sumter report directly to him, explaining that the command relationship was "not from disrespect [to Rutledge] but from the nature and necessity of the thing." However, Greene noted, "such matters as are worthy [of Rutledge's] notice or concern the interest or security of the State I communicate to him." Rutledge was comfortable with the arrangement.[19]

The harmony between Rutledge and Greene would be very useful when it came time to restore civil government. The safety that Greene gained by winning the Race to the Dan created an opportunity for Rutledge to go to Philadelphia to deliver an accurate report of the situation in the South and to lobby for additional aid. While Rutledge was away, Greene's successful prosecution of the "War of the Posts" led him on May 14 to write Rutledge that "From the State in which I find things and the confusion and persecution which I foresee, I could wish the Civil Government might be set up immediately ... to have the minds of the people formed to the Labels of Civil rather than Military authority." It was a prospect which Rutledge had long anticipated, and he was eager to make it a reality.[20]

Still, there were many practical matters to be overcome. Although Rutledge thought that reopening all branches of government "would have a great Effect, on our affairs particularly abroad," in August he decided he could not open the district courts "for want of Judges and Attorney General." Likewise, he delayed scheduling elections until prisoners and exiles could be returned, believing that to "exclude our worthy Friends" from potential seats in the legislature would be "ungenerous" to them and "injurious to the publick, to deprive it of their Abilities and Services."

It was not until the latter part of November that Rutledge ordered elections for the state legislature on December 17 and 18. He announced January 8, 1782 as the date for the new legislature to meet in Camden, but later accepted Greene's recommendation to change the location to Jacksonborough.[21] Ultimately, the first meeting of the South Carolina legislature since 1780 assembled on January 17 and adjourned on February 26.[22]

Rutledge challenged the assembly that "the interest and honor, the safety and happiness of our country depend, so much on the result of your deliberations that I flatter myself you will proceed in the weighty business before you, with firmness and temper, with vigor, unanimity and dispatch." Among the matters discussed were the raising and organizing of a state militia, devising a plan to punish those citizens disloyal to the Revolution in accordance with the degree of disloyalty, repealing the use of the Crown's tender and any monies in circulation at that time, formulating a debt-management plan and suspending taxation, and restoring civil, criminal, and admiralty forms of justice. Rutledge also praised Marion, Pickens, and Sumter, whose "enterprising spirit and unremitted perseverance under many difficulties are deserving of great applause" and congratulated Greene "on the pleasing change of affairs, which under the blessing of God,... and bravery of the great and gallant General Greene and the intrepidity of the officers and men under his command, have happily effected."[23]

Rutledge too would receive his share of praise for the leadership he had displayed in South Carolina's season of crisis. Moultrie declared in his *Memoirs* that Rutledge had done "every thing that could be done for the good of the country" and that it was crucial "to have a man of such great abilities, firmness, and decision amongst them."[24] Had Rutledge allowed himself to be captured at Charleston rather than going into exile, such capacity would have been lost. Perhaps the final victory would still have been gained, but Rutledge's leadership certainly contributed to it.

Crisis Leadership

Crisis leadership often is the result of a sudden crisis, such as fire or a shooting. Rutledge instead found himself immersed in a sustained crisis, which Michaela Kerrissey and Amy Edmondson describe as "an ongoing period of intense difficulty, trouble, or uncertainty."[25] In such situations, the primary goal is building resiliency and convincing people that the persistence and sacrifice required to meet the challenge is worth it. Rather than the "fast reactivity" required in a sudden crisis, Kerrissey and Edmondson argue that sustained crises require "intentional proactivity."

Rutledge modelled such intentional proactivity in several ways. He made two trips to Philadelphia to advocate for support. He built the organizational and logistical capacity necessary to sustain the meager forces South Carolina had in the field. He exercised decentralization through his partisan commanders. He invested the time and presence necessary to forge a relationship of trust and mutual support with Greene. He delayed his ardent desire to restore civil government until the conditions existed that would allow it to be successful. Kerrissey and Edmondson note that leadership in the midst of a sustained crisis requires a "different approach." As a one-man government in exile, Rutledge met that challenge.

Thomas Sumter and Transactional Leadership

Thomas Sumter was born on August 14, 1734, in Hanover County, Virginia. After having served in the French and Indian War, he relocated to Long Cane, South Carolina, to escape imprisonment for debt. He soon settled at a crossroads near Eutaw Springs and Nelson's Ferry along the Santee River and opened a store. There he acquired more property and slaves, and in 1767, he married a wealthy widow named Mary Cantey Jameson. The couple settled across the river at Jameson's Great Savannah plantation. As the rebellion gathered momentum, Sumter was elected to the First and Second Provincial Congresses.[1]

When the war broke out, Sumter raised a local militia group and was promoted to lieutenant colonel in 1776. After participating in several early campaigns, he resigned his commission in 1778 because of a lack of activity and returned to his plantation.

With the fall of Charleston in 1780, the British launched several incursions into the interior of South Carolina. During one such foray, Lieutenant Colonel Banastre Tarleton burned Sumter's plantation. Angered by this personal attack, Sumter responded by rallying a partisan force to help keep the Patriot cause alive through one of its lowest points in the war.

That summer, Sumter fought the British at Rocky Mount, Hanging Rock, and Fishing Creek, before being made a brigadier general on October 6, 1780. After an engagement at Fishdam Ford on November 9, Sumter enjoyed perhaps his finest hour, defeating Tarleton at Blackstock's Plantation on November 20. Sumter, however, sustained a wound during that engagement that kept him from active campaigning until early in 1781.

By then, Major General Nathanael Greene had arrived in South Carolina with the Third Continental Army in December 1780 and requested the cooperation of the South Carolina militias. Preferring to operate independently, Sumter was often an irritant to Greene and suffered a series of failures at Fort Granby, Belleville Plantation, and Fort Watson in February 1781.

It was after these setbacks that Sumter announced in March a plan to raise a regular, standing militia of 10-month enlistments. The plan became known as "Sumter's Law" and proposed a graduated system of paying officers and men in slaves that were anticipated to be captured from Loyalists. A colonel, for example, was "to receive three grown negroes and one small negro." A private was authorized "one grown negro." Each rank in between had its own allotment. Governor John Rutledge agreed to the plan, and Greene reluctantly accepted it, insisting that the Loyalists receive certificates for their seized property.[2]

For all its immorality, the economic incentives underpinning Sumter's Law were obvious. First of all, slaves were essential to South Carolina's agricultural economy, especially its labor-intensive production of rice.[3] As George Milligen-Johnston wrote in 1763, "the Negro slaves ... do all the Labour or hard Work in the Country, and are a considerable Part of the Riches of the Province."[4] To this demand, there was the additional factor of supply. Between 1700 and 1775, 40 percent of the Africans imported to North America passed through Charleston. South Carolina's population quickly became majority Black; so much so that in 1737 a Swiss immigrant remarked that "Carolina looks more like a Negro country than a country settled by white people."[5] By 1765, South Carolina's Black population of 90,000 was more than double its white population of 40,000. The result was a bustling slave market that made slaves an extremely valuable commodity. During the colonial period, the average price of a slave was 30 pounds sterling ($2,700). Skilled slaves sold for as much as 200 pounds sterling ($18,000).[6]

It is no surprise then that Sumter's Law had its intended effect in drawing recruits. In fact, Sumter's ranks were so swelled that he could not pay their promised bonuses. To pacify his complaining soldiers, Sumter resorted to plunder, such as in July 1781 when he ordered

Captain William Ransome Davis to seize the slaves, horses, salt, indigo, and medical supplies in and around Georgetown. In addition to the inherent moral bankruptcy of Sumter's Law, the raid revealed some of its other problems. Georgetown was Francis Marion's territory, and Sumter's incursion created operational friction and angst. While it "may Interfer with my Command," Marion lamented, "[I] suppose I must submit." When Greene belatedly learned of the situation, he noted, "General Sumter's taking the goods at Georgetown was certainly wrong, but it is now too late to prevent it."[7]

Thomas Sumter. (Artist, William Armstrong, c. 1835, National Portrait Gallery)

Transactional Leadership

Sumter's Law is an example of "transactional leadership" which involves exchanging things of value with subordinates to advance the leader's and the subordinate's interests. Both the leader and the subordinate may benefit from the project's overall success, but the differences in their individual interests require motivations to be tailored to what each hope to gain from the process and outcome. The relationship is "not that of collaboration toward a common goal but of barter—and barterers have a common transaction but different goals within that single transaction." Garry Wills explains that an employer and employee may have a mutually beneficial relationship, "but that does not mean they are working toward a common goal. The worker wants dignity, reward, good relations with his fellows and his work. The employers want the most work to be had, under such restrictions, for making and selling products and services that reward owners or shareholders of the business."[8] Both benefit from the business' successful operation, but for different reasons and as a result of different motivations.

As a *quid pro quo* exchange of carrots and sticks, transactional leadership is a difficult system to manage because it requires constant monitoring of behavior and regular re-negotiation of what items are valued. Sumter experienced this difficulty when his raids failed to capture the needed number of slaves, leaving one observer to report to Governor Rutledge that Sumter found himself commanding "the most discontented sett of men I ever saw."[9] As a result, Sumter had to resort to additional means of plunder to satisfy the demands of his men. As Sumter learned, it is hard to move to a self-sustaining leadership environment with transactional leadership, because the process must be renewed with each transaction.[10]

An alternative to transactional leadership is "transformational leadership," and in 1978, James MacGregor Burns described the contrast between the two styles in his pioneering work called *Leadership*. Burns explored the roles of leadership and followership, and argued that the most effective leaders were those who tapped into the motivations and needs of their followers. Thus, rather than the relationship of exchanges that characterizes transactional leadership, transformational leadership is the process whereby an individual engages with others to the point of creating a connection that raises the level of motivation and morality in both the leader and follower. The transformational leader responds to the needs and motives of followers in a way that allows them to achieve their fullest potential.[11]

This sense of fulfillment must transcend the typical needs associated with transactional leadership such as financial reward, and extend to intangible needs such as learning, self-worth, pride, competence, and serving others. Transformational leadership taps into what people find enjoyable about work or an activity, rather than merely its utilitarian value. It seeks to allow people to find motivation from an inner sense of purpose rather than from extrinsic factors.[12]

Francis Marion rejected Sumter's Law, stating that it was "inhuman, immoral, and violative of due process."[13] He went on to issue strict orders to protect slaves from falling victim to Sumter's seizures. Marion charged that he would "not suffer Negroes to be seized on or taken out of his Brigade."[14] This was, in fact, his attitude toward all seizures. "Any soldier taking any article from any plantation from white or black," he warned his men, "will be deemed a marauder & plunderer & shall suffer immediate death."[15]

Instead of the transactional leadership of Sumter, Marion led his men with a much more transformational style. The difference is evidenced in the observations of the British officer who was present for the celebrated "sweet potato dinner"; an event no doubt embellished by Pastor Weems but nonetheless instructive as a contrast between the effects of transactional and transformational leadership.

As Weems reports it, a British officer from Georgetown was conducted into Marion's secret camp to arrange for an exchange of prisoners. The officer was led to Marion, and the details of the exchange were soon settled. The visitor then prepared to leave, but Marion insisted, "Oh no! It is now about our time of dining; and I hope, sir, you will give us the pleasure of your company to dinner."

Looking around, the guest "could see no sign of a pot, pan, Dutch oven, or any other cooking utensil that could raise the spirits of a hungry man." Instead, there was only one of Marion's men tending to a heap of sweet potatoes roasting over some embers. On Marion's command, the partisan cook gathered some potatoes from the pile, blew and brushed off the ashes, and delivered them to Marion and his guest on a large piece of pine bark. As the soldier placed the meal between the two enemies, Marion said, "I fear, sir, our dinner will not prove so palatable to you as I could wish; but it is the best we have."

Midway through the meal the British officer broke into a laugh at the circumstances and marveled to Marion at the difference between their two camps. To the Briton's further surprise, Marion confessed that he and his men often subsisted on much less than what was now before them. When the visitor expressed his amazement that Marion could stand such conditions, Weems credits Marion with a poetic discourse on liberty, the heart, and freedom.

To the Briton's disbelief that Marion and his men sustained their support for the Patriot cause on the terms of "all fighting and no pay! and no provisions but potatoes!," Marion replied, "Why, sir, these things depend on feeling." "The heart is all," Marion continued, "and, when that is much interested, a man can do any thing." "I am in love," Marion declared, "and my sweetheart is liberty."

When the British officer returned to Georgetown, he reported his experience to Lieutenant Colonel John Watson, who noted that the man looked quite serious. "I have cause, sir, to look serious," said the officer. "I have seen an American general and his officers, without pay, and almost without clothes, living on roots and drinking water; and all for liberty! What chance have we against such men!" Weems adds that "the young officer was so struck with Marion's sentiments, that he never rested until he threw up his commission, and retired from the service."[16]

Of course, there will always be an element of transactional leadership present in the workplace. Individuals rightfully expect to receive pay and perks in exchange for a certain level of performance. But Joseph Badaracco cautions against creating a system in which people are "running faster and faster, like rodents on a treadmill to get larger and larger monetary pellets." Instead, he admonishes leaders to foster an environment in which people "work with devotion and passion to express who they are and what they really care about."[17] The transformational leadership style displayed by Marion is much more prone to foster such an environment than the transactional style embodied in Sumter's Law.

Francis Marion and Emotional Intelligence

Born in 1732 in Berkeley County, South Carolina, Francis Marion assumed management of the family plantation in 1750 after his father died. Marion gained valuable experience in irregular warfare as a lieutenant in the expedition against the Cherokees led by Lieutenant Colonel James Grant in 1761. At the conclusion of that campaign, Marion returned to farming and in 1773 purchased a plantation at Pond Bluff along the Santee River, four miles below Eutaw Springs. By the beginning of the American Revolution, Marion was a well-respected member of plantation society, exemplified by his being elected as a delegate to South Carolina's first Provincial Congress.

In 1775, Marion was selected as captain in the Second South Carolina Regiment of Infantry. He worked his way up through the officer corps and eventually became a lieutenant colonel and commander of the regiment.[1] Marion avoided capture when Charleston fell in May of 1780 and was ordered by Major General Horatio Gates to take command of the Williamsburg militia camped at Witherspoon's Ferry on Lynches Creek. Arriving on August 17, 1780, the day after Gates's army was decimated at the battle of Camden, Marion began a remarkable career as a partisan. One key to his extraordinary success was Marion's high degree of emotional intelligence; a combination of motivation, self-awareness, self-regulation, empathy, and social skills that allows leaders to effectively manage their emotions in all manners of situations.[2] Marion possessed each of these competencies in strong measure and used them to be a truly transformative leader.

Motivation

Daniel Goleman argues that all effective leaders are "driven to achieve beyond expectations—their own and everyone else's," and that their motivation comes not from pecuniary gain but from "a deeply embedded drive to achieve for the sake of achievement."[3]

Joseph Badaracco agrees, writing that "leaders have a deep conviction that they must make something happen and they devote themselves to making it happen—despite obstacles, frustrations, failures, and very steep costs."[4] "Because leadership is often a long, hard struggle against opposing forces," he continues, "it requires determination, commitment, strength, and sheer will." Under such circumstances, the leader must be able to muster "an almost superhuman intensity of focus and effort."[5] All this energy is driven by the leader's need to achieve. Marion displayed this high level of motivation immediately after the fall of Charleston in May 1780.

Although Marion escaped from Charleston before it fell, the city's surrender posed a new threat to his safety. Additional British troops could now be released to scour the countryside for suspected rebels and eradicate the uprising. In fact, Sir Henry Clinton soon sent three columns of men into the interior of South Carolina to strengthen British control. The situation worsened still for the Patriots when Lieutenant Colonel Banastre Tarleton was ordered to pursue what remained of the organized resistance. Tarleton caught up with Colonel Abraham Buford's 350 Virginia Continental dragoons at Waxhaws near the North Carolina border and decimated his enemy. One hundred and thirteen Virginians were killed and over two hundred were wounded, compared to just five British killed and fourteen wounded. In the wake of Tarleton's rampage, even Governor John Rutledge was forced to flee to North Carolina.[6]

Charleston's *Royal Gazette* boasted that there was "NOT A REBEL IN ARMS IN THE COUNTRY," and rumors circulated that the Continental Congress was preparing to cede the three southernmost colonies to Britain. On May 22, Clinton issued a proclamation offering pardon to anyone who professed allegiance to the Crown, and many people flocked to take the oath.[7]

Given such circumstances, Scott Aiken concludes, "History would not have condemned [Marion] had he, a supernumerary officer without a command, limping on an ankle not yet healed, faded into the woods of the South Carolina Lowcountry. He had already served in his state's militia against the Cherokees and earlier in the American Revolution."[8] Instead, Marion willingly accepted responsibility to make even greater contributions; in spite of the risks and sacrifices associated with his decision. He made his way to Hillsborough, North Carolina, the designated rendezvous point for Continental troops in the South after the fall of Charleston, arriving there sometime after July 27.[9]

Francis Marion. (Artist, P. P. Carter, South Carolina House Chamber Portraits, Columbia, SC)

Major General Horatio Gates, the commander of the Southern Department, gave Marion a cool reception, and Marion's prospects for being given significant responsibilities under Gates were slim. What seemed much more promising to Marion was news of the recent exploits of Thomas Sumter, and the defeat of a detachment of Tarleton's dragoons and Loyalist militia commanded by Captain Christian Huck at Williamson's Plantation on July 11.

Rather than while away his time under Gates's obvious disinterest, Marion asked to be released from the army and build off Sumter's partisan success as commander of the militia in the Williamsburg District. "Not unhappy"[10] to see Marion go, Gates released him, and Marion fortunately left the day before the disastrous battle of Camden. For Marion, it was a bold and uncertain move, and one for which John Oller notes there was "no script telling [Marion] what to do or where to go."[11]

Instead, it was Marion's motivation to serve the Patriot cause and his desire to achieve on its behalf that led him into a precarious future. In a description which Goleman would no doubt consider exemplary of the motivation required of an emotionally intelligent leader, Lieutenant Colonel Henry Lee described Marion as "enthusiastically wedded to the cause of liberty ... The commonwealth was his sole object; nothing selfish, nothing mercenary, soiled his ermine character."[12]

Self-awareness

Goleman describes self-awareness as "having a deep understanding of one's emotions, strengths, weaknesses, needs, and drives."[13] One of the most important—and encouraging—aspects of Goleman's research is that emotional intelligence can be learned and improved upon. That Marion improved his self-awareness based on introspection and reflection is evidenced by tactical improvements he made after the engagement at Black Mingo Creek.

On September 24, 1780, Marion left the Great White Marsh and traveled three days until at Lynches River, he received the latest intelligence about Colonel John Coming Ball's dispositions in the Williamsburg District. The report was that British security was lax. Marion immediately initiated a 12-mile night movement toward Ball's positions around Black Mingo Creek.[14]

Shortly before midnight, the Patriots were crossing Willtown Bridge, about a mile upstream from Ball's location. Although the riders approached under the cover of a very dark night, a British sentry heard the clamor of their horses' hooves as they crossed the loose planks of the bridge. He fired a shot that alerted the rest of Ball's men.[15]

With surprise lost, Marion ordered an immediate attack, and in just 15 minutes, he had routed the British, killing at least 3 and wounding or capturing 13 more. It was a clear Patriot victory, but Parson Weems lamented that "the surprise and destruction of the tories would have been complete, had it not been for the alarm given by our horses' feet in passing Black Mingo bridge, near which they were encamped." As a result, Weems reports that "Marion never afterwards suffered us to cross a bridge in the night, until we had first spread our blankets on it, to prevent noise."[16]

It should be noted that John Oller believes Marion had employed such a precaution in engagements prior to Black Mingo, and that Weems tells the tale as he did in order to "make a better story."[17] Perhaps Oller is correct, but the point remains the same. Whether at Black Mingo or elsewhere, Marion at some point learned the hard way that rickety planks create noise, and he implemented a countermeasure. Furthermore, Marion continued to glean lessons for future use. A month later, Marion achieved "one of his greater successes in the general region of the Santee River" with a victory at Tearcoat Swamp.[18] There, "using tactics proved at Black Mingo," Marion again divided his men into three groups and routed a British force commanded by Lieutenant Colonel Samuel Tynes.[19] Whether in failure or success, Marion continued to build his self-awareness and adjust and improve his tactics.

Self-regulation

The British opposing Marion held many advantages. Their leaders tended to have more experience and more formal training. They had more resources. They were a global power. Marion's self-awareness included knowledge of these disparities and led him to impose a degree of self-regulation with regard to the tactics he would pursue. Rather than confronting the British military preponderance head-on, Marion generally confined himself to tactics that involved surprise, mobility, and intelligence, and avoided decisive engagement. His limited manpower also necessitated that he preserve his force and avoid risking high numbers of casualties. Locked in a war of attrition, Marion had to sustain his ability to harass and disrupt the British while safeguarding his force's ability to continue to survive and fight.[20]

The engagement at Blue Savannah on September 4, 1780, is illustrative of the standard self-regulation Marion incorporated in his tactics. Marion had with him slightly over 50 men encamped at Port's Ferry on Britton's Neck. Opposing him were at least 250 British

Marion Crossing the Pee Dee. (Artist, William Ranney, 1850, Amon Carter Museum of American Art)

commanded by Major Micajah Ganey. On September 4, Ganey led his men from their camp on the Little Pee Dee River in an attempt to surprise Marion.[21]

Marion, however, had learned of the Loyalist mobilization and had begun his own march in search of Ganey. Since both forces wore homespun, Marion instructed his 50 or so men to place white cockades in their caps to distinguish friend from foe. To preserve secrecy, Marion did not tell his men their destination, but placed the capable Major John James and a group of select horsemen as an advanced guard.[22]

After about two hours of movement, one of James's scouts reported a Loyalist company of forty-five mounted men blocking the road. James ordered his men to attack, and the startled British scattered and fled. James lost one man wounded, and only fifteen men from Ganey's advance guard escaped; the rest were killed, wounded, or captured.

Marion learned from the prisoners that the main body of Loyalists was about three miles away and began moving in that direction. In about

10 minutes he ran into Major Jesse Barefield's men, who had been alerted of the action and were waiting in battle line. Barefield had a force of 200, and Marion wisely decided to break contact. As he did, he feigned fear and using his tactic of retreat, enticed Barefield to pursue.[23]

Marion halted his men at Blue Savannah, an open sandy swale surrounded by a screen of pine saplings and undergrowth, and set up an ambush. Thinking Marion was on the run, Barefield pressed onward without proper security into the ambush. As Marion's mounted men attacked, the unprotected Loyalist infantry broke and ran into the surrounding woods and the Little Pee Dee Swamp.[24]

Marion pursued the British until the edge of the swamp and then returned to camp. He knew that following the enemy into the swamp would be dangerous and time consuming, and he had the necessary self-regulation to know when to stop. Marion had suffered just 3 or 4 men wounded compared to 30 casualties among the British. At Blue Savannah, Marion successfully accomplished his mission to harass and attrite the British while preserving his own force. Remarking on this aspect of Marion's self-regulation, Lieutenant Colonel Henry Lee observed that Marion "risked the lives of his troops only when necessary."[25]

Empathy

The traditional yardstick for interacting empathetically with others is the Golden Rule's admonition to treat others as we would like to be treated ourselves. Marshall Goldsmith notes that a better standard might be to treat others as *they* would like to be treated. His logic is that we all have different levels of tolerance for life's inconsistencies, annoyances, and difficulties. If it is within our ability to absorb some circumstance, we sometimes have a hard time understanding why other people can't also just suck it up and deal with it. Real understanding of others requires us to see things not from our point of view but from the other person's. To that end, leaders must remember that they are leading other people; not themselves.[26] Marion displayed this level of empathy in how he led partisan soldiers.

Many of Marion's men were small farmers who lived along the Black and Pee Dee Rivers.[27] As such, they were beholden to the agricultural cycle for their livelihood and survival. They were also responsible for the safety of their families and the security of their property. Whenever they were in the field with Marion, his men had understandable concerns for their crops and loved ones. As William Simms explains, the planting of crops "though not allowed by the regular disciplinarian, was, in the mind of the militiaman, a duty quite as imperative as any that he owed to his family. Indeed, it was inseparable from his necessities that, when the Government did not give him bread, he must make it for himself. His family could not starve, and if he could fight without pay, it was not possible to do so without food."[28]

Marion understood these needs and allowed his men great discretion to come and go as they felt necessary to tend to their responsibilities at home. As a result, Hugh Rankin estimates that Marion seldom had the same people under his command for longer than two weeks.[29] This significant turnover created numerous difficulties for Marion in terms of training, readiness, and predictability, but he did not interfere with it because of his sensitivity to the situations of his men.

One example of this aspect of Marion's emotional intelligence occurred in late 1780 when British Major James Wemyss took advantage of Marion's absence to ransack the Williamsburg District, which was where many of Marion's men made their homes. At the time, Marion was in the middle of a successful offensive, but instead of pressing his advantage, he broke contact with the British and allowed his men to leave the field to check on their families. As Simms explains, in such cases, "the necessity of providing for, and protecting destitute families, starving wives and naked children, was more imperative than that of a remote and fancied liberty."[30]

By allowing his men the freedom to come and go, Marion was modelling empathy of the sort epitomized in Goldsmith's interpretation of the Golden Rule. Marion's personal commitment and endurance were extraordinary, remaining on the campaign trail continuously for most of two years. While he held himself to that high standard, he recognized that his men had different needs and expectations, and he understood that they would have to come and go based on their personal situations.[31] Such empathy placed a burden on Marion by limiting his freedom of action, but his men responded to his obvious concern for their needs by giving him their steadfast loyalty.

Social skills

Goleman describes social skill as "friendliness with a purpose; moving people in the direction you desire." He considers it "the culmination of the other dimensions of emotional intelligence," explaining for example that "people tend to be very effective at managing relationships when they can understand and control their emotions and emphasize with the feelings of others."[32] This synthesis is present in the way Marion responded to the personal situations of partisan soldiers. His mastery of social skills is also demonstrated in his dealings with the "conniving lieutenant" in early 1776 at Fort Johnson.

By this time Marion was a captain. Under his command was an unnamed lieutenant who previously served under other captains, all of whom the dramatic Parson Weems reports had "spoken of him as a slippery, worthless fellow, whom they knew not what to do with."[33] The lieutenant was, according to Weems, "destitute of soul as a monkey."[34]

The lieutenant became aware of a cockfight in Dorchester that he wanted to attend and, in order to obtain leave from the fort, concocted a story that he wished to visit his dying father. Marion quickly assented, telling the deceiver, "To be sure, lieutenant, go, by all means, go and wait upon your father; but return as soon as possible, for you see how much we have to do."[35]

As was his plan, the lieutenant abused Marion's trust, and it was some two weeks later before he returned to duty. Marion was at the time sitting with his officers. Rather than publicly giving the lieutenant the admonishment he deserved, Marion showed tremendous self-regulation and simply pretended not to notice the lieutenant. Embarrassed and trying to recover himself, the lieutenant said, "I am sorry, sir, to have overstayed my time so long; but—but I could not help it—but now I am returned to do my duty." By this time, Marion was wise to the charade and, with what Weems describes as "a most notifying neglect," replied, "Aye, lieutenant, is that you? Well, never mind it—there is no harm done—I never missed you."[36]

The lieutenant slinked away and soon found himself the source of his comrades' great amusement. He had to admit that in Marion he had met his match. "I was never at a loss before," he lamented, "to manage all other officers that were ever set over me. As for our colonel [William Moultrie], he is a fine, honest, good-natured old buck. But I can wind him round my finger like a pack thread. But as for the stern, keen-eyed Marion, I dread him."[37]

Marion knew exactly how to deal with a pompous and self-serving character like the lieutenant. Even after the initial rebuke, Marion kept him at arms' length and "when visited on business, he would receive and treat him with a formality sufficient to let him see that all was not right." But Marion's distance was not without purpose or empathy. Weems notes that Marion "wished his officers to be gentlemen. And whenever he saw one of them acting below that character, he would generously attempt his reformation."[38]

And so it was with in this case. Weems reports the lieutenant soon "became remarkably polite, and also attentive to duty. In short, no subaltern behaved better." As the lieutenant improved, so did his relations with those around him, to include with Marion, and the two grew to become both brothers-in-arms and friends.[39]

Even allowing for Weems's characteristic embellishments, Marion's treatment of the lieutenant illustrates how emotionally intelligent leaders use their social skills to meet people where they are. To some, a stern rebuke is needed where for others a word of encouragement is in order. Marion possessed the social skills needed to deal with people in a range of ways in order to bring out the best in them.

Marion certainly possessed significant intelligence and technical competencies. While leaders need these skills, Goleman considers them to be essentially just threshold capabilities. What is necessary for leadership excellence is the emotional intelligence that Goleman considers to be the "*sine qua non* of leadership." It was his possession of emotional intelligence that gave Marion a leadership advantage over opponents like Banastre Tarleton.

Isaac Shelby and Cooperation

During the colonial era, settlers in the area west of the Blue Ridge Mountains, in parts of Virginia, North Carolina, and modern-day Kentucky and Tennessee, carved out for themselves isolated, rugged communities on what was then the far frontier. The constant threat of Indian attack led the settlers to organize small companies for protection. The members were rough-hewn, independent-minded, daring outdoorsmen who resisted military discipline and fought to protect their family and home. The officers—men such as Isaac Shelby—were selected based on trust and merit, led by example, and were removed by acclamation when confidence in them was lost. Living on the frontier, these "Overmountain" communities were fairly isolated from the war being waged farther east. Even news of the fall of Charleston was slow to make its way across the mountains.[1]

With Charleston in their hands, the British pushed forces into the South Carolina interior, winning the stunning victory at Camden on August 16, 1780. Lord Charles Cornwallis next prepared to advance north into North Carolina. To do so, he would need to secure his left flank; a mission he assigned to one of Sir Henry Clinton's most trusted officers, Major Patrick Ferguson. Ferguson was a career soldier, a proven leader, and experienced in irregular warfare. As Cornwallis's "inspector of militia," Ferguson was in charge of organizing all Loyalist militia in South Carolina.[2]

Ferguson left Charleston with about 1,100 Loyalist troops, arriving at Gilbert Town (modern-day Rutherford, North Carolina) on

September 7. There he defeated a militia unit commanded by Colonel Charles McDowell, but also made a general nuisance of himself by harassing the local population and confiscating their property. While Ferguson was able to handle McDowell's isolated group with ease, he would be in far greater danger if the various Overmountain militias united against him. Desiring to dissuade such a course, on September 10, Ferguson paroled a Patriot militiaman and dispatched him with a warning to Colonel Isaac Shelby. If the Patriots did not cease their resistance to the British, Ferguson vowed to "march over the mountains, hang their leaders, and lay the country waste with fire and sword." As Robert Brown astutely notes, however, "the people Ferguson was trying to intimidate were exactly the kind of people that such demonstrations of bravado failed to impress."[3]

Shelby, the man to whom Ferguson sent his decree, was born in 1745 and lived in what was then Sapling Grove, North Carolina, and now is Bristol, Tennessee. His father Evan was the local militia commander, so Shelby was raised a soldier, lived in a fort, and served in his father's unit. Shelby's life followed a parallel course with his friend John Sevier, who was five years older than Shelby and lived nearby on the banks of the Holston River near what is now Kingsport, Tennessee. J. David Dameron considers Shelby and Sevier to be "two of the most naturally gifted and admired leaders on the frontier."[4] William Campbell, whose ruthless treatment of Loyalists had earned him the sobriquet of "the bloody tyrant of Washington County," commanded militia from Virginia. These Overmountain Men were joined by militia from Georgia, North Carolina, and South Carolina commanded by men like Benjamin Cleveland, Charles McDowell, Joseph Winston, William Chronicle, and James Williams.

Shelby had already brought his contingent of Overmountain Men into South Carolina to Musgrove's Mill on the Enoree River in the Spartan District in August of 1780. There Edward Musgrove operated a mill that had been occupied by a Loyalist force, much of which was quasi-regular Provincials. Shelby was joined by Georgia militia led by Lieutenant Colonel Elijah Clarke and South Carolinians led by Williams. The three Patriot groups had a combined strength of about two hundred men. The Loyalist force, commanded by Colonel Alexander Innes, was over twice that large.[5]

To overcome the odds, the Patriots developed a plan to deceive the Loyalists. On August 18, a small detachment of Georgians led by Captain Shadrach Inman forded the river, pretending to stumble into the enemy position. They then withdrew and led the pursuing British into an ambush where the rest of the Patriot force waited behind a breastwork of logs and dirt. The Patriots opened up a galling fire at close range, and the British charged with fixed bayonets. As the Patriots were being forced back, Innes was wounded, and the British momentum was broken. The Patriots rallied, and the British beat a hasty retreat. In the hour-long battle, the Patriots suffered a dozen casualties, but the British lost about sixty killed or wounded and seventy men captured. The Patriots considered pressing their advantage with a move against Ninety Six, but by then word reached them of the disastrous defeat that had occurred at Camden two days previously, and they instead withdrew to the north and west.[6]

Isaac Shelby. (Engraving by Durand after Mathew Harris Jouett, date unknown, Library of Congress)

In September, Ferguson received intelligence that Clarke was retreating toward Ninety Six, and he deployed his men to the southwest along the Green River to intercept him. Unable to locate Clarke, Ferguson called off his search upon hearing that the Overmountain Men were mobilizing.[7] On October 1, he issued another threatening proclamation from his position at Denard's Ford on the Broad River in Tryon County:

> Gentlemen:
> Unless you wish to be eat up by an inundation of barbarians, who have begun by murdering an unarmed son before the aged father, and afterwards lopped off his arms, and who by their shocking cruelties and irregularities, give the best

proof of their cowardice and want of discipline: I say, if you wish to be pinioned, robbed, and murdered, and see your wives and daughters, in four days, abused by the dregs of mankind—in short, if you wish or deserved to live and bear the name of men, grasp your arms in a moment and run to camp.

The Backwater men have crossed the mountains; McDowell, Hampton, Shelby, and Cleveland are at their head, so that you know what you have to depend upon. If you choose to be pissed upon forever and ever by a set of mongrels, say so at once and let your women turn their backs upon you, and look out for real men to protect them.[8]

Katherine White correctly judges that Ferguson had written an "insolent letter which caused his ruin."[9]

Indeed, "about 1500 good men, drawn from Washington, Surrey, Wilkes, Burk of North Carolina, and Washington County, Virginia" had already gathered near Gilbert Town, and they were expected "to be joined in a few days by Colonel Williams of South Carolina with about a thousand more" when on October 4, Colonels Shelby, Sevier, Cleveland, Campbell, Winston, and Hampton sent a joint letter to Major General Horatio Gates asking that either Brigadier General Willam Davidson or Colonel Daniel Morgan be appointed to lead them. In the meantime, Shelby nominated Campbell as temporary commander.[10]

Over the next two days, the leaders picked the 910 best men with the best horses, and then headed out to find Ferguson, following the general direction they thought he had taken. On their march they were joined at Cowpens by sixty Lincoln County, North Carolina men under Colonel Frederick Hambright as well as four hundred more South Carolinians led by Williams. It was a grueling and miserable trek. At one point Campbell, Sevier, and Cleveland felt a halt was in order to rest the men and horses, but Shelby, who had become the de facto leader of the ad hoc force, insisted on keeping moving. "I will not stop," he said, "Until night if I follow Ferguson into Cornwallis's lines."[11]

Ferguson knew the Overmountain Men were coming for him, but he did not know their exact strength. He also had no contact with a large detachment of his Tory militia led by Colonel Zacharias Gibbs and "Bloody Bill" Cunningham, even though they were sweeping through the area. These potential reinforcements, therefore, played no part in what was unfolding around them. Instead, Ferguson turned to Cornwallis, writing him on October 5 that "I am on my march towards you, by a road leading from Cherokee Ford, north of Kings Mountain. Three or four hundred good soldiers, part dragoons, would finish the business. Something must be done soon. This is their last push in this quarter and they are extremely desolate and awed. I wish for your Lordship's orders."[12] The next day, Ferguson remained confident, advising Cornwallis that "I have arrived at King Mountain and I have taken a post where I do not think I can be forced by a stronger enemy than that against us."[13]

Historians are uncertain why Ferguson decided to make a stand. He was less than a day's march from Cornwallis and could have easily escaped his pursuers had he continued on to Charlotte. Perhaps Ferguson expected Cunningham's force to return to him or that Cornwallis was going to send Tarleton to come to his aid. He may have just had such utter contempt for what he dismissed as "backwater banditti" that he did not give the matter much thought at all. Kings Mountain did afford Ferguson the room he needed to accommodate his entire force, and he was happy with it. Supposedly he declared that "This is Kings Mountain and I am king of this mountain."[14]

Whatever potential the position may have afforded the defender, Ferguson forfeited it by faulty terrain analysis. Apparently, Ferguson was so impressed by Kings Mountain's prominence that he positioned his 1,100 men on the bald "topographical crest" of the ridge. A topographical crest is a ridge's highest point. While it does allow long range views out into the distance, it also silhouettes its occupants against the sky, allowing them to be seen from afar. More importantly, it often provides limited fields of fire because attackers can approach the position masked by the terrain sloping sharply off of the peak. For that reason, the "military crest," located two-thirds of the way to the topographical crest, is the most advantageous defensive position, but Ferguson did not occupy it.[15]

To make matters worse, Ferguson took no steps to improve his position by building breastworks and abatis. Instead, he spent October 6 resting his men and even sent out two hundred of them on a foraging expedition, reducing his numbers still further. Ferguson's visible position and lax security resulted in the local inhabitants being well-aware of his location; information that quickly reached the approaching Patriot force.[16]

Battle of Kings Mountain, death of Ferguson. (Artist, Alonzo Chappel, 1863, Wikimedia Commons/Anne S. K. Brown Collection, Brown University)

Armed with this intelligence, in the morning hours of October 7, the Patriots crossed Ponder's Creek on the old colonial trail that is now South Carolina Highway 216. From there, they wound their way southward, crossed the lower branch of Kings Creek, and began their ascent up the ridge. After a gradual incline of some 2,500 feet, the road passes through a short plateau between two knobs. The northern slopes of Kings Mountain are visible from this position. While the thick forest prevented the Patriots from seeing the enemy, it also prevented the enemy from seeing them. Now knowing exactly where they were on the ground, the Patriots slipped down into a ravine below the road and finalized their preparations to attack.[17]

Shelby described the Patriot plan as being "to surround the mountain and attack the enemy from all sides." Once one unit made contact, others would pile on, forcing the enemy to collapse into an ever-tightening kill zone. The plan reflected the simplicity needed for execution by an ad hoc force. It was also a safe plan. Because Ferguson had positioned his men on the topographical crest, the advancing Patriots would be protected from fratricide by firing uphill until the summit was gained.[18]

To facilitate command and control, the Patriot leaders organized themselves into two forces of roughly equal size. A "Left Division" would surround the base of the mountain on the north side, and a "Right Division" would surround it on the south side. The Left Division consisted of some 440 men from the commands of Shelby, Williams, Lacey, Candler, Cleveland, Hambright, and Chronicle. The Right Division consisted of some 470 men from the commands of Campbell, Sevier, McDowell, and Winston. As the columns prepared to move forward, their respective commanders delivered inspirational speeches. Colonel Cleveland perhaps captured the nature of the attack best, telling his men "When you are engaged, you are not to wait for the word of command from me. I will show you by example how to fight; I can undertake no more. Every man must consider himself an officer, and act from his own judgment."[19]

As the Patriots advanced, they encountered sporadic fire from British pickets. Shelby counselled his men to hold their fire and continue moving forward. Campbell, realizing surprise had been lost, ordered his division to assault. It was roughly 3:00pm. For the first 20 minutes of the battle, Campbell's Right Division bore the brunt of the fighting as the other units were still farther back. As Campbell's men neared the crest, Ferguson ordered Captain Abraham DePeyster to launch a bayonet charge that pushed the Virginians and North Carolinians back, but Campbell rallied his men and attacked again. This attack too was repulsed. A third Patriot attack was met by an especially strong British counterattack that did much damage to Campbell's force, but, fearing the threat developing on the other side of his position, Ferguson ordered DePeyster to retreat. Although repulsed, Campbell had created an opportunity for Shelby's men to near the summit in their sector, but they too were pushed back by British bayonets.[20]

In spite of the strength of the British defense, the Patriots remained remarkably adaptive and resilient. With their larger units broken, small teams and individuals followed Cleveland's admonition to "act from [their] own judgment." A swarming effect resulted, with the ad hoc groups supporting each other as they advanced up the mountain. Expert marksmen like Josiah Culbertson steadily picked off British leaders, creating havoc in Ferguson's ranks.[21] In contrast, because of their positions on the topographical crest, Loyalists such as Drury Mathis found that they "were very generally overshooting the Americans."[22]

Hand-to-hand fighting raged, but the Patriots gained an advantage around 3:30 when the Left Division units commanded by Chronicle and Hambright finally reached their assault positions on the extreme northeast corner of the mountain. Chronicle was killed rallying his men to advance, but Hambright assumed overall command and pressed the attack.

While the terrain was too steep and the fire too great for the Left Division to seize the heights, the constant pressure applied there forced Ferguson to reinforce the northeast and weaken other sectors. The Right Division took advantage of the situation and rushed to the summit. Soon Patriots from all sides pressed forward, and Ferguson found himself pushed back into a small enclave at the northeast end of the mountain. Ferguson fought on manfully, ultimately leading a hastily organized force of himself, two mounted Tory officers, and a dozen Loyalist foot soldiers in a final assault.

As he launched this attack, Ferguson was killed by a volley of Patriot fire, and British resistance soon collapsed. Many British soldiers were unnecessarily killed before Patriot officers gained control over the passions of their men, and DePeyster was able to surrender the shattered remnants of Ferguson's command. In addition to Ferguson, the British suffered 157 killed and 163 wounded, and 698 captured. The Patriots lost just 28 killed and 62 wounded; less than 10 percent of their force.[23]

The Patriot victory was important both for its symbolic and its practical value. Symbolically, Dameron declares that Ferguson had made himself "the embodiment of everything the American Patriots abhorred" and representative of "an illusive [sic] and oppressive evil." "In his death," Dameron continues, "the Patriots saw hope and freedom."[24]

Practically, the Patriot victory reversed the trajectory of the British campaign. "Added to the depression and fear it communicated to the loyalists upon the borders, and to the southward," wrote Tarleton, "the effect of such an important event was sensibly felt by Earl Cornwallis at Charlotte town." "The total ruin of his militia," Tarleton continued "presented a gloomy prospect at the commencement of the campaign," and led Cornwallis to evacuate Charlotte and retreat to Winnsboro, South Carolina, where he established a defense and contemplated his new uncertain situation.[25] Dameron is among many who consider Kings Mountain to be "the turning point in the Revolutionary War."[26] Clinton more eloquently termed the British defeat there to be "the first link of a chain of evils that followed each other in regular succession until they at last ended in the total loss of America."

This incredible outcome is even more remarkable when one considers that the Patriot force was a loose association of men from Virginia, South Carolina, North Carolina, and what are now the states of Kentucky and Tennessee under 11 different leaders. That this eclectic gathering could, in a matter of days, coalesce into an effective fighting force is an example of "unity of effort" and a testimony to the leadership of Shelby and his fellows.

Unity of Effort

Dating back to at least 1921, US Army doctrine has cited nine "principles of war" as being fundamental to successful military operations. Early versions of the principles included "unity of command," but the changes to the nature of military operations in the post-Cold War era prompted military leaders to increasingly pursue unity of *effort* rather than unity of *command*. The 1993 version of FM 100–5, *Operations*, the Army's capstone field manual, explained that "unity of command means that all the forces are under one responsible commander. It requires a single commander with the requisite authority to direct all forces in pursuit of a unified purpose." Unity of effort, the manual notes, is something else. It "requires coordination and cooperation among all forces—even though they may not be of the same command structure—toward a commonly recognized objective.... Unity of effort—coordination through cooperation and common interests—is an essential component to unity of command."[27]

The globalized era and the changing nature of society have also affected the ability of non-military leaders to leverage unity of command in its traditional hierarchal form. Instead, they must recognize the large degree of free will that various stakeholders wield in any situation and seek the function provided by unity of effort. To do so, they must draw heavily on their conceptual and interpersonal skills. Shelby and the other officers and men at Kings Mountain were ahead of their time in coming to this realization and proved expert at achieving unity of effort.

Nathanael Greene and Strategic Leadership

Nathanael Greene was born in 1748 in Warwick, Rhode Island, to a prosperous Quaker family. Despite having a father who eschewed book learning, Greene was an avid reader whose private collection of books included military writings. Before the American Revolution, Greene was a forge-master and merchant.

Greene's personal alienation with the British can be traced to February 17, 1772, when Lieutenant William Dudingston seized the *Fortune*, a sloop owned by Nathanael Greene & Company and captained by Greene's cousin Rufus. The *Fortune* was bearing undeclared rum, and Dudingston sent the vessel and its cargo to Boston for trial. Greene and many other Rhode Islanders felt that Dudingston exceeded his authority in sending a vessel outside of the colony for trial. Greene's anti-British sentiment grew further still with the passage of the Intolerable Acts in 1774. In response, he helped organize a state militia group known as the Kentish Guards. Greene was saddened that he was not selected as an officer in the new unit and blamed the rebuff on a limp he had incurred in childhood.

Greene's disappointment would not last long. In May 1775, right after the battles of Lexington and Concord, the legislature of Rhode Island established an "Army of Observation" and sent it to Boston. Greene was made the army's commander and a brigadier general. What engendered this remarkable reversal of Greene's military fortunes is "an intriguing historical question" to which John Buchanan muses the "answer may never be found." But what matters, concludes Buchanan "is that the Rhode Island Assembly, for whatever reason had chosen most wisely."[1]

In June, the Second Continental Congress established the Continental Army and appointed Geoge Washington to be its commander. Greene was among the 16 other generals appointed. Washington had originally favored Greene to command the Southern Department, but the Continental Congress instead appointed Horatio Gates to the post on July 25, 1780.

Greene remained with Washington, and quickly became a valuable member of his councils of war and took part in the major battles in the North. At Trenton, Greene led one of the American columns and he performed admirably at the battle of Princeton. At Brandywine, he may have saved the army by thwarting a British flank attack. In December, he camped with the rest of the army at Valley Forge. With each battle, Greene learned more, and Washington's confidence in him and their friendship grew.

In March 1778, Greene reluctantly left the line to become the army's quartermaster general. Under difficult conditions he did an excellent job, establishing a transportation system and field depots, and clothing the soldiers. Despite being a staff officer, Greene still was able to command troops at the battle of Monmouth and the battle of Rhode Island. He resigned as quartermaster in August 1780, after sharply criticizing Congress. When Gates and his Southern command was destroyed at the battle of Camden that same month, Congress gave Washington the authority to appoint a new commander of the Southern Theater. On October 14, in one of his wisest decisions during the war, Washington chose Greene.

As Greene traveled south to his new position, he applied his keen quartermaster's eye to the river systems along the way and detached surveyors to study them further. His primary interest was in supply routes, but the intelligence he gathered about fords would also help him maneuver in his campaign against the British. Greene arrived in Charlotte, North Carolina, on December 2, 1780, and formally took command from Gates the following day.[2]

Greene found many problems in his new command, not the least of which was the fact that his combined force of Continentals and militia numbered barely more than 2,000 men, with few having any proven reliability in combat. It was therefore startling when Greene divided his small force into three parts. Brigadier General Daniel Morgan was dispatched west with about 600 men to operate in the vicinity of the British outpost at Ninety Six. Lieutenant Colonel Henry Lee took his Legion of 280 eastward to cooperate with Francis Marion along the coast. The remaining few hundred remained with Greene at his new headquarters in Cheraw Hills, South Carolina. Russell Weigley notes that such strategic "unorthodoxy" placed Greene at odds with Washington's cherished principle of concentration, but Greene was driven to such a measure by his need for provisions, and his partisan bands helped provide

Nathanael Greene. (Artist, Charles Wilson Peale, 1783, Wikimedia Commons)

him protection. The move also had the pleasant outcome of tempting Lord Charles Cornwallis to divide his superior force, making it possible for Greene to operate under somewhat more agreeable odds.[3]

In following Greene's lead, Cornwallis kept part of his force with him to watch Greene and dispatched the rest under Lieutenant Colonel Banastre Tarleton to deal with Morgan. In a battle that must have surpassed Greene's highest hopes, Morgan soundly defeated Tarleton at Cowpens on January 17, 1781. A frustrated Cornwallis then chased Greene and Morgan throughout North Carolina until the Patriots reached safety across the Dan River in Virginia.

Greene rested and refitted, and then returned to North Carolina, where he next met Cornwallis at Guilford Court House on March 15. Cornwallis won the bloody slugfest, but was left without adequate provisions, significantly reduced numbers, and besieged by partisan enemy forces that prevented him from dispatching forage parties. Unable to risk another battle, he limped his way to Wilmington, where he had access to resupply from the sea.[4]

Greene then turned south, reentered South Carolina, and by the spring had embarked on the so-called War of the Posts. After the fall of Charleston, the British had established a supply line that pushed inland from Charleston and Georgetown. A series of relatively isolated posts both guarded the supply line and gave British forces bases from which to operate.

This dispersal made sense when the garrisons were first created, because there was no real American army in the South to threaten them. Now with the maturation of the partisan forces as well as his own army, Greene had a new opportunity. He hoped that by nearly simultaneously attacking several key posts he could prevent the posts from reinforcing each other. Without their posts to guard their supply line, the British would be forced back to Charleston.[5]

When Greene set his sights on the central post at Camden, Cornwallis decided not to oppose him and instead departed North Carolina for Virginia. He left Lieutenant Colonel Francis Lord Rawdon in command in South Carolina, and Rawdon soon found himself overwhelmed by both the partisans and Greene. Marion, Lee, Sumter, and Pickens steadily gobbled up Fort Watson, Fort Motte, Orangeburg, Georgetown, and Augusta, Georgia. For his part, Greene engaged the British at Hobkirk's Hill, Ninety Six, and Eutaw Springs, which on September 8, 1781, was the final major engagement in South Carolina. Greene technically lost all three of those battles, but in each, the British lost irreplaceable manpower, allowing Greene to win the strategic battle of attrition. The war dragged on for another year, but for the most part, the British in the South were loosely confined to Charleston, which they abandoned in December 1782.[6]

Although Greene is decidedly underrepresented in popular history, his brilliance as a strategist is profound. Allan Millett and Peter Maslowski declare that "Greene's operations rank with Washington's performance at Trenton and Princeton as the war's most brilliant campaigns."[7] Indeed, Greene is a remarkable portrait of the strategic leader.

Strategic Leadership

Strategic leadership "is the process used by a leader to affect the achievement of a desirable and clearly understood vision."[8] To do so, strategic leaders develop "strategy," which, Arthur Lykke explained in a 1989 article, is the sum of ends, ways, and means. In Lykke's formula, "ends" are the "objectives towards which one strives." "Ways" are "courses of action." "Means" are "instruments by which some end can be achieved."[9] Although Greene was in the field over 200 years before Lykke wrote his article, Greene seemed to intuitively understand strategy in similar fashion.

Modern-day observers routinely describe Greene's Southern campaign using Lykke's vocabulary. John Gordon, for example, notes that "Greene's sense of strategy—of how to apply limited resources in order to attain a specific end, of how to reach a final goal or outcome that would yield what the Americans needed in the South—had been unfailing."[10] Joel Woodward concludes that "ultimately, Nathanael Greene succeeded because he matched his means to his ends."[11] "Greene," Woodward continues, "applied his available resources using synchronization and operational mobility to achieve his desired end state of a protracted campaign that wore down British strength and will."[12]

Ends

In appointing Greene to his new command, Washington had little to offer in the way of strategic advice. "Uninformed as I am of the enemy's force in that quarter, of our own, or of the resources [that you will have available]," admitted Washington, "I can give you no particular instructions, but must leave you to govern yourself entirely according to your own prudence and judgment, and the circumstances in which you find yourself."[13] Left to his own devices, Greene discerned that the proper end was simply to gain time. Such an end is conducive with a strategy of exhaustion in which "the objective is not to destroy the enemy but gradually to destroy his will and capacity to resist."[14] But while exhausting the enemy, the leader must also sustain the will to fight among his own command. In recognition of this important consideration, Greene acknowledged shortly after assuming command that "Every Thing here depends on opinion. If you lose the Confidence of the People, you lose all support."[15] Thus Greene's strategy was pursuant to the dual ends of weakening Cornwallis's force and preserving his own.

Ways

The "way" Greene would accomplish this end was to give battle only on his terms; to avoid decisive engagement through many of the tactics of unconventional war that would later be espoused by Mao Tse-tung.[16] Noting that Morgan deserves credit for the victory at Cowpens, historians often explain Greene's underrated reputation as a general with the fact that he never won a battle.[17] In reality, that was Greene's strategic way. He modestly and simply captured the process by which he weakened British will while maintaining American resiliency in a letter to French ally, the chevalier de La Luzerne: "we fight, get beat, rise and fight again."[18] Of course, the principal factor that drove Greene to such a way was his paucity of means. Indeed, Greene lamented, "I have been obliged to practice that by finesse which I dared not attempt by force."[19] In the final analysis, Maurice Matloff summarizes that "Greene had lost battles, but won a campaign. In so doing, he paved the way for the greater victory to follow at Yorktown."[20]

Means

By temperament, Greene would have preferred to have a body of American regulars who had the discipline, unit cohesion, and officer leadership necessary to defeat the British on equal terms. He knew, however, that when he assumed command, he lacked such a force and would continue to lack it for the immediate future. Instead, Greene found in North Carolina a force of just 1,482 men fit for duty, only a fraction of whom were Continentals. They were poorly trained and equipped, and save for some limited successes in backcountry actions, had largely been defeated in the last six months of fighting. Cornwallis, on the other hand, commanded an army of disciplined British regulars some three times greater than Greene's and was fresh from the victory at Camden. Greene knew that he needed time to recruit and train men, to gather supplies, and to build confidence.[21]

To gain that time, Greene would rely on irregulars like Francis Marion to keep Cornwallis occupied. He wrote Marion on December 4, "Until a more permanent Army can be collected than is in the Field at present, we must endeavor to keep up a Partizan War and preserve the Tide of

Sentiment among the People as much as possible."[22] Greene also knew, however, that he could not give Cornwallis a free hand against the much smaller partisan bands. It was in part to relieve that pressure that Greene advanced his small Continental force into Cheraw Hills and divided his force, sending Morgan toward Ninety Six. Greene also ordered Lieutenant Colonel Henry Lee and his Legion to join forces with Marion.[23] The result was a mutually supporting relationship of which Bruce Lancaster quipped, "without Greene, Marion could not have existed. Without Marion, Greene could hardly have survived."[24]

Marion reveled in the role he played within Greene's larger strategy, and his attacks on the British supply lines had multiple-order effects. Obviously, they disrupted the British ability to logistically support on-going operations. Moreover, the constant threats caused Tarleton and other British commanders to divert soldiers from offensive operations in order to guard baggage trains and depots. Finally, the supplies that Marion captured helped equip his men and the Continental Army.[25]

It is for this careful weaving of ends, ways, and means that Theodore Thayer subtitled his biography of Greene "Strategist of the American Revolution."[26] Many other observers note Greene's unique and singular contributions. Lawrence Babits declares that "demoralized American forces received their most important reinforcement when Major General Nathanael Greene rode into Charlotte on 2 December 1780."[27] As Fletcher Pratt puts it, "Nathanael Greene made himself master of the circumstances he found, and left to the American Army a tradition it has never quite lost, of considering each problem in the light of its surrounding conditions."[28]

Yet, Greene's example provides lessons that stretch beyond the military. The US Army War College argues that "the strategic paradigm comprised of 'ends, ways, and means' has almost universal applicability."[29] Like Greene, leaders of all sorts are faced with the daunting task of bringing some order to the complex and ambiguous nature of strategic planning. The ends, ways, and means methodology is a proven technique to create such a process.

Daniel Morgan and Team Building

Military historian Russell Weigley effusively declares Daniel Morgan to be "a superb battle captain, an inspiring leader who was able to draw from his troops battlefield performances unexcelled and perhaps unequalled by any other officer of the American cause."[1] Those who knew Morgan in his early years may have found it difficult to imagine such praise. Born in 1736, most likely in Hunterdon County, New Jersey, Morgan had what was assumed to have been a difficult childhood, and when he was about 17 years old, he left home without his parents' knowledge or permission and moved to Virginia. Young Morgan could barely read and write, enjoyed fighting and strong drink, and was generally considered to be coarse and rough-hewn. After jobs preparing land for planting and as the superintendent of a sawmill, Morgan became a wagoner and hauled supplies over the mountains to settlers. He served in that capacity during the French and Indian War, including as part of British Major General Edward Braddock's ill-fated expedition into western Pennsylvania in 1755. From that experience, Morgan acquired the nickname of "The Old Wagoner."

While hauling supplies in the spring of 1756, a disputed incident occurred that resulted in Morgan striking a British officer. For the offense, Morgan was assigned 400 lashes, but by his count he received only 399. Later, Morgan delighted in telling the tale and insisting he was a British "creditor to the amount of one lash."[2] It was also while serving with the British that Morgan obtained a large scar on his cheek; the result of a ball entering the back of his neck, passing through his mouth, taking out his left rear teeth, and finally exiting through his upper lip.[3] The combination of Morgan's height of over six feet, his great strength, his backcountry ways, his picturesque past, and his scar made him an imposing figure.[4]

When the Revolutionary War broke out, Morgan raised a company of riflemen and led them from Frederick County, Virginia, to Boston, Massachusetts. From there, Morgan and his men went with General Benedict Arnold into Canada in the winter of 1775, and Morgan was captured at Quebec. After being exchanged, Morgan distinguished himself at Saratoga. After reaching the rank of colonel, he ultimately left the army. Lawrence Babits explains that Morgan suffered from failing health and took a leave of absence to return to Virginia.[5] Others such as John Moncure argue that Morgan felt unappreciated as others were promoted ahead of him and resigned his commission in a pique. Either way, when Morgan learned of the Patriot defeat at Camden in August of 1780, he hurried south to join General Nathanael Greene, the newly appointed commander of the Southern Theater. Upon arrival, Morgan found that he had been promoted to brigadier general.[6] He was then 44 years old; older than many other senior officers in the Continental Army.

Wasting no time, Greene boldly divided his army, sending Morgan and a large detachment west of the Catawba River to take command of all militia forces in the South Carolina upcountry. Moncure assesses that "A better commander could not have been chosen for the foray into South Carolina. Morgan was a commander of proven courage, and he had an uncanny understanding of the psychology of soldiers and a firm grasp of tactical principles."[7] With one wing in Morgan's capable hands, on December 20, Greene marched with the rest of the army into South Carolina and camped along the upper Pee Dee River.

Moving westward, Morgan arrived at Grindal's Shoals on December 25, and Greene was in camp by December 26.[8] Lord Charles Cornwallis was located between the two Patriot forces at Winnsboro, South Carolina, and thus able to use what military theorists would later call "central position" to deal with each enemy sequentially to prevent them from massing. Cornwallis decided to go after Morgan first, assigning the task to his most aggressive officer, Lieutenant Colonel Banastre Tarleton.

As Tarleton moved west to find Morgan, Morgan arranged a rendezvous of his regulars and militia at Cowpens, a road intersection north of modern-day Spartanburg, South Carolina. By the time Tarleton found him, Morgan had occupied an excellent location and was well-prepared for the attack.

According to Major Edward Giles, Morgan's aide, the Patriot forces consisted of 290 Maryland and Delaware Continental light infantry, 350 South Carolina and Georgia militia under Andrew Pickens, 170 Virginia militia under a Major Francis Triplett, and William Washington's cavalry, estimated to be around 82. An unknown number of additional militia men arrived over the evening before the battle. Against this total of at least 892, Tarleton mustered as many as 1,150 men.[9] In addition to the possible numerical advantage, John Gordon assesses that "Tarleton's force contained some of the most proven British units in America."[10]

Daniel Morgan. (Artist unknown, c. 1780. National Portrait Gallery, Smithsonian Institution)

Morgan offset this disadvantage by deploying his forces with an astute understanding of their strengths and weaknesses. Up to this point, the Patriot militia had been of uncertain reliability. At Camden, for example, they had turned and run when the British bayonets came bearing down on them, leaving the Continental regular soldiers in dismay. At Cowpens, Morgan expected that Tarleton would mount an aggressive charge that would again test the militia's mettle. Thus, Morgan arrayed his forces to, as Moncure describes, "behave as a shock absorber" in three successive lines, with each line being stronger than the former.[11]

Morgan assigned a very limited and defined role to the militia in this scheme of maneuver. Knowing that in battle, militiamen responded to the enthusiasm of the moment rather than disciplined instinct born of years of drill and training, Morgan appealed to them based on the values they held dear and realistic expectations. Thomas Young recalled Morgan instructed the militia to "just hold up your heads, boys, three fires, and you are free, and when you return to your homes, how the old folks will bless you, and the girls kiss you, for your gallant conduct."[12]

Morgan's front line consisted of South Carolina and Georgia riflemen positioned behind a set of scattered trees. With fires accurate to 300 meters, these skirmishers would target British officers and then fall back to join the main militia line. As the British continued their advance, they would be met by Morgan's second line, consisting of South Carolina militia under Colonel Andrew Pickens. These men would fire the three volleys described by Young and then retire from the field by moving around the left flank of the Continentals. Since this withdrawal was all part of the plan, the panic that had plagued the Patriots at Camden would be avoided. The impetuous Tarleton, however, was expected to believe the Patriot defense was folding and rush forward, where he would be met by a third line commanded by Lieutenant Colonel John Eager Howard and consisting of Maryland, Delaware, and Virginia Continentals and Virginia militia and State Troops. Behind a gully to the left of Howard's line, Lieutenant Colonel William Washington's Continental Light Dragoons and mounted militia waited in reserve.[13]

Just before dawn on January 17, 1781, Tarleton appeared before the American front line. As was his nature, he ordered an immediate attack. The first two Patriot lines performed their assigned tasks, and, as expected, Tarleton interpreted their planned retreat as the beginning of a rout and rushed headlong into the Continental line. An intense battle was soon joined, and, in the confusion, Howard's men fell back, only to reform a new line designated by Morgan. There they delivered devastating fire into the advancing British. Morgan then launched a double envelopment with Washington's cavalry striking from the left and Pickens's reformed militia hitting from the right.

The entire battle lasted less than an hour and was a resounding victory for the Americans. William Sherman estimates Tarleton suffered 100 killed, 200 wounded, and 529 captured or missing.[14] Other sources claim the British sustained as high as 90 percent total casualties and prisoners.[15] Sherman places the American losses between 127 and 148 killed and wounded.[16]

Cowpens would not be the sum of Morgan's novel tactic. Rod Andrew writes that it would become the "standard American practice whenever

Battle of Cowpens. (Artist, F. Kemmelmeyer, 1809, Wikimedia Commons)

patriot militia and Continentals fought together," and it was repeated at places like Guilford Court House and Eutaw Springs.[17] Moncure declares that "The Cowpens may be one of the most important battles ever fought on American soil from the standpoint of the tactical lessons one can learn from it." He adds, however, that even beyond these tactical considerations, the battle "stands as a superb laboratory for analysis of the psychological factor in war."[18] It is in this latter realm that the battle also illustrates the leadership "law of the niche."

The Law of the Niche

The law of the niche is one of John Maxwell's "seventeen indisputable laws of teamwork." According to this law, "all players have a place where they add the most value," and it is the responsibility of the leader to put people in such situations where they can maximize their effectiveness. James Collins describes the same situation by likening an organization to a bus. The leader's task, Collins explains, is to get "the right people in the right seats."[19] That is what Morgan did in his use of the militia at Cowpens. If that does not happen—"when people aren't where they do things well"—Maxwell cautions, "things don't turn out well."[20] That is what happened with the militia at Camden. The whole idea of the law of the niche is to understand the places and the people available to fill them, and to then align the two in a way that maximizes effectiveness. Misplacement leads to frustration and failure. On the other hand, having the right people in the right places multiplies the overall effectiveness of the team.[21]

In order to put people in the places that best utilize their talents and maximize the team's potential, Maxwell says leaders must know the team, know the situation, and know the player.[22] To that extent, a leader's ability to follow the law of the niche would require many of the characteristics Daniel Goleman argues comprise emotional intelligence. Like Francis Marion, Morgan possessed a high degree of emotional intelligence, and like Marion, he used that advantage to thwart the less well-equipped Tarleton.

Thaddeus Kosciuszko and Planning Branches and Sequels

Thaddeus Kosciuszko was born on February 12, 1746 in the Polish-Lithuanian Commonwealth (present-day Belarus).[1] In 1765, he enrolled as a cadet in the inaugural class of the military academy in Warsaw, and after graduating a year later, became a lieutenant and a student instructor.[2] When civil war broke out in the Polish-Lithuanian Commonwealth in 1768, Kosciuszko went to Paris, France, where he embraced the Enlightenment philosophies of Montesquieu, Voltaire, and Rousseau that were then sweeping through Europe.[3] Feeling in concert with the revolutionary colonists, Kosciuszko left for America and enlisted in the Continental Army after his arrival on August 30, 1776.[4]

Initially, Kosciuszko served as a volunteer aide to Benjamin Franklin, but in October Kosciuszko was reassigned as a colonel of engineers.[5] In 1777, he was ordered to report to Major General Horatio Gates at Fort Ticonderoga, New York. Kosciuszko went on to help design the defenses at Saratoga and those surrounding West Point.[6] In 1780, he was transferred with Gates to the Southern Theater.[7] Although Gates was a friend and mentor to Kosciuszko, when Major General Nathanael Greene succeeded Gates on December 2, 1780, Kosciuszko joined the new commander and continued as his chief of engineers.[8]

As the quartermaster general of the Continental Army, Greene had relied on rivers to transport the men and materiel of war. Now on his way south to his new command, Greene wrote General George Washington that "On my arrival at Hillsborough, I intend to have all the rivers examined in order to see if I cannot ease this heavy business by water transportation." As part of that effort, on December 3, Greene ordered Kosciuszko to "explore the navigation of the Catawba river from mill creek below the forks up to Oliphant mill." The specificity of Greene's instructions shows his appreciation for riverine navigation. "Report to me," he told Kosciuszko, "its particular situation as to the depth of water, the rapidity of the stream, the rocks, shoals or falls you may meet with and every other information necessary to enable me to form an accurate opinion of the transportation which may be made on the river in the different seasons of the year. It is of the utmost importance that your report to me should be very particular and as early as possible." With Captain Thompson as a guide, Kosciuszko set out in a canoe, avoiding Tories who were "as thick as the trees," to return with the information Greene required. In addition to Kosciuszko's exploration of the Catawba, Greene sent Brigadier General Edward Stevens to survey the Yadkin and Lieutenant Colonel Edward Carrington, his new quartermaster, to explore the Dan.[9]

In addition to needing to understand the topography, another problem facing Greene at his new headquarters was that the army had only three days' worth of provisions on hand. To exacerbate the situation, the surrounding region had already been stripped of whatever it could supply.[10] Thus, after Kosciuszko had returned from his exploration of the Catawba, on December 8 Greene ordered him to survey the Pee Dee "from the mouth of little River twenty or thirty miles down" in search of a place "that would afford a healthy camp & provisions in plenty." Major William Polk of the North Carolina Continental Line accompanied Kosciuszko on this reconnaissance.[11]

Greene anxiously awaited Kosciuszko's return, writing Colonel Thomas Polk, the North Carolina commissary general, on December 15 that it was "impossible to leave this camp as early as I intended as Col. Kosciuszko has made no report yet respecting a position upon the Pedee." When Kosciuszko returned the next day, he brought the news that the Cheraws region, just across the South Carolina border where Hick's Creek emptied into the Pee Dee, had been untouched by the war and could subsist the army. The population there was also decidedly supportive of the Patriot cause. Greene accepted Kosciuszko's recommendation and moved his command to Hick's Creek. When he arrived there on December 26, Greene found that not just his logistics, but that his operational flexibility had been improved as well. He was now in a position from which he could attack Camden, march on Charleston, or aid Brigadier General Francis Marion's partisan efforts. While Greene studied his options, Kosciuszko set about the fortify the camp.[12]

By this time, it had become obvious to Greene that rivers would play a critical role in the campaign, and he began to plan accordingly. On January 1, 1781, he ordered Kosciuszko to move to Cross Creek with all the officers he could find "to assist you in procuring a number of tools suitable for constructing a number of boats [and] ... engage all the carpenters you can find you may think necessary to dispatch the construction of the boats. Confiding in your zeal and activity I persuade myself you will make all the dispatch the business will admit as the safety and support of the Army depend upon your accomplishing this business."[13] Pursuant to Greene's instruction, throughout January Kosciuszko superintended the construction of a small fleet of flat-bottomed boats.

Thaddeus Kosciuszko. (Artist, Henry H. Houston, c. 1796, National Portrait Gallery, Smithsonian Institution)

While Kosciuszko labored with his project, Greene shared the information with Morgan. In a January 19 letter that Theodorus Bailey Myers labels "Greene Predicts Cowpens," Greene warned Morgan "As the rivers are subject to sudden and great swells, you must be careful that the enemy do not take a position to gain your rear, when you can neither retreat by your flank or front. The Pedee rose 25 feet for the last week in 30 hours." To mitigate this threat, Greene advised Morgan that "I am preparing boats to move always with the army. Would one or two be of use to you? They will be put upon four wheels, and may be moved with little more difficulty than a loaded wagon."[14] Of course, by the time Greene wrote this letter, unbeknownst to him, Morgan had already dealt Cornwallis a decisive defeat at Cowpens on January 17, lending even more value to Greene's preparations.

After his victory, Morgan hastened to retreat to North Carolina and reunite with Greene. "It was at this moment also," writes Andrew Waters "that rivers took center stage for Morgan needed to escape across the Broad and Catawba Rivers as soon as possible."[15] Blazing the way, Kosciuszko moved ahead of the Americans, charting their course with Cornwallis in hot pursuit. This Race to the Dan led Greene's army through North Carolina and across the Dan River into the safety of Virginia. It is a fascinating tale during which James Pula describes Kosciuszko as "appear[ing] to be everywhere, handling the myriads of details necessary for success, planning lines of march, gathering and dispatching crucial boats, and seeking little known short cuts."[16] As tempting as it is to explore Kosciuszko's exploits outside of South Carolina, they are beyond the scope of this book. One example will suffice and that is Morgan's transfer of his army across the Yadkin River at Trading Ford on February 3 "on boats which had previously been collected." John B. O. Landrum notes that "it was General Greene's foresight on his way South that caused these boats in be in the place."[17] This broad "foresight" of Greene and Kosciuszko's fulfillment of it are brilliant illustrations of a leader's responsibility to plan and prepare for "branches and sequels."

Branches and Sequels

Because of the inherent unpredictability of the future, many plans require adjustment early in the process of their execution. Branches and sequels provide the flexibility needed to preserve freedom of action in rapidly changing conditions. "Branches" are planned contingencies that provide a range of alternatives often built into the basic plan. They add flexibility by anticipating situations that could alter the basic plan.[18] Greene communicated one branch that involved the Pee Dee River in his December 29, 1780 letter to Morgan that Myers labels "A Parting Caution."

If Cornwallis, who was then at Camden, moved not toward Morgan but instead toward Greene at Cheraw, Morgan was to "endeavor to cross the river and join us."[19]

Cornwallis did, however, go after Morgan, rendering such a contingency unnecessary. Instead, what followed the battle at Cowpens was a "sequel" to the original plan. "Sequels" anticipate and plan for subsequent actions based on the possible outcomes of the current action; whether that be success, failure, or something in between.[20] At Cowpens, the outcome was a case of remarkable tactical success, but one that operationally was still fraught with danger if Cornwallis could catch up to Morgan.

This disaster was avoided because Greene had begun his forward thinking as soon as he learned he would be taking command of the Southern Theater. He gained an appreciation of the topography that convinced him of the criticality of rivers. He used Kosciuszko to both gather intelligence for him and build the boats that would give the army the mobility it needed. Therefore, at the conclusion of the battle at Cowpens, Greene could immediately launch a sequel that would end with his army safely beyond British reach on the north side of the Dan and a hapless Cornwallis 240 miles from his supply base at Camden.

Leaders must be able to operate on the time continuum. They must be able to meaningfully act in the present based on what is known, but they also must be able to project into the future to prepare for new actions based on potential outcomes of current actions. Leaders with this ability to anticipate model Wayne Gretzky's explanation that "A good hockey player plays where the puck is. A great hockey player plays where the puck is going to be."[21] Greene had the foresight to look beyond the present state of affairs and begin thinking about sequels to the tactical battle between Morgan and Cornwallis. In Kosciuszko, Greene had a skilled engineer who could animate his foresight.

Henry Lee and Negotiation

Henry Lee was born into the famous Lee family in Leesylvania, Virginia, in 1756. He began his military career in 1776 as a captain in the Fifth Troop of Light Horse of the Virginia State Troops, which soon was incorporated in the First Continental Light Dragoons in George Washington's Continental Army. In January 1778, Lee was surprised by Lieutenant Colonel Banastre Tarleton at Spread Eagle Tavern, near Valley Forge, Pennsylvania. Lee acted quickly, foiling the attack by barricading his men in the tavern. Congress recognized this "brave and prudent officer," promoting him to major.[1] Around this time, Lee acquired the sobriquet of "Light Horse Harry" in recognition of his formidable skills as an equestrian.

In February 1780, Lee formed a Legionary Corps, and by November of that year the corps had grown to three mounted troops and three dismounted or infantry troops. "Lee's Legion," as it became known, acted as the 18th-century equivalent of a combined arms unit today. Lee continued to perform well in Washington's army in partisan actions and was promoted to lieutenant colonel.

Lee and his Legion were detached to General Nathanael Greene's Southern command when Greene marched south late in 1780. In January 1781, Greene sent Lee to South Carolina to cooperate with Francis Marion. Lee and Marion quickly formed a bond and a plan to attack the British forces in Georgetown, however, the two-pronged assault was mistimed and failed. Greene soon recalled Lee when, after the British defeat at Cowpens, Lord Charles Cornwallis made a determined effort to catch and destroy Greene's Continental Army in North Carolina.[2] The Legion played an active role in the Race to the Dan campaign and at its climax at the battle of Guilford Court House on March 15, 1781.

When Cornwallis moved north into Virginia, Greene returned to South Carolina, and Lee was again detached to join Marion with the goal of cutting the British supply lines to Camden, Ninety Six, Augusta, and other backcountry posts. Together, Marion and Lee laid siege to and captured Fort Watson in April and Fort Motte in May. Lee then moved independently to capture Fort Granby and joined Colonel Andrew Pickens to take the forts at Augusta. At Fort Watson, Fort Motte, Fort Granby, and Augusta, Lee showed a willingness to negotiate. His efforts at Fort Granby are perhaps his most profitable example.

Fort Granby was one of the series of British forts that extended into the interior of South Carolina and became the focus of the War of the Posts in the spring of 1781. It was located where the road between Ninety Six and Camden reached the Congaree River, where today is the city of Cayce below Columbia. The fort was a rectangular redoubt built around a house and outbuildings; it had bastions and strong parapets and was surrounded by a ditch protected by abatis.[3] It was garrisoned by about 300 Provincials and Loyalist militia under the command of Major Andrew Maxwell of Maryland.[4]

Thomas Sumter had unsuccessfully attacked Fort Granby in February. With a woefully insufficient force, Sumter first tried to deceive Maxwell with "Quaker Guns," logs painted black to resemble cannon. This trick had been successfully used by Colonel William Washington at Rugeley's Mill near Camden in December 1780, but this time, Maxwell, aware of Sumter's approach and his lack of artillery, did not fall for it. His ruse frustrated, Sumter began to lay siege. When he learned that a sizeable force commanded by Lieutenant Colonel Welbore Ellis Doyle was on its way to relieve Granby, Sumter abandoned the siege and withdrew to the south.

After his successful cooperation with Marion to secure Fort Watson on April 23 and Fort Motte on May 12, Lee pushed west in support of operations Greene planned for Ninety Six. As he approached Fort Granby, Lee sent forward instructions to advise Maxwell that "the army will be near the fort by twelve o'clock on the 15th, and if he shall obstinately persist in holding the post, he must abide the consequences, as he will never receive but one summons for its surrender."[5]

Lee knew he was up against a formidable position. He described Fort Granby as "being completely finished, with parapet encircled by fosee and abbatis, and being well-garrisoned, it could not have been carried without considerable loss, except by regular approaches; and in this way would have employed the whole force of Greene for a week at least, in which period lord Rawdon's interposition was practicable."[6] Thus, when Lee arrived "in the neighborhood of the fort" on May 14, he proceeded with deliberate care. Writing in his *Memoirs* in the third person, Lee reports that, "relying upon the information of his guide, he began to erect a battery in the margin of the woods to the west of the fort." An "uncommonly foggy" morning allowed this work to be done without Maxwell's attention.[7]

Henry Lee. (Artist, James Herring, c. 1834, National Portrait Gallery, Smithsonian)

If Lee had reverence for the Loyalist position, he had nothing but chagrin for its commander. He appraised Maxwell to be "neither experienced in his profession, nor fitted by cast of character to meet the impending crisis" and considered him "disposed to avoid, rather than to court, the daring scenes of war." Lee was also aware of Maxwell's reputation as an opportunistic plunderer who "held with him in the fort his gathered spoil."[8]

Having thus sized up the competition, Lee "determined to try the effect of negotiation with this pliable antagonist; and prepared a summons, couched in pompous terms, calculated to operate upon such an officer as Maxwell was represented to be." Lee made the final preparation of advancing his infantry to secure the key terrain in front of the fort, and then dispatched Captain Joseph Eggleston to deliver the surrender demand. After a brief consultation with some of his officers, Maxwell agreed to capitulate but requested four terms. In confirmation of his notoriety as a freebooter, his first demand was that "private property of every sort, without investigation of title, should be conferred to its possessor." To this he added that the garrison be allowed to go to Charleston as prisoners until exchanged, that the militia be accorded the same treatment as the regulars, and that an escort be provided to ensure safe passage to Charleston. The assiduous Eggleston did not feel he had the authority to grant Maxwell's first demand, so he requested guidance from Lee. Lee agreed to it but "with the single exception of all horses fit for public services." He then instructed Eggleston "to expedite the conclusion of the business."[9]

Although Maxwell personally had no objection to Lee's modification, his Hessian officers did, so Eggleston returned to Lee to sort out this latest development. At that same time, Lee received intelligence that Lord Rawdon was advancing with reinforcements toward Fort Motte. Lee knew that if Maxwell were to gain this knowledge, he would very likely be emboldened to stand and fight. To prevent that from happening, Lee quickly acquiesced to excluding the horses. Thus, the capitulation was signed, and the fort occupied before noon. An exasperated Rawdon halted his advance, "yielding up with much reluctance his anxious desire to defend his line of posts, already broken through in its weakest points, and about to be assailed throughout." With Fort Granby in hand, Lee was off to Augusta.[10]

Negotiating

Sun Tzu was a military theorist during the period of the Warring States in ancient China. In his classic *The Art of War*, he writes that "those who win every battle are not really skillful—those who render others' armies helpless without fighting are the best of all."[11] Lee fulfilled Sun Tzu's admonition by using negotiation at Fort Granby. Sumter had earlier tried the same technique and failed. Information, negotiating from a position of strength, and appreciating the importance of timing, were what made the difference with Lee.

Perhaps Sun Tzu's most famous maxim is "So it is said that if you know others and know yourself, you will not be imperiled in a hundred battles; if you do not know others but know yourself, you win one and lose one; if you do not know others and do not know yourself, you will be imperiled in every single battle."[12] Maxwell knew Sumter and knew himself better than Sumter knew himself or Maxwell. Maxwell knew Sumter was approaching and knew he lacked artillery. Therefore, he was not impressed by Sumter's Quaker gun ruse. Maxwell also knew he had reinforcements nearby. Sumter, on the other hand, failed to appreciate his own weakness relative to Maxwell's.

In contrast, Lee enjoyed great information superiority over Maxwell. Lee fully understood the strength of Fort Granby and treated it with respect. Armed with information from a guide, however, he did avail himself of what advantages the terrain allowed. Even more importantly, he understood Maxwell and all his character flaws. Lee knew Maxwell was no hero and that he was motivated by plunder. Thus, Lee had information he could exploit. Maxwell was seemingly devoid of information. A fog kept him from noticing Lee's placement of his artillery until it was a *fait accompli*, and Lee even knew of Rawdon's advance before Maxwell did.

This information advantage allowed Lee to negotiate from a position of strength. Some of that strength was based on the astute placement of his artillery and infantry, but the preponderance was the psychological advantage that Lee enjoyed. He knew that what mattered to Maxwell was his ill-gotten gains, not his devotion to the cause. The Hessian mercenaries also lacked the sense of nationalism that motivated the Patriots to fight. To the Hessians, their horses were what mattered. Lee had taken the measure of his competition and knew exactly how to exploit it.

But Lee's carefully arranged advantage was threatened by Rawdon's advance. Lee had to close the deal not just before Rawdon arrived, but even before Maxwell knew help was on the way. Thus Lee, who no doubt could have used the Hessian horses for his own cavalry, wasted no time with lesser things. He agreed to the Hessian modification to his original offer with the urgency required to secure the bigger prize, which was the fort itself.

Men like Sun Tzu and Lee see negotiations as a means of gaining military victory. The other party in the negotiation is, in Lee's words, to be compelled to "surrender," and in Sun Tzu's to be rendered "helpless." Leaders in the business of influencing those under their care to follow them use a much softer form of negotiation. In those cases, the desire is to create a win-win situation in which all parties feel good about what they perceive as a mutually beneficial outcome.[13] This dynamic is especially prevalent in transactional leadership in which "leaders exchange things of value with their subordinates to advance their own as well as their subordinates' agenda." Transactional leaders wield influence because subordinates see it as in their best interest to do what it is that the leader wants.[14] Lee's conduct at Fort Granby is even illustrative in this context. Maxwell wanted his plunder more than he wanted Fort Granby. Lee wanted Fort Granby more than he wanted Maxwell's plunder. The negotiation represented an exchange of what both men relatively valued the most, and, to that extent, was a win-win.

Hezekiah Maham and Innovation

Hezekiah Maham was born on June 26, 1739, and became a successful planter in St. Stephen's Parish, South Carolina. When the American Revolution began, he was representing St. Stephen's in the Second Provincial Congress. He was active in the militia from early 1776 and was promoted to the rank of major in a state regiment of light dragoons in 1779. After the fall of Charleston in May 1780, Maham joined Francis Marion's brigade and served as a commander of cavalry.

By the spring of 1781, General Nathanael Greene's South Carolina strategy had evolved into the War of the Posts. The British had established a supply line that pushed inland from Charleston and Georgetown. A series of relatively isolated posts both guarded the supply line and gave British forces bases from which to operate. Greene hoped that by nearly simultaneously attacking several key posts he could prevent the posts from reinforcing each other. Without their posts to guard their supply line, the British would be forced back to Charleston.[1] One such post was Fort Watson, a strategic location that stood on the road to Nelson's Ferry.

Fort Watson was manned by a force of 114 British Regulars and Loyalists normally under the command of Lieutenant Colonel John Watson. Watson had left the fort on March 5, however, on a joint operation with Lieutenant Colonel Welbore Ellis Doyle designed to destroy Marion's camp on Snow's Island. In Watson's absence, command of Fort Watson fell to Lieutenant James McKay.[2] Greene sent Marion and Lieutenant Colonel Henry Lee to reduce this strongpoint.

Although Lee's Legion numbered 300 and Marion had 80 men of his own, Fort Watson, was "a tough nut to crack." Marion had resisted Greene's encouragement to attack it in January, deeming the defenses too formidable, and Brigadier General Thomas Sumter had failed miserably when he tried in February. A conventional assault would be suicidal, so to reduce Fort Watson would require a siege; a tactic with which Marion had little familiarity.[3]

Fort Watson was relatively small—50 by 55 feet—but what it lacked in size was more than compensated for by the terrain. The fort was built on top of a 23-foot-high pyramid-shaped Indian temple mound and surrounded by three rows of abatis. The British had cleared away all the trees and brush around the fort to rob the attackers of cover and to provide the defenders with excellent fields of fire.[4]

Marion and Lee arrived at Fort Watson on April 15, surrounded it, and promptly demanded that McKay surrender. With plenty of food and ammunition, and confidence in the strength of his position, McKay refused, telling the Patriots that "if they wanted [Fort Watson], they must come take it."[5]

At first Marion tried to reduce the fort by cutting it off from its water supply at Scott's Lake. Marion positioned riflemen between the fort and the lake to interdict any watering parties, but rather than challenge Marion, McKay began digging a well at the base of the hill inside the abatis. On April 18, the British struck water, thwarting Marion's plan.[6]

Fort Watson normally had two 3-pound cannons, but Watson had taken these with him when he left in March. Lee realized that if the Patriots could get a cannon, they would have a great advantage. He asked Greene to supply one, boasting that he would use it to "finish the business" in "five minutes" and promptly return it. Greene agreed and dispatched a six-pounder, but the infantry transporting it got lost and returned to Camden.[7]

Having anticipated a quick victory, the Patriot ranks soon became restless with the siege. The digging was slow and difficult. Morale declined, and men began to desert, in spite of Marion's threats of capital punishment. Moreover, cases of smallpox began to appear. Lee's men had been inoculated, but Marion's had not, and the disease cut a three-fold swath through Marion's ranks. Some healthy men fled to avoid it. Others such as Samuel Jenkins, who had been with Marion since August 1780, caught it. Still others such as Jenkins's brother Britton, carried infected comrades home.[8]

In the midst of this deteriorating situation, Maham approached Marion and Lee with an idea. Maham proposed building a log tower some 30 feet high to enable marksmen to shoot down into the fort. It would be an immense undertaking, but Marion determined it was worth a try.[9]

The Patriots gathered axes from the nearby plantations and began cutting pine saplings that could be fashioned into slender poles. These were carried to a position just outside of British rifle range, and the Patriots began assembling the logs into an oblong tower on the afternoon of August 21. A floor was built at a point higher than the British fort and the front protected with a wall of logs. The tower was completed under cover of darkness and moved to its final position with a party of Captain William McCottry's riflemen at its apex. McCottry was a wise choice for this assignment. He was himself an expert marksman, and his company became known as "McCottry's Rifles" in honor of their skills.[10] A contingent of Maryland Continentals posted themselves behind a nearby breastwork to protect the tower from attack.[11]

As dawn began to break on the eighth day of the siege, McCottry's men initiated the attack, raining a shower of bullets down on Fort Watson that drove the defenders to seek cover and rendered them unable to return effective fire. With the enemy so occupied, one group from Lee's Legion led by Robert Lee and another group of militiamen led by Ensign Baker Johnson advanced with little difficulty. Edward McCrady reports that "such was the effect of the riflemen upon the top of the tower, having complete command of every part of the fort, that the besieged found it impossible to resist the lodgement effected by the attacking party."[12] Under such protection, Lee and Johnson's men quickly reduced the three abatis and began hacking away at the logs forming the wall of the stockade.[13] Behind Lee and Johnson was an assault element comprised of infantrymen led by Captain Patrick Carnes. "Helmets down and bayonets fixed," Carnes's men stood "ready to charge through the opening and storm the fort."[14] A final assault, however, proved unnecessary. Finding that "a majority of the men [had] grounded their arms and refused to defend the post any longer," McKay had little recourse but to surrender.[15]

Marion was quick to give Maham credit for the Patriot victory, writing Greene that Maham "had, in a particular manner, a great share of the success by his unwavering diligence in erecting the tower which principally occasioned the reduction of the fort."[16] Later, "Maham's Tower," as the structure became known, was copied to capture Fort Cornwallis in Augusta, Georgia, and during the siege of the star fort at Ninety Six. Even in the American Civil War, Federal forces used such a structure to fire on the besieged Confederates at Vicksburg.[17]

Innovation

Maham's initiative at Fort Watson illustrates the role innovation plays in leadership. Maham knew that carrying on with the unsatisfactory status quo was not an acceptable option. The formidable British defense had not only defied the Patriot efforts to defeat it, attrition and the lack of progress were dangerously threatening the morale of Marion's partisans. Indeed, some initiatives such as trying to cut off the British water supply and employing cannons had been attempted, but the failure of these relatively conventional efforts had sapped the Patriot will. It was "at this low point during the siege of Fort Watson" that Scott Aiken proclaims, "low country innovation thankfully came to the rescue in the form of the Maham tower."[18]

Maham understood that change was required. In so doing, he illustrates James Kouzes and Barry Posner's argument that leaders must move beyond "habitual thinking patterns" in order to start imaging "truly novel alternatives."[19] Similarly, Peter Northouse writes that to counter the ordinary, leaders must "act to expand the available options to long-standing problems" and "change the way people think about what is possible."[20] Kouzes and Posner agree, adding that "change is the work of leaders. It's what they do ... They experiment. They tinker."[21] "Innovation and leadership," they argue, "are nearly synonymous."[22]

By this point in the siege of Fort Watson, one can imagine some partisan soldiers dejectedly surveying the British defenses with a degree of resignation and grudging acceptance. In contrast, Maham's response to the situation met the challenge Kenneth Blanchard poses in *Leading at a Higher Level* to go beyond "problem spotting" and actually engage in "problem solving."[23] Rather than bemoaning the problem, Maham energetically set out to solve it.

Such problem solving requires initiative, creativity, and originality to transcend the standing perspective, understanding, and information. This skill set is often described as "thinking outside the box." "Making extraordinary things happen in organizations," Kouzes and Posner argue, "demands a willingness to try new things and take chances with new ideas."[24] Clearly Maham exhibited this skill and will in constructing his tower.

But such individual initiative would be meaningless in problem-solving without leadership that is willing to create "an organizational climate that releases the knowledge, experience, and motivation that reside in people"; a process Blanchard refers to as "empowerment." One can only imagine the initial reaction of Marion when Maham first approached him with the idea of building a tower, but Aiken credits Marion for a characteristic "acceptance and use of unique weapons."[25] In fact, Lee recalls that Maham approached Marion and "suggested a plan, which was no sooner communicated than adopted."[26] Such a supportive organizational climate illustrates the contention of Kouzes and Posner that "the more trusted people feel, the better they innovate."[27] Both men deserve credit for showing good leadership: Maham for his creative application of problem-solving to produce change and Marion for supporting him through it.

Rebecca Motte and Leadership by Example

Rebecca Brewton Motte, born June 15, 1737, was the daughter of Robert Brewton, a Charleston goldsmith whose father came to South Carolina from Barbados. On June 11, 1758, Rebecca married Jacob Motte, Jr., a prominent plantation owner, politician, and member of the General Assembly. He served several times in the Royal Assemblies between 1760 and 1775, in the Second Provincial Congress, and the First, Second, and Third General Assemblies between 1775 and 1780.[1]

Rebecca had seven children by Jacob, three of whom died in their youth. Two daughters, Elizabeth and Frances, would successively marry Thomas Pinckney, who was an aide to Major General Horatio Gates during the war and later governor of South Carolina. Jacob and Rebecca acquired Fairfield Plantation on the lower Santee River around 1758.[2] When Jacob died in January 1781, Rebecca inherited Fairfield, other properties, and 244 slaves.

Motte was already quite wealthy before Jacob died, having previously inherited a significant portion of her brother Miles Brewton's estate. Brewton was a prominent mercantile businessman and slave dealer. He owned as many as eight ships and eventually became "South Carolina's largest slave dealer."[3] In 1765, he began the construction of the lavish and still standing Brewton House on King Street in Charleston. He also purchased a number of plantations totaling over 12,000 acres, including Mount Joseph Plantation in 1773 or 1774 near the confluence of the Congaree and Wateree Rivers.[4] He was elected to the second Provincial Congress, but in August 1775, he, his wife, and family were on their way to Philadelphia when all were lost at sea.[5]

Sometime after Brewton's death, Motte moved to Charleston and settled into the Brewton House. She was there when the British threatened Charleston in 1780, and she offered her slaves to the Patriot cause to assist in the construction of defenses around Charleston.[6] When the British occupied Charleston, the Brewton House was seized and used as a headquarters by British commanders. Motte remained in the house briefly, and tradition has it that she used her female slaves to slip messages about British activities in Charleston to Francis Marion.[7]

Motte's daughters were also with her at the Brewton House, and to protect their virtue she moved to Mount Joseph, along the Congaree River, in the summer of 1780, where she built a new mansion. The road from Charleston to Camden passed nearby this location, rendering it potentially useful to the British as a supply depot. In early 1781, they seized the property; fortified it by adding palisaded walls, earthworks, and an outlying ditch; and it became known as "Fort Motte."[8]

While Marion and Lieutenant Colonel Henry Lee were laying siege to Fort Watson, Nathanael Greene was marching for Camden, arriving near there on April 19. Greene took up a position on Hobkirk's Hill, just north of Camden, and there clashed with Lieutenant Colonel Francis Lord Rawdon on April 25. Rawdon scored a tactical victory but having lost nearly a third of his men in the process, he ultimately decided to abandon Camden in order to consolidate his forces. He began a movement south towards Nelson's Ferry along the Santee River.[9] After the fall of Fort Watson, Lee and Marion stayed close to Greene, on the north side of the Santee until they received a much needed six-pounder cannon. Then they crossed the river and began the siege of Fort Motte on May 6.[10]

Marion had some 150 men, and Lee's Legion consisted of perhaps 100 dragoons and 148 infantry.[11] The Americans also had the 6-pounder cannon under the command of Captain Ebenezer Finley and an escort of as many as 115 North Carolina Continentals under Major Pinkethan Eaton.[12] It was a small force arrayed against a formidable defense which Marion described to Greene as being "obstinate, and strong."[13]

Opposing the Americans was a detachment of 184 British regulars, Hessians, and Provincials, collectively under the command of Captain-Lieutenant Charles McPherson. The British consisted of 80 officers and men of the 2nd Battalion, 84th Regiment of Foot, under the command of

Captain Neil Campbell. The newly raised and green-jacketed Hessians included 59 officers and men of Frederick Starcloff's troop of Light Dragoons under the command of Corporal John Ludvick. There were also some 45 Provincials under the command of Loyalist Levi Smith, who had not officially been commissioned as their leader. Included in the total mix of defenders were an unknown number of dragoons who had arrived with supplies and two cannon the day before Marion and Lee did.[14]

Marion and Lee immediately began formal siege operations, but word of Rawdon's abandonment of Camden instilled a sense of urgency to capture Fort Motte before he could arrive with reinforcements. Both sides could see Rawdon's campfires on the High Hills of Santee and assumed he was fast approaching. For the Americans, this development meant there would be no time to employ a Maham's Tower, as had been done at Fort Watson. For the British, the knowledge that help was on the way strengthened their resolve. Buoyed by this optimism, McPherson rejected two demands that the fort surrender. Undeterred, Lee and Marion developed a very pragmatic solution to their problem. They would compel the British to surrender by firing flaming arrows to set the house's roof on fire.

Sometime shortly before or right after the arrival of Marion and Lee, McPherson had ordered the Motte contingent out of the fort and exiled them back across the vale to their old "overseer's" house.[15] When Lee arrived, Motte invited him to stay there as well. Motte proved to be a gracious host. Lee writes that not just he, "but every officer of his corps, off duty, daily experienced her liberal hospitality, politely proffered, and as politely administered." Lee recalled "her richly-spread table presented with taste and fashion all the luxuries of her opulent country, and her

Mrs. Jacob Motte (Rebecca Brewton). (Artist, Jeremiah Theus, c. 1758, Wikimedia Commons)

Mrs. Motte Directing General Marion and Colonel Lee to Burn her Mansion to Dislodge the British. (Artist, John Blake White, c. before 1859, US Senate)

sideboard offered without reserve the best wines of Europe." For Lee, it was an "antiquated relic of happier days." In addition to such sociability, Lee notes that Motte's "active benevolence found its way to the sick and wounded; cherishing with softest kindness infirmity and misfortune, converting despair into hope, and nursing debility into strength."[16]

In the midst of such refinement, it was determined that the more polished Lee would be a better candidate to discuss the plan of attack with Motte than would be the rough-hewn Marion. Although a stalwart Patriot, the widow could ill-afford to lose her home. Nonetheless, she not only acquiesced to Lee's proposal, legend has it that she proclaimed that "if it were a palace, it should go."[17] As Lee records it, "with a smile of complacency this exemplary lady listened to the embarrassed officer, and gave instant relief to his agitated feelings, by declaring, that she was gratified with the opportunity of contributing to the good of her country, and that she should view the approaching scene with delight."[18]

The exact weapon and tactic employed in carrying out the plan is open to some debate. Lee rather fancifully credits Motte herself with providing the bow and arrow—family heirlooms imported from India in his version of the story.[19] One of Marion's privates, Nathan Savage, claimed that instead of bows and arrows, he made a ball of rosin and brimstone which he set on fire and slung on top of the roof. The more likely scenario and one described by a British officer is that the arrows were fired from muskets.[20]

Regardless of the actual means of delivery, the tinder-dry shingles on Motte's roof were soon set ablaze. Lee relates that "The first arrow struck, and communicated its fire; a second was shot at another quarter of the roof, and a third at a third quarter; this last also took effect; and like the first, soon kindled a blaze."[21] British efforts to put the fire out were stymied by canister fire from the Patriot's six-pounder cannon, and at 1:00pm on May 12, the British surrendered.[22] With that matter resolved, the erstwhile enemies cooperated to extinguish the flames.

Then in what John Gordon describes as being "in best plantation style," Motte remarkably invited both the British and Patriot officers to "a sumptuous dinner."[23] "Soothing in the sweets of social intercourse," Lee claims the feast served to placate "the ire which the preceding conflict has engendered." "Conversing with ease, vivacity, and good sense" throughout the meal, Lee credits the gracious Motte with "obliterate[ing] our recollection of the injury she had received."[24]

Motte's willingness to sacrifice her house was far from the only service she rendered the Patriot cause. After the war, she was awarded over 600 pounds for the rice, beef, pork, corn, and fodder she supplied the troops from 1778 through 1783.[25] Nonetheless, she would spend much of the rest of her life repaying debts caused by the war.

Leadership by Example

Motte's heroism and selflessness exemplify "leadership by example." In employing this leadership style, leaders not only show their subordinates "what right looks like," they reaffirm their commitment to the organization's values by demonstrating that their words match their deeds and aligning actions and values.[26] In so doing, they build the credibility that James Kouzes and Barry Posner consider to be "the foundation of leadership."[27]

Such credibility comes when followers see that the leader is "personally passionate and enthusiastic about the work."[28] Motte modelled this commitment not just by her willingness to sacrifice her house, but by her almost cheerful attitude to making such a costly offering. By Pastor Weems's account, Motte declared, "God forbid I should bestow a single thought on my little concerns, when the independence of my country is at stake."[29] Weems, of course, is a chronic embellisher, but in this case his poetic license is a useful indicator of the impact such a gesture would have on the soldier witnesses who were also making heroic sacrifices for the cause.

Kouzes and Posner also insist that leadership by example—or what they call "modelling the way"—enhances a leader's moral authority.[30] Evidence that Motte's behavior had this effect can be gleaned from the hagiographic manner in which Lee describes her "ease, vivacity, and good sense," and by the fact that even the British soldiers rallied to help put out the flames.[31]

Finally, good leadership by example elicits something from the follower and helps him understand something about himself.[32] The wonderful meal that Motte served to both victor and vanquished after the battle had this effect. It gave an opportunity, as Lee eloquently expresses, for hard-bitten soldiers to pause and reflect, to process recent events, and to perhaps find some humanity amid the ravages of war. Not unsurprisingly, Weems exuberantly declares that "for my life I could not keep my eyes from her" and marveled how, "catching her amiable spirit, we seemed to have entirely forgotten our past animosities."[33]

Leading by example goes beyond merely doing what is supposed to be done. Everyone should be doing that. Leading by example is a way a leader influences others by using herself to elicit a desired behavior response. Motte's example of personal sacrifice, magnanimity, and grace certainly had that effect.

William Moultrie and Servant Leadership

William Moultrie was born in Charleston, South Carolina, on November 23, 1730, the second son of Dr. John Moultrie and his wife, Lucretia Cooper. Moultrie's biographer, C. L. Bragg, describes him as being "brought up in a relatively sophisticated southern society that highly valued literacy," and Moultrie apparently received a good education.[1] His marriage into the wealthy St. Julien family secured Moultrie's wealth and social standing, and he obtained a 1,020-acre estate called North Hampton from his brother-in-law. As a planter, Moultrie accumulated even more wealth through the cultivation of rice and indigo. He was also active in politics, being elected to the South Carolina Commons House of Assembly in 1752.[2]

In addition to planting and politics, Moultrie began what Bragg terms "a military apprenticeship" with his appointment as aide-de-camp to Governor William Henry Lyttleton in 1759. Moultrie accompanied Lyttleton on his ill-advised expedition against the Cherokees, and while his involvement was nominal, Moultrie was exposed to the hardships of war and the vagaries of militiamen.[3] He played a larger role in Lieutenant Colonel James Grant's expedition against the Cherokees in 1761, where Moultrie served as a captain in a regiment commanded by Lieutenant Colonel Henry Laurens. In addition to Laurens, Moultrie's experience fighting the Cherokees brought him in contact with such figures as Francis Marion, Isaac Huger, Christopher Gadsden, and Andrew Pickens, who would all play important roles in the coming war with Britain.[4]

When he returned home, Moultrie resumed his seat in the Commons House of Assembly. He also continued his militia service, being promoted to major in 1773 and colonel in 1774.[5] As tensions mounted with Britain, the Council of Safety ordered Moultrie on September 14, 1775, to dispatch 150 men to capture Fort Johnson on the east end of James Island. Upon completing this mission, Moultrie set out to improve the fort's defenses. It was also at this time that Moultrie may have been inspired to create the "Moultrie" or "Liberty" Flag that would later become famous.[6]

Even more important than Fort Johnson was Sullivan's Island which guarded the northern shore of the entrance to Charleston Harbor. The Patriot defenders began rafting thousands of palmetto logs there to build what became Fort Sullivan, and on January 10, 1776, the Council of Safety ordered Moultrie to detach a force there to protect the workers. When a fleet of over 50 vessels commanded by Commodore Sir Peter Parker and bearing soldiers led by Major General Sir Henry Clinton appeared outside the harbor on June 1, Major General Charles Lee, commander of the Southern Department, declared the fort to be a veritable "slaughter pen" that would not last half an hour against a British attack. He urged abandoning the island, but, buoyed by Moultrie's confident reports, Governor John Rutledge told Moultrie, "General Lee wishes you to evacuate the fort. You will not do so without an order from me. I would sooner cut off my right hand than write one."[7]

On June 28, 1776, the British attacked, and Moultrie and his men repelled a bombardment from the sea against Fort Sullivan and a land assault across Breach Inlet on the other side of the island. The British retreated, and Moultrie was promoted to brigadier general by a grateful Continental Congress. Fort Sullivan was also renamed Fort Moultrie in his honor. While Moultrie continued to defend Charleston, Major General Benjamin Lincoln, Lee's successor, joined forces with the French in a failed effort to capture Savannah, Georgia. On October 9, 1779, Lincoln hurried back to Charleston, while the British reinforced their army in Georgia.

On February 11, 1780, 2,000 British grenadiers and light infantry commanded by Clinton landed on Simmons (now Seabrook) Island to begin their campaign to take Charleston.[8] By March 30, Charleston was under siege. The Patriot situation steadily deteriorated until

Lincoln surrendered on May 12. Under the terms of surrender, 5,600 Continental soldiers and sailors, Moultrie among them, became prisoners of war on parole until duly exchanged.[9]

While the enlisted Continental soldiers were confined to barracks in the city of Charleston, the officers were sent to Hadrell's Point, a mile or so across the cove from Sullivan's Island on the mainland at Mount Pleasant. Moultrie was the senior officer at Hadrell's Point, and the British allowed him the freedom to travel to Charleston as he pleased to check on the welfare of the men. Lincoln also assigned Moultrie the responsibility of arranging quarters for the officers until they were exchanged. Moultrie found housing for himself with Charles Cotesworth Pinckney at Snee Farm, the plantation of Pinckney's uncle located some five miles from Hadrell's Point in Christ Church Parish.[10]

William Moultrie. (Artist, Charles Willson Peale, 1805. National Portrait Gallery, Smithsonian Institution; transfer from the National Gallery of Art: gift of the A. W. Mellon Educational and Charitable Trust, 1842)

In early June, Lincoln departed for Philadelphia under the terms of his parole, and Moultrie became the de facto commanding officer. With this development, Bragg notes that Moultrie also became "the principal advocate for the captive Continental force—not just for his fellow parolees at Hadrell's Point, but also for the enlisted men in Charlestown."[11] Among the areas that demanded Moultrie's attention in the fulfillment of this immense responsibility were provisions, discipline, diplomacy, and fair treatment.

Before Lincoln departed, he appointed Captain Charles Turner to be deputy commissary general for prisoners. Almost immediately, food became a serious problem, and Moultrie began advocating for improvements. On May 28, he wrote to Turner that "we have almost been starved" and inquired "what instructions you have, relative to the prisoners."[12] On June 16, Moultrie informed Brigadier General James Patterson, then the British commandant of Charleston, of the irregular food supply and requested him to "allow the officers at Hadrell's-point, to be supplied with provisions weekly."[13]

Although Moultrie maintained amicable terms with Patterson, Moultrie had a tense relationship with Turner. Much of the problem was due to Moultrie not fully understanding the financial difficulties under which Turner labored, but for his part, Turner also considered himself beyond Moultrie's authority. The two men squabbled for four months which further strained an already precarious supply system.[14] Nonetheless, Moultrie's entreaties to both Patterson and Turner are indicative of his advocacy on behalf of his fellow prisoners.

In addition to obtaining supplies, Moultrie was tasked with maintaining discipline among the prisoners. This proved a difficult undertaking, with Moultrie declaring that the officers at Hadrell's Point "were very ungovernable indeed." While Moultrie was willing to assign some of the blame to close-quarters living among men from different backgrounds, he also reported finding "some of them to be very uncouth gentlemen." Disputes, duels, disorderly conduct, and uncivil behavior were all too common.[15] To restore discipline, Moultrie advised Brigadier General Lachlan McIntosh, the senior American residing at Hadrell's Point, that "should any disorders happen, you will apply them to me, and I will immediately order a court martial to be held."[16]

On the other hand, Moultrie was quick to defend those under his care when he perceived an injustice was being done. In one such case, Dr. John Houston, a Continental officer paroled in Charleston but given permission to travel to Georgia on private business, was arrested by the Crown's chief justice there on charges of treason. In a letter of June 30, Moultrie appealed to Royal Governor James Wright on Houston's behalf. Although he received no reply to his letter, Moultrie reports "Doctor Houston was immediately released."[17]

Moultrie's diplomatic skills were tested surrounding the independence celebration at Haddrell's Point on July 4. The British had graciously allowed music and illuminations, but Patterson declared reports of firearms being discharged to be "an indecent abuse of lenity." He therefore ordered Moultrie to ensure "the officers do immediately, and without exception, deliver up all their fire-arms to the commanding officer at Fort Arbuthnot [as the British had renamed Fort Moultrie in honor of Admiral Mariot Arbuthnot, commander of the British fleet]."[18]

Moultrie had been present at the celebration and recalled "no indecent abuse, or gross outrage," but upon investigation, did confirm firearms had been discharged. This, he assured Patterson in a July 7 letter, represented "no intended affront, but to that exhilaration of spirit which in young men is so frequently the effect of convivial entertainments."[19] Through adroit negotiation, Moultrie was able to convince Patterson to allow the Americans to keep their pistols, but Patterson insisted upon "immediately withdrawing the indulgence granted them, of being allowed their fowling-pieces."[20]

Moultrie faced a greater challenge when Lieutenant Colonel Nisbet Balfour replaced Patterson in August. Moultrie described Balfour as a "proud and haughty Scot, [who] carried his authority with a very high hand; his tyrannical disposition, treated the people as the most abject slaves."[21] Nonetheless, Balfour was one of the most trusted subordinates of Lord Charles Cornwallis.[22]

Moultrie and Balfour quickly clashed over the British prison ships that had come into increased use to house the influx of prisoners after the American defeat at Camden. Bragg describes conditions aboard these ships as "horrific beyond most imagination" and notes that more Americans died of starvation and disease aboard the ships than died in battle.[23] On August 29, Moultrie read in the newspaper that Cornwallis had ordered 33 prominent Charlestonians to the prison ship *Lord Sandwich* on suspicion of plotting insurrection. Among the accused were Thomas Heyward, Jr., a signer of the Declaration of Independence, and Christopher Gadsden, the lieutenant governor. Moultrie demanded the prisoners return to their paroles to which Balfour replied that he "would do as he pleased with the prisoners ... and not as General Moultrie pleases."

Moultrie pressed Balfour with accusations of other violations of the articles of capitulation, and Balfour responded equally contemptuously. Undeterred, Moultrie forwarded his complaints to the Continental

Congress in Philadelphia in March where it was determined "that outrages abhorrent to Civilized Nations have been practiced and sanctioned by the British General Cornwallis and the Officers and Men which compose the banditti under his command." In June, Congress resolved to retaliate by treating British and German prisoners "in a manner as will be most conformable to the usage which American soldiers in captivity receive from the enemy."[24]

In addition to the vexations imposed upon him by Balfour, Moultrie was offered self-serving temptations to abandon the Patriot cause. Lord Charles Greville Montague, former royal governor of South Carolina and long-time acquaintance of Moultrie, told Moultrie "You have fought bravely in service of your country ... You have had your share of hardships and difficulties ... younger hands should now take the toil from you."[25] Montague then suggested Moultrie leave the Continental Army and go with him to command a regiment in Jamaica to fight the French and the Spaniards. Moultrie rejected the offer out of hand. "Great God!" he wrote Montague, "is it possible that such an idea could arise in the breast of a man of honor?"[26] But given the near contemporaneous treason of Benedict Arnold, Montague's proposal was not unprecedented. The difference, Henry William DeSaussure notes, was that "while in Arnold [the British] found a traitor, in General Moultrie they met a true patriot who rejected with scorn the offers to abandon that struggle for liberty and independence."[27]

Moultrie would have one last major confrontation with Balfour in March 1778. Fledgling talks of prisoner exchanges, notwithstanding, Balfour notified Moultrie of Cornwallis's decision "to send all the prisoners of war here, forthwith to some one of the West-India islands."[28] Moultrie responded with considerable restraint but with clear purpose. "I must request you will be so kind as to inform me," he asked Balfour, "whether you deem the capitulation dissolved?" Then, after briefly alluding to the on-going talks of exchange, he advised Balfour that "the sending of us to the West-India islands cannot expedite the exchange one moment, neither can the measure alleviate the distresses of those of your officers who are prisoner, as you must be well assured such treatment as we receive will be fully retaliated by Gen. Washington."[29] Before the matter went further, however, the articles of exchange for the Southern Department were finally agreed upon on May 3.[30]

In a final cruelty, Balfour issued an edict on June 27 that banished from Charleston the wives and families of those who had refused allegiance to the Crown. Thus, in July, Moultrie and his family, along with some 90 other Continental officers and militia with their families, set sail for Philadelphia. Many of the parolees had incurred serious financial hardship during their captivity and were now nearly destitute. When Moultrie received an August 13 letter from 24 former prisoners asking him to present their grievances to Congress, Moultrie was quick to act on their behalf. Congress responded with firewood and three months of back pay.[31] On February 19, 1782, Moultrie was formally exchanged and released from parole in a deal for Major General John Burgoyne that included Moultrie and Pinckney, 32 other officers, and 433 rank and file.[32] Moultrie finally returned to Charleston on December 14, 1782, entering the city with Major General Nathanael Greene as the British evacuated.[33]

Servant Leadership

Moultrie's conduct as a prisoner of war is an excellent example of "servant leadership," an idea popularized by Robert Greenleaf who published *Servant Leadership* in 1977. Servant leadership is a leadership approach in which the leader meets the subordinate's legitimate needs—which might include such concerns as training, encouragement, resources, or help with personal issues—in order to allow the subordinate to better focus on and accomplish the organizational mission.[34] While the traditional authoritarian leader asks, "What can the organization do for me?," the servant leader asks, "What can I do for the organization?"

Greenleaf made no attempt to provide a universal checklist or a formula for becoming a servant leader. Instead, he wanted each person and organization to apply the principles and values in ways that were meaningful to them.[35] In *Seven Pillars of Servant Leadership*, James Sipe and Don Frick attempt to "constellate ... and expand upon" Greenleaf's insights in defining a servant leader as "a *person of character* who *puts people first*. He or she is a *skilled communicator, a compassionate collaborator* who has *foresight*, is a *systems thinker*, and *leads with moral authority*." The italicized words and phrases make up Sipe and Frick's seven pillars which in turn generate 21 traits or competencies.[36]

Sipe and Frick describe character as "operative values" or "values in action."[37] In putting their values in action, Sipe and Frick argue that "Servant-Leaders maintain integrity."[38] One instance of Moultrie demonstrating this attribute was in his refusal of Montague's offer to forsake the Patriot cause for personal gain.

When a servant leader "puts people first," Sipe and Frick write that they "express genuine care and concern for others."[39] Moultrie's actions on behalf of his fellow prisoners demonstrate such service. His efforts to provide his fellows with food, shelter, and financial support are examples.

A skilled communicator "influences others with assertiveness and persuasion rather than power and position."[40] As a prisoner, Moultrie was certainly void of power and position relative to Balfour, but Moultrie effectively advocated for his fellow prisoners and argued their cases.

For Sipe and Frick, a compassionate collaborator "relates well to people of diverse backgrounds and interests" and "manages disagreements respectfully, fairly, and constructively."[41] Moultrie displayed these characteristics in his dealings with Patterson. The compromise resolution to the Fourth of July celebration is an example.

A servant leader with foresight "imagines possibilities, anticipates the future, and proceeds with clarity and purpose."[42] Such foresight was necessary as the British and Americans began to discuss exchange protocols, and Moultrie was able to articulate to Balfour the negative impact that relocating the American prisoners to the West Indies would have on that process.

According to Sipe and Frick, systems thinking requires the servant leader to "think and act strategically, manage change effectively, and balance the whole with the sum of its parts."[43] As the de facto commanding officer of the American prisoners at Charleston, Moultrie thought and acted strategically by focusing on the clear outcome of safeguarding the lives of his men. He managed change between a fairly agreeable commander in Patterson and a hostile one in Balfour. He understood that the whole prisoner system was the sum of such parts as food, shelter, and supplies. A very finite example of a system Moultrie created was the one addressing discipline.

A servant leader who exhibits moral authority is "worthy of respect, inspires trust and confidence, and establishes quality standards for performance."[44] In response to the assessment that American soldiers held prisoner during the Korean War were unprepared and ill-equipped to deal with the type of treatment imposed upon them by the communists, on August 17, 1955, President Dwight Eisenhower signed "Executive Order 10631—Code of Conduct for members of the Armed Forces of the United States." The order states that "All members of the Armed Forces of the United States are expected to measure up to the standards embodied in this Code of Conduct while in combat or in captivity."[45] One of the Code's mandates is "If I am senior, I will take command." Moultrie did that. The last article of the Code states, "I will never forget that I am an American fighting man, responsible for my actions, and dedicated to the principles which made my country free. I will trust in my God and in the United States of America."[46] Moultrie did that too.

Andrew Pickens and Personal Leadership

Andrew Pickens was born in Paxtang Township, Pennsylvania, and his family migrated to Waxhaw Creek, South Carolina, around 1752. His first experience of warfare was as a lieutenant in Lieutenant Colonel James Grant's expedition against the Cherokees in 1761. While Grant led a regiment of British regulars, Pickens served in the provincial regiment commanded by Lieutenant Colonel Henry Laurens. Pickens reported that in the campaign "I learned something of brittish cruelty which I always abhorred."[1]

In 1763, Pickens moved to the Long Cane region, and he soon established himself as a justice of the peace, elder in the Presbyterian Church, respected war veteran, and substantial landowner. He was also becoming increasingly invested in establishing the peace and order necessary for the backcountry to realize its economic potential.[2] It is unclear if Pickens played a part in the "Regulator" movement that surfaced in late 1766 to counter the rampant crime plaguing the backcountry, but Rod Andrew, Pickens's excellent biographer, notes that Pickens "certainly … represented the type of settler who would have supported and might have participated in it."[3]

Many citizens of the backcountry were either ambivalent to the Patriot cause or fully loyal to the Crown. Pickens, however, was wholeheartedly among the Patriots. Thus, in November of 1775 he found himself with a force of 560 men under the command of Major Andrew Williamson defending the garrison at Ninety Six against well-over 1,500 Loyalist militia commanded by Patrick Cunningham and Joseph Robinson.

Ultimately, the siege turned into a stalemate, but the Patriots emerged from it with a renewed resolve to address the Loyalist presence in the backcountry. Pickens was almost certainly a part of the ensuing Snow campaign that smashed the Tory resistance over the course of the winter.[4]

While the Patriots in Charleston were repulsing the first British attack there in the summer of 1776, Pickens and his backcountry colleagues were engaged in a series of battles against the Cherokees. In August, Pickens had the misfortune of walking into an Indian ambush and quickly became surrounded. In a desperate battle immortalized as the "Ring Fight," Andrew writes that Pickens and his men survived when they "should not have," and as a result, Pickens "began acquiring an aura of invincibility." His champions report that from that point forward, the Indians began referring to him as "Sky-a-gun-sta" or "Great Warrior." In subsequent fighting, the whites inflicted significant damages on the Cherokees that compelled them to negotiate a treaty with the South Carolina government in 1777.[5]

The Patriot successes of 1776 against the British at Charleston and against the Cherokees in the backcountry led to three years of relative calm in South Carolina. During that period, Pickens was elected justice of the peace for the Ninety Six District and as one of the district's 10 representatives in the General Assembly which sat from 1776 to 1778. The Patriot effort to solidify control in the South was interrupted in March of 1778 when the British inaugurated a new strategy of focusing on that theater. Pickens, now a colonel, was part of the campaign in Georgia that failed to bring to bay Tory Colonel Thomas Brown in the summer of 1778, as well as the Patriot victory at Kettle Creek on February 14, 1779, that Andrew deems "the key event in reversing British gains in upper Georgia."[6]

When General Sir Henry Clinton began his siege of Charleston in March 1780, Pickens was part of Brigadier General Andrew Williamson's effort to serve as a diversion in the backcountry. When Charleston fell on May 12, many of the demoralized militia accepted the same British terms of parole offered to the troops that had surrendered there and returned to their homes. Pickens was among them. Facing no organized Patriot resistance, Lieutenant Colonel Banastre Tarleton and his Legion rode roughshod throughout the backcountry and also emboldened the local Tory population to engage in vandalism and violence. In the last week of November 1780, while Pickens was away, a British-Tory force looted his plantation and abused his family. Andrew argues that although "every American source cites [this raid] as the cause of Pickens's renouncing his parole," Pickens was already preparing to rejoin the Patriot cause.[7] Either way, in December, Pickens led a loosely organized militia group of his Long Cane fellows north to join the Continental forces commanded by Brigadier General Daniel Morgan.

Gen. Andrew Pickens. (Engraving by J. B. Longacre after painting by Sully, between 1820 and 1869, Library of Congress)

Pickens commanded the South Carolina militia in Morgan's brilliant victory at Cowpens on January 17, 1781, and was promoted to brigadier general on January 25. During the War of the Posts, Pickens joined with Elijah Clarke and Henry Lee to help secure Augusta, Georgia, for the Patriot cause on June 5, 1781. Pickens was also part of the unsuccessful siege of the British fort at Ninety Six from May 22 to June 19, 1781. He then led his brigade at Eutaw Springs on September 8, 1781; a tactical draw but strategic Patriot victory that proved to be the last major battle between the British and Patriots in South Carolina.

The next month the British surrendered at Yorktown, but that certainly did not mean that the backcountry was suddenly safe and peaceful. Pickens remained busy with the lingering security threats posed by Tories, Cherokees, and vengeful Whigs. In a brutal campaign in South Carolina and Georgia that lasted until the fall of 1782, order was restored and the threat of organized cooperation between the Cherokees and Tories was eliminated. The ruthless tactics employed by Pickens would alarm modern sensibilities, but there was no such outcry at the time.[8]

The conclusion of these important military duties allowed Pickens to focus on his political ones. He was elected to the House of Representatives from the Ninety Six District for the third time in November 1782. Military activities had prevented Pickens from serving on the two previous occasions, but he now immersed himself with his fellow legislators in resolving the unfinished business of the war. He continued to serve in the House until 1788 and then in the State Senate, representing the Pendleton District from 1790 to 1793. In 1793, he went to the United States House of Representatives, where he served until 1795. Returning to South Carolina, he served in the General Assembly from 1796 to 1799. Pickens came out of retirement at the onset of the War of 1812 to serve again briefly in the General Assembly. When he died on August 11, 1817, he was viewed by his contemporaries as the embodiment of the patriotism and virtue that had established the new republic.[9]

Pickens lived a remarkable lifetime of broad and varied accomplishments, but for the purposes of this study, it is in the post-war period that his leadership attributes are of particular interest. The fledgling days of the republic were unsettled and evolutionary. Not only was America trying to rebuild a society shattered by war, Andrew notes it was "also trying to construct an entirely new political order without kings or hereditary lords—a republic where liberty and order were protected by men selected to lead because of their 'virtue' rather than their lineage."[10] Pickens was one such man.

Personal Power

In order to lead, leaders must influence their followers, and this influence comes from applying the power that the leader has.[11] The leader can gain that power from both his position and his person. Positional power is the power the leader derives from the rank or position he holds in the organization.[12] It was the sort of power that was the accepted norm before the Revolution.

In those days, leadership in South Carolina at the state and national levels was largely positional, reserved exclusively for the elite "gentlemen of rank" who occupied the upper strata of the society.[13] Consider, for example, some of the men with whom Pickens served as part of Grant's expedition against the Cherokees in 1761: Henry Laurens, wealthy owner of a thriving import-export business and slave merchant, commanded the provincial regiment as a lieutenant colonel. William Moultrie, who had married into great wealth and then purchased a large rice plantation, was a captain. Son of a wealthy planter, Isaac Huger was just 18 years old and newly returned from Europe where he had been sent for his education, when he was made a lieutenant. On the political side, that same year John Rutledge, who would become South Carolina's wartime governor, was beginning his career representing Christ Church in the provincial assembly. A lawyer and wealthy landowner, Rutledge is described by one study as bearing a political philosophy "typical of his class ... He believed that those with wealth and social standing, men with the greatest stake in society, had the duty to govern."[14] In contrast, men without pedigree or formal education were simply not entrusted to offices beyond the local level, and Pickens, Andrew notes, "did not have a good education, great wealth, or even average speaking ability."[15]

Lacking the positional characteristics of the gentry, Pickens instead led by personal power; that is, he rose to higher levels of leadership by his personal characteristics and how his fellow men considered him.[16] Whereas positional power promotes the *compliance* of followers, personal power transcends mere tangible action and promotes the intangible *commitment* of followers.[17] It "allows the leader to influence not just the followers' behavior, but their thinking as well through an appeal to personal attitudes, beliefs, and values."[18] Consider, for example, the situation in which Pickens found himself in in December 1780 as he led his group of volunteers north from Long Cane to join Daniel Morgan. With the collapse of South Carolina's Whig government in May, Patriot militiamen no longer received formal pay or any of the other incentives commonly used to gain compliance in the exercise of positional leadership. Like Pickens, they were leaving their homes and families to serve a cause in which they believed, and Pickens could only sustain their commitment "by [the] force of personality and persuasion" required of personal leadership.[19]

The leader earns this personal power by gaining the trust, admiration, and respect of the followers. Because personal power is "derived from the followers," Glenn Klann reminds leaders that "followers can withdraw this power just as easily as they give it."[20] Pickens, Andrew writes, was "seen as honest, steady in times of uncertainty, and adept at leading other men in war.... He was exactly the kind of man that the fledgling republican state of South Carolina needed in its attempts to shore up liberty and order."[21]

Followers give leaders personal power when leaders act in ways that are important to the followers.[22] Specifically, leaders receive this personal power when they act as good role models, display high competence, or show special consideration for those they are leading. Robert Greenleaf argues that such personal power amounts to a "moral principle ... which holds that the only authority deserving one's allegiance is that which is freely and knowingly granted by the led to the leader in respect to, and in proportion to, the clearly evident servant stature of the leader."[23]

Rather than parlaying his military fame into financial gain through opportunistic land deals as so many of his contemporaries did after the war, Pickens followed Greenleaf's prescription and selflessly served in one capacity after another.[24] Andrew points to Pickens's public service during the crisis surrounding the War of 1812 as a notable example. "Coming as it did roughly a decade after his 'retirement,'" Andrew argues, "it was easy for [Pickens's contemporaries] to conclude that his willingness to return to Columbia had nothing to do with ambition and everything to do with patriotism in time of war."[25] The relationship between such example and impact is captured in William Martin's 1843 reminiscence of Pickens: "And to see the homage paid to Virtue! What a strong incentive to imitate it!"[26]

Personal power of the sort wielded by Pickens is divided into two categories: expert power and referent power.[10] Expert power is based on the knowledge and expertise one has in relation to followers. It is being the subject-matter expert. The more knowledge, skills, talents, and proficiencies leaders have, the more power they can leverage.

Pickens certainly had abundant expert power based on his knowledge of the Indian trade and his familiarity with backcountry land and geography. For these reasons, Andrew declares that "if one wanted to do business in the most westerly portions of [South Carolina], Andrew Pickens was a good man to know."[27]

But it was in the area of referent power, which Klann describes as "the power generated by relationships—the brick and mortar of solid organizations,"[28] that Pickens excelled. Pickens's expert power notwithstanding, Andrew notes that "the most fundamental reason for the amount of public trust placed in Pickens, however, had to do with his generation's understanding of virtue and what was required to make a republic work."[29] Leaders gain referent power based on the strength of the personal bonds and relationships they develop with their followers. Andrew posits that "the Revolutionary generation had ... inherited a classical republican tradition that said that republics, and therefore liberty, were impossible unless some men could be counted on to rise above their own selfish interests." "The state," Andrew continues, "must find virtuous men who devoted themselves to the welfare and liberties of their fellow citizens." In Pickens, post-Revolution South Carolina found such a man.[30]

Conclusion

While this book relates an historical event, it does so in the context of leadership, so its conclusions will focus in that area. Maurice Matloff noted that the American Revolution began what he called the "democratization of war."[1] His observation certainly has leadership implications. Democratization generally involves a transition from authoritarianism to choice. Peter Northouse notes that "leadership is not a linear, one-way event but rather an interactive event."[2] He contrasts leadership with coercion which, like authoritarianism, involves the use of power and restraint to force followers to behave in a certain way. Instead of coercion, Northouse explains that leaders use influence to work with followers to achieve a common goal.[3] In such a relationship, the followers have a choice, and the task of the leader is to influence them to make the choice he desires. This intersection of leadership, choice, and influence certainly is one of the themes represented by these *Profiles in Leadership*.

As a leader, Henry Laurens sought to influence fellow South Carolinians facing the most fundamental choice of the day: to seek independence or to remain loyal to the Crown. It was a choice Laurens had grappled with on a personal level, overcoming his initial preference for reconciliation. Using steps that were compatible with John Kotter's eight-stage process of creating major change, Laurens and the Council of Safety led the majority of South Carolinians to choose independence.

Richard Furman's leadership task was like Laurens's, but instead of the entire colony, Furman's focus was on the backcountry. There much of the population was predisposed to a strong Tory sentiment, and Furman used charismatic leadership to try to influence them to choose unity with the low county.

William Jasper's choice was of a personal nature. He had to decide whether to remain behind the safety of Fort Sullivan's walls or risk his life to recover the fallen flag. The choice he made inspired many of his comrades to choose to redouble their efforts to defend against the British attack.

John Rutledge also faced at least two key personal choices. The first was to either surrender with Charleston or to flee and form a government-in-exile. The second was whether to restore civil government even as fighting continued or to wait until peace had been achieved. In both cases, Rutledge had to make pragmatic decisions, but his decisions empowered others to make choices. Had he not been willing to accept a certain level of suboptimization, he would have limited the choices available to his followers.

The transactional leadership of Thomas Sumter epitomizes follower choice, even if it does not necessarily reflect a high order of leader influence. By its very nature, transactional leadership presents followers with a personal choice that they can accept or decline based on self-interest. Each transaction must be re-negotiated, and the follower can make a new choice based on the terms the leader offers. As Sumter found out, the leader's ability to influence is determined by his ability to offer items of utilitarian value to the follower. In transactional leadership, it is the item offered in exchange more so than the leader that is influencing the follower's choice.

Francis Marion realized that his militia men were continually faced with the choice to either remain in the field or return home. He refused to use the promise of plunder to influence his men's choice and instead used transformational leadership to create a connection between his men and the Patriot cause and between his men and himself as their leader. As a result, most of Marion's men made a deep and enduring choice that transcended the fickle and temporal choices of transactional leadership.

Isaac Shelby and the Overmountain Men had a choice to stay in their relatively isolated communities or to come to fight in South Carolina. Having decided to come to South Carolina, they had the choice to informally cooperate with each other or to operate parochially. They choose cooperation, voluntarily following natural leaders who influenced by example, proven competence, trust, and inspiration.

Nathanael Greene had to make choices regarding ends, ways, and means. His options were informed by the limitations of his situation, but Greene wisely made choices that were realistic and practical, rather than wishful and unsupportable. In determining his end, Greene had to choose between trying to destroy the enemy or simply gaining time. He chose a strategy of exhaustion that would weaken the British forces while preserving his own. For his ways, Greene chose to give battle only on his own terms, relying on finesse rather than force. For his means, Greene had to choose between his proclivity for Continental regulars and the ready availability of the partisan militia. Although Greene lamented his hope that "the good lord deliver us" from a militia he considered ill-disciplined and unreliable, he had to confess that "the support of the militia is the very ground work of our Independence for the regular force can never maintain our cause independent of them."[4] Every choice Greene made was based on a realistic appraisal of his situation.

Daniel Morgan's choice revolved around how to employ his militia. Understanding their capabilities and limitations, Morgan chose a role for the militia that was "doable" for them and supportive of his overall tactical plan. Given this manageable task, the militia, which in other battles had turned and run, chose to do what Morgan asked them to do at Cowpens. Indeed, the outcome was so positive that other Patriot commanders chose a similar role for the militia in subsequent battles.

Thaddeus Kosciuszko obtained information that was critical to Nathanael Greene's ability to make operational choices. Kosciuszko's reconnaissance of the Cheraws allowed Greene to choose a better camp for his army. Kosciuszko's preparation of boats and other efforts to enhance mobility allowed Greene to choose an advantageous sequel to the victory at Cowpens. Perhaps unique among the profiles, Kosciuszko's role was more follower than leader, but he shows how a good follower can help his leader make wise choices.

Henry Lee's use of negotiation gave his adversaries a choice. They could either accept Lee's terms and surrender or take their chances in battle. Lee was careful to create conditions that influenced his enemy to make a choice advantageous to the Patriot position. In a sense, surrendering was an advantageous choice for the British as well in that, by it, they avoided what they perceived as a worse outcome from fighting.

Hezekiah Maham had the choice of accepting the status quo and conventional thinking or using innovation and originality to create positive change. As the commander and the man with overall responsibility for the operation's success or failure, Francis Marion also had a choice. He could either play it safe with the traditional methods or take a risk with Maham's untested idea. Both men demonstrated that some choices are based on unknowns.

Rebecca Motte faced the stark choice of allowing her house to be burned or not. Her precommitment to the Patriot cause made obvious for her a choice that would have caused most others untold distress. Instead, Motte's values led her to have already made the overarching choice that she merely held in abeyance until the time came to put it into action.

William Moultrie was given a choice by Lord Charles Greville Montague to abandon the Patriot cause and fight with the British in Jamaica or to remain a prisoner. Rather than take the opportunity to relieve himself from his deprivations, Moultrie rejected the treasonous offer. He chose instead to continue serving his fellow prisoners by advocating for their fair treatment.

Andrew Pickens had the choice to follow the example of many of his contemporaries and parlay his military fame into financial gain. Instead, he chose a life of public service after the war. The people of South Carolina responded to Pickens's decision by choosing to give their trust to a man whose power rested on his person rather than his position.

In discussing the dynamic of choice in the context of leadership and followership, much of the literature uses phrases like ownership, empowerment, and buy-in. Bob Chapman and Raj Sisodia have settled on the phase "responsible freedom" to describe the phenomenon. "Freedom," they argue, represents "the opportunity to exercise personal choice, to have ownership of the work you do and the decisions you make." "Responsibility" involves "ensuring that personal choice is exercised with care and concern for other people and the requirements of the organization."[5] When the Patriots in South Carolina choose to fight for their independence, they did so with full awareness of the risks and rewards that hung in the balance. In many ways, it was their ability to pursue their choice with responsible freedom that secured their victory.

Endnotes

Overview of the American Revolution in South Carolina and the Southern Campaign, 1775–1783

1. Robert Middlekauff, *The Glorious Cause: The American Revolution, 1763–1789* (New York, NY: Oxford University Press, 1982), 434–35; Jim Piecuch, *Three Peoples, One King: Loyalists, Indians, and Slaves in the Revolutionary South, 1775–1782* (Columbia: University of South Carolina Press, 2008), 36–37. In his book, Piecuch argues that truly there were many Loyalists in South Carolina, however, very early in the war the Americans began a campaign of harassment and cruelty, which intimidated the Loyalists from rallying to the British forces when they finally arrived in force in 1780.
2. Keith Krawczynski, *William Henry Drayton, South Carolina Revolutionary Patriot* (Baton Rouge: Louisiana State University Press, 2001), 153–95. In this book, we use the terms Whigs, Americans, and Patriots interchangeably as supporters of the rebellion against the British Crown. Supporters of the crown were called Loyalists or Tories.
3. Jerome A. Greene, *Historic Resource and Historic Structure Report, Ninety Six: A Historical Narrative* (Denver Colorado: Denver Service Center, National Park Service, 1979), 66–75; Jim Piecuch, *South Carolina Provincials: Loyalists in British Service During the American Revolution* (Yardley, PA: Westholme Publishing, 2023), 42.
4. William B. Wilcox, ed., *The American Rebellion: Sir Henry Clinton's Narrative of His Campaigns, 1775–1782* (New Haven, CN: Yale University Press, 1954), 25–27.
5. *Encyclopedia of the American Revolution*, 2nd ed., Volume 2, s. v. "Moore's Creek Bridge"; David K. Wilson, *The Southern Strategy: Britain's Conquest of South Carolina and Georgia, 1775–1780* (Columbia: University of South Carolina Press, 2005), 25–32.
6. William Moultrie, *Memoirs of the American Revolution so far as it Related to the States of North and South Carolina, and Georgia* (New York, NY: David Longworth, 1802), 141–43.
7. Letter of a surgeon with the British Fleet, July 9, 1776, Peter Force ed., American Archives, 4th Series, quoted from, Henry Steele Commager, and Richard B.

Morris, eds., *The Spirit of 'Seventy-Six: The History of the American Revolution as Told by Participants* (Edison, NJ: Castle Books, 2002), 1,066–67; Moultrie, *Memoirs*, 179.
8. *Encyclopedia of the American Revolution*, 2nd ed., Volume 1, s. v. "Charleston Expedition of Clinton in 1776"; Wilson, *Southern Strategy*, 40–58.
9. Kenneth Coleman, "Georgia in the American Revolution, 1775–1782" in Kenneth Coleman, gen. ed., *A History of Georgia* (Athens: The University of Georgia Press, 1991, second edition), 72–76; "The Battle of the Rice Boats," available https://revolutionarywar.us/year-1776/battle-of-rice-boats/. Accessed April 12, 2024.
10. John W. Gordon, *South Carolina and the American Revolution: A Battlefield History* (Columbia: University of South Carolina Press, 2003), 48; John Hairr, *Colonel David Fanning: The Adventures of A Carolina Loyalist* (Erwin NC: Averasboro Press, 2000), 36.
11. Ibid., 52–53.
12. Piecuch, *Three Peoples*, 71–73.
13. Ibid., 94.
14. Gregory D. Massey, *John Laurens and the American Revolution* (Columbia: University of South Carolina Press, 2000), 130–32.
15. Walter Edgar, *South Carolina: A History* (Columbia: University of South Carolina Press, 1998), 231.
16. Wilson, *Southern Strategy*, 67–69.
17. Stephen Conway, *The British Army 1714–1783: An Institutional History* (Philadelphia, PA: Pen & Sword Press, 2021), 34; Stephen Conway, "British Governments and the Conduct of the American War," in H. T. Dickinson, ed., *Britain and the American Revolution* (London: Addison Wesley Longman Limited, 1998), 155–79.
18. Letter Lord George Germain to General Sir Henry Clinton, March 8, 1778. K. G. Davies, ed., *Documents of the American Revolution 1770–1783*, Volume 15 (Dublin: Irish Academic Press, 1976), 60–61.
19. *Encyclopedia of the American Revolution*, 2nd ed., Volume 2, s. v. "Savannah Georgia"; Wilson, *Southern Strategy*, 74–77.
20. *Encyclopedia of the American Revolution*, 2nd ed., Volume 1, s. v. "Kettle Creek, Georgia"; Piecuch, *South Carolina Provincials*"; Wilson, *Southern Strategy*, 87–88.
21. Moultrie, *Memoirs*, 291–95; Lawrence S. Rowland, Alexander Moore, and George C. Rogers, Jr., *The History of Beaufort County, South Carolina, Volume 1, 1514–1861* (Columbia: University of South Carolina Press, 1996), 216–19.
22. Wilson, *Southern Strategy*, 91–98.
23. David Mattern, *Benjamin Lincoln and the American Revolution* (Columbia: University of South Carolina Press, 1998) 73–74; Wilson, *Southern Strategy*, 123–31.
24. *Encyclopedia of the American Revolution*, 2nd ed., Volume 1, s. v. "Savannah, Georgia"; Wilson, *Southern Strategy*, 133–92.
25. Wilson, *Southern Strategy*, 167–68.
26. John Buchanan, *The Road to Guilford Courthouse: The American Revolution in the Carolinas* (New York, NY: John Wiley & Sons, 1997), 27; Carl P. Borick, *A Galant*

Defense: The Siege of Charleston, 1780 (Columbia: University of South Carolina Press, 2003), 28; Wilson, Southern Strategy, 198–99.
27. Mattern, Benjamin Lincoln, 92; Wilson, Southern Strategy, 207.
28. Buchanan, Guilford Courthouse, 50–53; Borick, Galant Defense, 71–85.
29. Borick, Galant Defense, 148; Encyclopedia of the American Revolution, 2nd ed., Volume 1, s. v. "Monck's Corner, South Carolina."
30. Johann Ewald Diary, quoted in Mattern, Benjamin Lincoln, 104.
31. Wilson, Southern Strategy, 224.
32. Borick, Gallant Defense, 177–78.
33. Wilson, Southern Strategy, 234–35.
34. Mattern, Benjamin Lincoln, 108.
35. Buchanan, Guilford Courthouse, 48, 129.
36. Wilson, Southern Strategy, 258–61.
37. John S. Pancake, This Destructive War: The British Campaign in the Carolinas (University, AL: The University of Alabama Press, 1985), 80–81.
38. Alexander Innes to Charles Cornwallis, June 8, 1780, in, Ian Saberton, ed., The Cornwallis Papers, Volume 1 (Uckfield, East Sussex, England: The Naval & Military Press, 2010), 111. Hereinafter, CP and Volume.
39. Encyclopedia of the American Revolution, 2nd ed., Volume 1, s. v. "Clinton–Cornwallis Controversy."
40. Clinton in Willcox, American Rebellion, 174–75.
41. Borick, Gallant Defense, 237–38.
42. Francis Rawdon to Charles Cornwallis, July 7, 1780, in Saberton, CP, Volume 1: 193–94.
43. Kenneth Coleman, The American Revolution in Georgia, 1763–1789 (Athens: University of Georgia Press, 1958). Reissued 2021, online, https://ugapress.manifoldapp.org/read/the-american-revolution-in-georgia-1763-1789/section/591084e9-4ca1-4d65-98dc-abd3bc1334a7. Chapter 8, accessed January 25, 2024.
44. Hugh F. Rankin, The North Carolina Continentals (Chapel Hill: The University of North Carolina Press, 1971), 239.
45. Terry W. Lipscomb, Battles, Skirmishes, and Actions Which Took Place In South Carolina During the American Revolution (Columbia: South Carolina Department of Archives and History, c. 1991), 7–8.
46. Walter Edgar, Partisans and Redcoats: The Southern Conflict That Turned the Tide of the American Revolution (Columbia, SC: Harper Collins, 2001), 58–59, 81–85; Michael C. Scoggins, The Day It Rained Militia: Huck's Defeat and the Revolution in the South Carolina Backcountry, May–July 1780 (Charleston, SC: The History Press, 2005).
47. Encyclopedia of the American Revolution, 2nd ed., Volume 2, s. v. "Rocky Mount, South Carolina."
48. Encyclopedia of the American Revolution, 2nd ed., Volume 1, s. v. "Hanging Rock, South Carolina."; Anne King Gregorie, Thomas Sumter (Columbia, SC: R. L. Bryan Company, 2000), 80, 90–93.

49. Jim Piecuch, *The Battle of Camden: A Documentary History* (Charleston, SC: The History Press, 2006); Steven D. Smith, James B. Legg, and Tamara S. Wilson, *The Archaeology of the Camden Battlefield: History, Private Collections, and Field Investigations* (Columbia: South Carolina Institute of Archaeology and Anthropology, 2008).
50. Cornwallis quoted in Buchanan, *Guilford Courthouse*, 169.
51. Quoted from George F. Scheer and Hugh F. Rankin, *Rebels and Redcoats: The American Revolution Through the Eyes of Those Who Fought and Lived It* (New York, NY: Da Capo Press, Reprint, 1957), 411.
52. John Oller, *The Swamp Fox: How Francis Marion Saved the American Revolution* (New York, NY: Da Capo Press, 2016), 60, 70–71, 79–81; Steven D. Smith, *Francis Marion and the Snow's Island Community: Myth, History, and Archaeology* (Asheville, NC: United Writers Press, Inc., 2021).
53. Buchanan, *Guilford Courthouse*, 178–79; John Buchanan, *The Battle of Musgrove's Mill* (Yardley, PA: Westholme Press, 2022).
54. Robert Brown, *Kings Mountain and Cowpens: Our Victory Was Complete* (Charleston, SC: The History Press, 2009), 47–48.
55. Buchanan, *Guilford Courthouse*, 225–37; Lyman C. Draper, *King's Mountain and Its Heroes: History of the Battle of King's Mountain* (Johnson City, TN: The Overmountain Press, 1881, Reprint 1996).
56. Clinton in Wilcox, ed., *American Rebellion*, 228; Scheer and Rankin, *Rebels and Redcoats*, 421.
57. Gregoire, *Sumter*, 113.
58. Ibid., 116–17.
59. *Encyclopedia of the American Revolution*, 2nd ed., Volume 1, s. v. "Blackstock's Plantation, South Carolina"; Gregorie, *Sumter*, 94–95, 100–3, 121–23.
60. Buchanan, *Guilford Courthouse*, 288.
61. Letter, *Nathanael Greene to Edward Stevens, December 1, 1780*. Richard K. Showman, gen. ed., *The Papers of Nathanael Greene*, Volume 6 (Chapel Hill: The University of North Carolina Press, 1991), 513. Hereinafter *GP* and Volume.
62. Lipscomb, *Battles*, 10–11.
63. Stephen E. Haller, *William Washington: Cavalryman of the Revolution* (Bowie, MD: Heritage Books, Inc., 2001), 68.
64. Piecuch, *Three Peoples*, 239.
65. William Thomas Sherman, *Calendar and Record of the Revolutionary War in the South, 1780–1781*. 10th edition (Seattle, WA: Gun Jones Publishing, 2018), 339–40.
66. Lawrence Babits, *A Devil of a Whipping: The Battle of Cowpens* (Chapel Hill: The University of North Carolina Press, 1998), 150; Sherman, *Calendar*, 358, 361.
67. Babits, *A Devil of a Whipping* (for battle narrative), 151, Sherman, *Calendar*, 362, for British casualty figures.
68. Letter, Cornwallis to Clinton, January 18, 1781, in Davies, ed., *Documents*, Volume 20: 33–34; Hugh F. Rankin, "Charles Lord Cornwallis: Study in Frustration," in,

George Athan Billias, ed., *George Washington's Opponents* (New York, NY: William Morrow and Company, Inc., 1969), 210.
69. Quoted in Rankin, "Study in Frustration," 210.
70. Letter, Greene to ? January 1 to 23, 1781, in *GP*, Volume 7: 175. This letter could have been written before or after the battle of Cowpens, but it does clearly show that Greene had a solid understanding of both his and his enemy's situation.
71. Rankin, *North Carolina Continentals*, 274–76.
72. Ibid., 281.
73. Buchanan, *Guilford Courthouse*, 358.
74. Ibid., 360.
75. Rankin, *North Carolina Continentals*, 290.
76. *Encyclopedia of the American Revolution*, 2nd ed., Volume 1, s. v. "Guilford Court House, North Carolina."
77. Ibid., 473; Buchanan, *Guilford Courthouse*, 380.
78. Letter, William Dickson to Robert Dickson, November 30, 1784, quoted in Scheer and Rankin, *Rebels and Redcoats*, 452.
79. Rankin, *North Carolina Continentals*, 314–16.
80. Letter, Nathanael Greene to George Washington, March 29, 1781, in *GP*, Volume 7: 481.
81. *Encyclopedia of the American Revolution*, 2nd ed., Volume 2, s. v. "Southern Campaigns of Nathanael Greene."
82. Lipscomb, *Battles*, 12–14.
83. Smith, *Snow's Island*, 126–32.
84. Gregorie, Sumter, 136–43.
85. John Buchanan, *The Road to Charleston: Nathanael Greene and the American Revolution*. (Charlottesville: University of Virginia Press, 2019), 75; Pancake, *This Destructive War*, 190–91.
86. Smith, *Snow's Island*, 146.
87. Samuel Mathis, quoted in Scheer and Rankin, *Rebels and Redcoats*, 456–57.
88. Buchanan *Road to Charleston*, 93–103; *Encyclopedia of the American Revolution*, 2nd ed., Volume 1, s. v. "Hobkirk's Hill."
89. Letter, Nathanael Greene to Samuel Huntington, April 27, 1781, *GP*, Volume 8: 157.
90. Gregorie, *Sumter*, 157–58.
91. Steven D. Smith, *The Battles of Fort Watson and Fort Motte, 1781* (Yardley, PA: Westholme Press, 2024).
92. Robert Dunkerly, Robert and Eric K. Williams, *Old Ninety Six: A History and Guide* (Charleston, SC: The History Press, 2006), 65–66.
93. Roderick MacKenzie, *Strictures on Lt. Col. Tarleton's History of the Campaigns of 1780 and 1781, in the Southern Provinces of North America* (London: R. Faulder, 1787), 149.
94. Buchanan, *Road to Charleston*, 126–37.
95. Ibid., 155.

96. Ibid., 154–55; Greene, *Ninety Six: A Historical Narrative*, 159.
97. MacKenzie, *Strictures*, 158.
98. Buchanan, *Road to Charleston*, 172–74.
99. Robert E. Lee, *The Revolutionary War Memoirs of General Henry Lee* (New York, NY: De Capo Press, 1998), 386.
100. Buchanan, *Road to Charleston*, 176.
101. Oller, *Swamp Fox*, 172–77.
102. Ibid., 199–201; Steven D. Smith and James Legg. *Running the Gauntlet: Locating the Battle of Parkers Ferry, South Carolina August 30, 1781*. Columbia: South Carolina Institute of Archaeology and Anthropology, 2019, 11–17.
103. Buchanan, *Road to Charleston*, 218–21.
104. Ibid., 2019, 230–33.
105. Ibid., 2019, 237.
106. Rankin, "Study in Frustration" 213.
107. Letter, Henry Clinton to George Germain, May 22, 1781, in Davies, ed., *Documents*, Volume 20: 147.
108. Rankin, "Study in Frustration," 214–16.
109. Letter, Cornwallis to Clinton, August 22, 1781, *CP*, Volume 6: 27–28.
110. Dan L. Morrill, *Southern Campaigns of the American Revolution* (Baltimore, MD: The Nautical & Aviation Publishing Company of America, 1993), 178.
111. Rankin, "Study in Frustration," 217.
112. Germain quoted in Scheer and Rankin, *Rebels and Redcoats*, 497.
113. John Hairr, *Colonel David Fanning*, 131–43; Rankin, *North Carolina Continentals*, 364–65.
114. Buchanan, *Road to Charleston*, 245–48.
115. Ibid., 259.
116. Ibid., 260.
117. Terry Golway, *Washington's General: Nathanael Greene and the Triumph of the American Revolution* (New York, NY: Henry Holt and Company, 2005), 287, 290, 295.
118. Buchanan, *Road to Charleston*, 264.
119. *Encyclopedia of the American Revolution*, 2nd ed., Volume 1, s. v. "Southern Campaigns of Nathanael Greene."
120. Golway, *Washington's General*, 298–99.
121. Clinton in Wilcox, *American Rebellion*, 356.
122. Letter, Germain to Clinton, January 2, 1782, in Davies, ed., Documents Volume 21: 27–28.
123. *Encyclopedia of the American Revolution*, 2nd ed., Volume 1, s. v. "Georgia Expedition of Wayne."
124. Oller, *Swamp Fox*, 222–23.
125. Lipscomb, *Battles*, 22.
126. Buchanan, *Road to Charleston*, 315–16.
127. Oller, *Swamp Fox*, 231–33; Steven D. Smith, *Archaeological Evaluation of Wadboo Plantation, 38BK464* (Columbia: South Carolina Institute of Archaeology and Anthropology, 2008), 9–11.

128. Buchanan, *Road to Charleston*, 327–28.
129. American Battlefield Trust. "Dills Bluff Battle of James Island," available https://www.battlefields.org/learn/revolutionary-war/battles/dills-bluff. Accessed May 17, 2024.
130. Golway, *Washington's General*, 304.
131. *Encyclopedia of the American Revolution*, 2nd ed., Volume 2, s. v. "Peace Negotiations."

Henry Laurens and Creating Change

1. David Duncan Wallace, *The Life of Henry Laurens* (New York, NY: Russell and Russell, 1915), 15.
2. Ibid., 16.
3. Ibid., 45.
4. Ibid., 125.
5. Ibid., 95.
6. Rod Andrew, *The Life and Times of General Andrew Pickens: Revolutionary War Hero, American Founder* (Chapel Hill: University of North Carolina Press, 2017), 15.
7. Wallace, *Life of Henry Laurens*, 101.
8. Andrew, *Life and Times of Pickens*, 17–18.
9. John Kotter, *Leading Change* (Boston, MA: Harvard Business School Press, 1996), 21.
10. Ibid., 4.
11. Ibid., 45.
12. Jack Rosenthal, "A Terrible Thing to Waste," *New York Times*, July 31, 2009, available https://www.nytimes.com/2009/08/02/magazine/02FOB-onlanguage-t.html. Accessed October 2, 2024.
13. Kotter, *Leading Change*, 65.
14. Wallace, *Life of Henry Laurens*, 214.
15. Ibid., 68 and 71.
16. Ibid., 71.
17. "Papers of the First Council of Safety of the Revolutionary Party in South Carolina, June–November, 1775 (Continued)," *The South Carolina Historical and Genealogical Magazine*, Volume 1, No. 1 (Jan., 1900), 75.
18. Kotter, *Leading Change*, 71.
19. "Papers of the First Council of Safety," 75.
20. John W. Gordon, *South Carolina and the American Revolution* (Columbia: The University of South Carolina Press, 2003), 20.
21. Kotter, *Leading Change*, 71.
22. Andrew, *Life and Times of Pickens*, 45.
23. "Papers of the First Council of Safety," 42.
24. Kotter, *Leading Change*, 71.
25. Terry Lipscomb, *South Carolina Becomes a State: The Road from Colony to Independence* (Columbia: South Carolina Department of Archives and History, 1976), 13–14.

26. See for example Kotter, *Leading Change*, 90, and James Kouzes and Barry Posner, *The Leadership Challenge* (San Francisco, CA: Jossey-Bass, 2012), 139–51.
27. Kotter, *Leading Change*, 114–15.
28. Lipscomb, *South Carolina*, 16–17.
29. Kotter, *Leading Change*, 122–24.
30. Lipscomb, *South Carolina*, 10–11.
31. Gordon, *South Carolina*, 32.
32. Ibid., 55.
33. Peter Northouse, *Leadership: Theory and Practice* (Thousand Oaks, CA: Sage Publications, 2004), 8.

Richard Furman and Charismatic Leadership

1. James Rogers, *Richard Furman: Life and Legacy* (Augusta, GA: Mercer University Press, 1985), 21.
2. John W. Gordon, *South Carolina and the American Revolution* (Columbia: The University of South Carolina Press, 2003), 18.
3. Ibid., 18–19.
4. Robert Baker and Paul Craven, *History of the First Baptist Church of Charleston: 1682–2007* (Springfield, MO: Particular Baptist Press, 2007), 163.
5. Ibid., 163. The tea was eventually sold by South Carolina to help defray Revolutionary War expenses.
6. Rogers, *Richard Furman*, 25.
7. Rod Andrew, *The Life and Times of General Andrew Pickens: Revolutionary War Hero, American Founder* (Chapel Hill: University of North Carolina Press, 2017), 24.
8. Ibid., 24.
9. Ibid., 24–25; Rogers, *Richard Furman*, 27.
10. Rogers, *Richard Furman*, 27–28.
11. Andrew, *The Life and Times Pickens*, 22.
12. Rogers, *Richard Furman*, 28 and Andrew, *Life and Times of Pickens*, 39–40.
13. Rogers, *Richard Furman*, 29–30.
14. Rogers, *Richard Furman*, 29–30 and Andrew, *Life and Times of Pickens*, 40–51.
15. Rogers, *Life and Times of Pickens*, 267–73.
16. Ibid., 29–30.
17. Ibid., 30.
18. Ibid., 39.
19. Ibid., 30 and 38.
20. Baker and Craven, *First Baptist Church of Charleston*, 167–68.
21. Ibid., 168–69.
22. Rogers, *Richard Furman*, 40.
23. Ibid., 43.
24. Peter Northouse, *Leadership: Theory and Practice* (Thousand Oaks, CA: Sage Publications, 2004), 171–72.

25. Ibid., 171.
26. Jay Conger, *The Charismatic Leader: Behind the Mystique of Exceptional Leadership* (San Francisco, CA: Jossey-Bass, 1989), 33.
27. Northouse, *Leadership*, 171–72.
28. Conger, *Charismatic Leader*, 33–34.
29. Rogers, *Richard Furman*, 29.
30. Northouse, *Leadership*, 172.
31. Rogers, *Richard Furman*, 273.
32. Northouse, *Leadership*, 172.
33. Rogers, *Richard Furman*, 273.
34. Conger, *Charismatic Leader*, 34.
35. Rogers, *Richard Furman*, 273.
36. Northouse, *Leadership*, 172.
37. Baker and Craven, *First Baptist Church of Charleston*, 169.
38. Loizos Heracleous and Laura Alexa Klaering, "Charismatic Leadership and Rhetorical Competence: An Analysis of Steve Jobs's Rhetoric," *Group & Organization Management*, 2014, Volume 39(2), 135.
39. Rogers, *Richard Furman*, 210.
40. Heracleous and Klaering, "Charismatic Leadership," 134.

William Jasper and Heroic Leadership

1. Some sources suggest Jasper was of German ancestry. Sam Bauman, "The True Story Behind the Sgt. Jasper Ceremony." wtoc.com, assessed September 29, 2024.
2. Sgt. William Jasper Memorial Ceremony Honors Military, available https://savannahsaintpatricksday.com/sgt-william-jasper-memorial-ceremony-honors-military/. Accessed July 10, 2024.
3. William Moultrie, *Memoirs of the American Revolution so far as it Related to the States of North and South Carolina, and Georgia* (New York, NY: David Longworth, 1802), 90–91.
4. John W. Gordon, *South Carolina and the American Revolution: A Battlefield History* (Columbia: The University of South Carolina Press, 2003), 42–43.
5. Nic Butler, "Who was Sgt. William Jasper?", Weblog for the Mayor's "Walled City Task Force, June 22, 2015, available https://walledcitytaskforce.org/2015/06/22/who-was-sgt-william-jasper/. Accessed July 10, 2024.
6. Gordon, *South Carolina*, 43–44.
7. Peter Horry and Mason Locke Weems, *The Life of General Francis Marion* (Winston-Salem, NC: John F. Blair Publisher, reprint 2004), 34.
8. Kevin Dougherty and Steven D. Smith, *Leading Like the Swamp Fox: The Leadership Lessons of Francis Marion* (Philadelphia, PA: Casemate Publishers, 2022), xvi.
9. *Appletons' Cyclopaedia of American Biography*, Volume 6 (New York, NY: D. Appleton & Sons, 1889), 421.

10. Steven D. Smith, *Francis Marion and the Snow's Island Community: Myth, History, and Archaeology* (Asheville, NC: United Writers Press, 2021), xi, 237, 238, 259.
11. Charles Jones, Jr. "Sergeant William Jasper. An Address Delivered before the Georgia Historical Society, in Savannah, Georgia, on the 3rd of January, 1876" (Albany, GA: J. Munsell, printer, 1876), 22.
12. Ibid., 23.
13. John Keegan, *The Mask of Command* (New York, NY: Elisabeth Sifton Books, 1987), 10–11.
14. Ibid., 351.
15. Ibid., 351.
16. Chris Lowney, *Heroic Leadership: Best Practices from a 450-Year-Old Company That Changed the World* (Chicago, IL: Loyola Press, 2005), 14.
17. Ibid., 243.
18. Jones, "Sergeant William Jasper," 19.
19. Ibid., 6.
20. Ibid., 10.
21. Ibid., 23.
22. Lowney, *Heroic Leadership*, 242.
23. Ronald Reagan W. "Speech for Commencement by Ronald Reagan, May 15, 1993," The Citadel Archives Digital Collections, available https://citadeldigitalarchives.omeka.net/items/show/1075. Accessed October 3, 2004.

John Rutledge and Crisis Leadership

1. John Buchanan, *The Road to Charleston: Nathanael Greene and the American Revolution*. (Charlottesville: University of Virginia Press, 2019), 208.
2. Ibid., 208–9.
3. Ibid., 209.
4. Ibid., 210.
5. C. L. Bragg, *Crescent Moon over Carolina: William Moultrie & American Liberty* (Columbia: The University of South Carolina Press, 2013), 170.
6. Ibid., 171.
7. Ibid., 138.
8. Ibid., 135.
9. Ibid., 140.
10. Ibid., 141.
11. Ibid., 142.
12. Ibid., 146.
13. Ibid., 146.
14. Ibid., 148.
15. Ibid., 148.
16. Ibid., 149.

17. Ibid., 151 and Buchanan, *Road to Charleston*, 207.
18. Buchanan, *Road to Charleston*, 207–8.
19. Bragg, *Crescent Moon*, 151.
20. Ibid., 154.
21. Ibid., 160.
22. Buchanan, *Road to Charleston*, 291 and 298–99.
23. Resolution of the South Carolina General Assembly, February 16, 2007, available https://www.scstatehouse.gov/sess117_2007-2008/sj07/20070216.htm. Accessed July 10, 2024.
24. Moultrie, William. *Memoirs of the American Revolution so far as it Related to the States of North and South Carolina, and Georgia* (New York, NY: David Longworth, 1802), 105–6.
25. Michaela Kerrissey and Amy Edmondson, "Leading Through a Sustained Crisis Requires a Different Approach," *Harvard Business Review*, June 20, 2023, available https://hbr.org/2023/06/leading-through-a-sustained-crisis-requires-a-different-approach. Accessed October 4, 2024.

Thomas Sumter and Transactional Leadership

1. Anne King Gregorie, *Thomas Sumter* (Columbia, SC: The R. L. Bryan Company, 1931), 29–31.
2. Ibid., 148–49.
3. Walter Edgar, *South Carolina: A History* (Columbia: University of South Carolina Press, 1998), 66; William Scarborough, *The Allstons of Chicora Wood* (Baton Rouge: Louisiana State University Press, 2011), 1.
4. Edgar, *South Carolina*, 63.
5. Peter Wood, *Black Majority; Negroes in Colonial South Carolina from 1670 through the Stono Rebellion* (New York, NY: Knopf, 1974), 132.
6. Edgar, *South Carolina*, 80.
7. Hugh F. Rankin, *Francis Marion: The Swamp Fox* (New York, NY: Thomas Y. Crowell, 1973), 231–32.
8. Gary Wills, *Certain Trumpets: The Nature of Leadership* (New York, NY: Simon & Schuster, 1994), 120.
9. John Buchanan, *The Road to Charleston: Nathanael Greene and the American Revolution*. (Charlottesville: University of Virginia Press, 2019), 88.
10. Peter Northouse, *Leadership: Theory and Practice* (Thousand Oaks, CA: Sage Publications, 2004), 178.
11. Ibid., 170.
12. James Kouzes and Barry Posner, *The Leadership Challenge* (San Francisco, CA: Jossey-Boss, 2012), 171–72.
13. Philip Foner, *Blacks in the American Revolution* (Westport, CT: Greenwood Press, 1976), 65.

14. Benjamin Quarles, *The Negro in the American Revolution* (Chapel Hill: The University of North Carolina Press, 1996), 103.
15. William Boddie, *Traditions of the Swamp Fox: William Willis Boddie's Francis Marion* (Spartanburg, SC: The Reprint Company for the Williamsburgh Historical Society, 2000), xv.
16. Peter Horry and Parson M. L. Weems, *The Life of General Francis Marion: A Celebrated Partisan Officer, in the Revolutionary War, against the British and Tories in South Carolina and Georgia* (Philadelphia, PA: J. P. Lippincott, 1854, Reprint, Winston-Salem, NC: John F. Blair, 2000), 141–44.
17. Joseph Badaracco, *Questions of Character: Illuminating the Heart of Leadership Through Literature* (Boston, MA: Harvard Business Review Press, 2006), 87.

Francis Marion and Emotional Intelligence

1. Robert Bass, *Swamp Fox: The Life and Campaigns of General Francis Marion* (Orangeburg, SC: Sandlapper Publishing, 2000), 22.
2. Daniel Goleman, "What Makes a Leader?" *Harvard Business Review*, Volume 82, 2004: 82-91.
3. Ibid., 88.
4. Joseph Badaracco, *Questions of Character: Illuminating the Heart of Leadership Through Literature* (Boston, MA: Harvard Business Review Press, 2006), 117.
5. Ibid., 170.
6. Hugh F. Rankin, *Francis Marion: The Swamp Fox* (New York, NY: Thomas Y. Crowell, 1973), 46–48.
7. Ibid., 48–49.
8. Scott Aiken, *The Swamp Fox: Lessons in Leadership from the Partisan Campaigns of Francis Marion* (Annapolis, MD: Naval Institute Press, 2012), 61–62.
9. Rankin, *Francis Marion*, 57.
10. Aiken, *Swamp Fox*, 45.
11. John Oller, *The Swamp Fox: How Francis Marion Saved the American Revolution* (New York, NY: Da Capo Press, 2016), 57.
12. Aiken, *Swamp Fox*, 43.
13. Goleman, "What Makes a Leader?" 84.
14. Aiken, *Swamp Fox*, 115.
15. Ibid., 115.
16. Peter Horry and Parson M. L. Weems, *The Life of General Francis Marion: A Celebrated Partisan Officer, in the Revolutionary War, against the British and Tories in South Carolina and Georgia* (Philadelphia, PA: J. P. Lippincott, 1854, Reprint, Winston-Salem, NC: John F. Blair, 2000), 108.
17. Oller, *Swamp Fox*, 73.
18. John Gordon, *South Carolina and the American Revolution* (Columbia: The University of South Carolina Press, 2003), 117.

19. Bass, *Swamp Fox*, 76.
20. Aiken, *Swamp Fox*, 47.
21. Aiken, *Swamp Fox*, 111.
22. Ibid., 112; Bass, *Swamp Fox*, 49.
23. Aiken, *Swamp Fox*, 112.
24. Ibid., 112; Bass, *Swamp Fox*, 50–51.
25. Aiken, *Swamp Fox*, 45.
26. Marshall Goldsmith, *What Got You Here Won't Get You There: How Successful People Become Even More Successful* (New York, NY: Hyperion, 2007), 207–8.
27. Aiken, *Swamp Fox*, 6.
28. William G. Simms, *The Life of Francis Marion: The "Swamp Fox"* (New York, NY: G. F. Cooledge & Brother, 1844), 234.
29. Rankin, *Francis Marion*, 123.
30. Simms, *Life of Francis Marion*, 140.
31. Aiken, *Swamp Fox*, 49.
32. Goleman, "What Makes a Leader?" 90.
33. Horry and Weems, *Life of Marion*, 25.
34. Ibid., 26.
35. Ibid., 26.
36. Ibid., 26–27.
37. Ibid., 27.
38. Ibid., 27.
39. Ibid., 28.

Isaac Shelby and Cooperation

1. Pat Alderman, *One Heroic Hour at King's Mountain* (Johnson City, TN: The Overmountain Press, 1968), 3.
2. John W. Gordon, *South Carolina and the American Revolution: A Battlefield History* (Columbia: University of South Carolina Press, 2003), 112–13.
3. Robert Brown, *Kings Mountain and Cowpens: Our Victory Was Complete* (Charleston, SC: The History Press, 2009), 47–48.
4. J. David Dameron, *King's Mountain: The Defeat of the Loyalists, October 7, 1780* (Cambridge, MA: Da Capo Press, 2003), 24–25.
5. Gordon, *South Carolina*, 108.
6. John Buchanan, *The Battle of Musgrove's Mill, 1780* (Yardley, PA: Westholme Press, 2022), 55–56.
7. Dameron, *King's Mountain*, 30.
8. Robert Dunkerly, *The Battle of Kings Mountain: Eyewitness Accounts* (Charleston, SC: History Press, 2007), 135–36.
9. Katherine White, *The King's Mountain Men: The Story of the Battle, with Sketches of the American Soldiers who Took Part* (Baltimore, MD: Clearfield Company, 2001), 4.

10. Ibid., 4–5.
11. Alderman, *One Heroic Hour*, 32–33; Brown, *Kings Mountain*, 60.
12. Dameron, *King's Mountain*, 40; Dunkerley, *Battle of Kings Mountain*, 136.
13. Dunkerley, *Battle of Kings Mountain*, 136.
14. Dameron, *King's Mountain*, 4; Brown, *Kings Mountain*, 57–58.
15. Brown, *Kings Mountain*, 58.
16. Ibid., 58; Dameron, *King's Mountain*, 43–44.
17. Dameron, *King's Mountain*, 44.
18. Brown, *Kings Mountain*, 60–61.
19. Dameron, *King's Mountain*, 45–46.
20. Ibid., 57–60.
21. Ibid., 60–61.
22. Brown, *Kings Mountain*, 73.
23. John Buchanan, *The Road to Guilford Courthouse: The American Revolution in the Carolinas* (New York, NY: John Wiley & Sons, 1997), 225–37; Dameron, *King's Mountain*, 60–76; Brown, *Kings Mountain*, 75–83.
24. Dameron, *King's Mountain*, 77–78.
25. Ibid., 87.
26. Ibid., 88.
27. FM 100-5, *Operations* (Washington, DC: Headquarters, Department of the Army, 1993), 2–5 and 13–14.

Nathanael Greene and Strategic Leadership

1. John Buchanan, *The Road to Guilford Courthouse* (New York, NY: John Wiley & Son, 1997), 265.
2. Kevin Dougherty and Steven D. Smith, *Leading Like the Swamp Fox: The Leadership Lessons of Francis Marion* (Havertown, PA: Casemate, 2022), 40–42.
3. Russell Weigley, *The American Way of War* (New York, NY: Macmillan Publishing, 1973), 29.
4. Ibid., 32.
5. Scott Aiken, *The Swamp Fox: Lessons in Leadership from the Partisan Campaigns of Francis Marion* (Annapolis, MD: Naval Institute Press, 2012), 162; Weigley, *American Way of War*, 33.
6. Dougherty and Smith, *Leading Like the Swamp Fox*, 42–43.
7. Allan Millett and Peter Maslowski, *For the Common Defense: A Military History of the United States of America* (New York, NY: The Free Press, 1984), 72.
8. Roger Magee, ed., *Strategic Leadership Primer* (Carlisle, PA: US Army War College 1998), 3.
9. Arthur F. Lykke Jr., "Defining Military Strategy = E + W + M," *Military Review* 69, No. 5 (1989), 4.
10. John W. Gordon, *South Carolina and the American Revolution: A Battlefield History* (Columbia: University of South Carolina Press, 2003), 177.

11. Joel Woodward, "A Comparative Evaluation of British and American Strategy in the Southern Campaign of 1780–1781" (master's thesis, US Army Command and Staff College, Fort Leavenworth, KS, 2002), 79.
12. Ibid., 83.
13. Washington to Major-General Greene, October 22, 1780, in Worthington Chauncey Ford, ed., *The Writings of George Washington*, Volume 9 (New York, NY: Putman's Sons, 1890), 9–10.
14. John Alger, *Definitions and Doctrine of the Military Art* (West Point, NY: Department of History, United States Military Academy, 1979), 8.
15. James Haw, "'Every Thing Here Depends Upon Public Opinion': Nathanael Greene and Public Support in the Southern Campaigns of the American Revolution," *South Carolina Historical Magazine*, Vol. 109, No. 3 (July 2008), 212.
16. Weigley, *American Way of War*, 36.
17. Millett and Maslowski, *Common Defense*, 72.
18. Terry Golway, *Washington's General: Nathanael Greene and the Triumph of the American Revolution* (New York, NY: Macmillan, 2005), 271.
19. Weigley, *American Way of War*, 36.
20. Maurice Matloff, *American Military History* (Washington, DC: Office of the Chief of Military History, US Army, 1969), 93.
21. Gordon, *South Carolina*, 125–26.
22. Gregory Massey and Jim Piecuch. *General Nathanael Greene and the American Revolution in the South* (Columbia: University of South Carolina Press, 2012), 120.
23. Gordon, *South Carolina*, 126–27.
24. Bruce Lancaster, "'Heroic Huguenot,' Review of The Swamp Fox" *Saturday Review* (January 31, 1959): 33.
25. Ibid., 28.
26. Theodore Thayer, *Nathanael Greene: Strategist of the American Revolution* (New York, NY: Twayne Publishers, 1960).
27. Lawrence E. Babits, *A Devil of a Whipping: The Battle of Cowpens*. Chapel Hill: The University of North Carolina Press, 1998, 5.
28. Fletcher Pratt, *Eleven Generals; Studies in American Command* (New York, NY: William Sloane, 1949), 36.
29. Magee, *Strategic Leadership Primer*, 3.

Daniel Morgan and Team Building

1. Russell Weigley, *The American Way of War: A History of the United States Military Strategy and Policy* (Bloomington: Indiana University Press, 1977), 30.
2. Lawrence E. Babits, *A Devil of a Whipping: The Battle of Cowpens* (Chapel Hill: The University of North Carolina Press, 1998), 23–24. Many other sources relate the story as involving 500 assigned lashes and Morgan receiving 499.

3. Ibid., 23.
4. Babits, *A Devil of a Whipping*, 24; John Moncure, *The Cowpens Staff Ride and Battlefield Tour* (Fort Leavenworth, KS: US Army Command and General Staff College, 1996), 44.
5. Babits, *A Devil of a Whipping*, 24.
6. Moncure, *Cowpens Staff Ride*, 44.
7. Ibid., 44.
8. Sherman, *Calendar and Record of the Revolutionary War in the South, 1780–1781*. 10th edition (Seattle, Washington: Gun Jones Publishing, 2018), 339–340.
9. Babits, *A Devil of a Whipping*, 150; Sherman, *Calendar*, 358–362.
10. John W. Gordon, *South Carolina and the American Revolution: A Battlefield History* (Columbia: University of South Carolina Press, 2003), 133.
11. Moncure, *Cowpens Staff Ride*, 48.
12. Ibid., 47.
13. Ibid., 47–48.
14. Sherman, *Calendar*, 362.
15. Allan Millet and Peter Maslowski, *For the Common Defense: A Military History of the United States of America* (New York, NY: The Free Press, 1984), 72.
16. Sherman, *Calendar*, 362.
17. Rod Andrew, *The Life and Times of General Andrew Pickens: Revolutionary War Hero, American Founder* (Chapel Hill: University of North Carolina Press, 2017), 147.
18. Moncure, *Cowpens Staff Ride*, 43.
19. James Collins, *Good to Great* (New York, NY: Harper Business, 2001), 13.
20. John Maxwell, *The 17 Indisputable Laws of Teamwork* (Nashville, TN: Thomas Nelson, Inc, 2001), 33–34.
21. Ibid., 33.
22. Ibid., 34–36.

Thaddeus Kosciuszko and Planning Branches and Sequels

1. Alex Storozynski, *The Peasant Prince: Thaddeus Kosciuszko and the Age of Revolution* (New York, NY: Thomas Dunne Books, 2009), 2.
2. Storozynski, *Peasant Prince*, 10–11.
3. Ibid., 12.
4. Ibid., 17–18.
5. Ibid., 20.
6. For Kosciuszko's work at Saratoga see ibid., 32–39. For West Point, see ibid., 52–70.
7. Ibid., 87.
8. Ibid., 96–97.
9. Miecislaus Haiman, *Kosciuszko in the American Revolution* (New York, NY: Polish Institute of Arts and Science in America, 1943), 104.

10. Edwin Bearss, *The Battle of the Cowpens: A Documented Narrative & Troop Movement Maps* (Washington, DC: Office of Archeology and Historic Preservation, US Department of the Interior, 1967), 1.
11. Haiman, *Kosciuszko*, 105.
12. Storozynski, *Peasant Prince*, 97.
13. Strorozynski, *Peasant Prince*, 97.
14. Theodorus Bailey Myers, ed., *Cowpens Papers: Being Correspondence of General Morgan and the Prominent Actors* (Charleston, SC: The News and Courier, 1881), 23.
15. Andrew Waters, *To the End of the World: Nathanael Greene, Charles Cornwallis, and the Race to the Dan* (Yardley, PA: Westholme Publishing, 2020), xviii.
16. Quoted in Storozynski, *Peasant Prince*, 97.
17. J. B. O. Landrum, *Colonial and Revolutionary History of Upper South* Carolina (Greenville, SC: Shannon & Co, 1897), 306.
18. Joint Publication 5-0, *Joint Planning* (Washington, DC: Office of the Joint Chiefs of Staff, 2020), IV-38.
19. Myers, *Cowpens Papers*, 11.
20. Joint Publication 5-0, IV-39.
21. Quoted in Rob-Jan De Jong, *Anticipate: The Art of Leading by Looking Ahead* (New York, NY: AMACOM, 2015), 83.

Henry Lee and Negotiation

1. *Encyclopedia of the American Revolution*, 2nd ed., Volume 1, s. v., "Henry Lee,"; Michael Schelhammer, "10 Fateful Hits and Misses," online *Journal of the American Revolution*, September 19, 2013, available https://allthingsliberty.com/2013/09/10-fateful-hits-misses/. Accessed November 17, 2020.
2. John Oller, *The Swamp Fox: How Francis Marion Saved the American Revolution* (New York, NY: Da Capo Press, 2016), 115–17.
3. "Sketch of the Works at Fort Granby," in Dennis M. Conrad, Roger N. Parks, Martha King Richard Showman, eds., *The Papers of General Nathanael Greene*, Volume 8 (Chapel Hill: University of North Carolina Press, 1995), 265.
4. Mark Boatner, *Encyclopedia of the American Revolution* (New York, NY: David McKay Company Inc., 1963), 377.
5. Henry Lee, *The Campaign of 1781 in the Carolinas: With Remarks, Historical and Critical on Johnson's Life of Greene* (Philadelphia, PA: E. Littell, 1824), 367.
6. Robert E. Lee, ed., *The Revolutionary War Memoirs of General Henry Lee* (New York, NY: De Capo Press, 1998), 349.
7. Ibid., 350.
8. Ibid., 350.
9. Ibid., 351.
10. Ibid., 352.
11. Sun Tzu, *The Art of War*, Thomas Cleary, trans. (Boston, MA: Shambhala, 1988), 67.

12. Ibid., 82.
13. Stephen Covey, *The 7 Habits of Highly Effective People* (New York, NY: Simon & Schuster, 1989), 207.
14. Peter Northouse, *Leadership Theory and Practice* (Thousand Oaks, CA: Sage Publications, 2004, 178.

Hezekiah Maham and Innovation

1. Scott Aiken, *The Swamp Fox: Lessons in Leadership from the Partisan Campaigns of Francis Marion* (Annapolis, MD: Naval Institute Press, 2012), 162
2. John Oller, *The Swamp Fox: How Francis Marion Saved the American Revolution* (New York, NY: Da Capo Press, 2016), 147.
3. Ibid., 145.
4. Ibid., 147; Steven D. Smith, *The Battles of Fort Watson and Fort Motte* (Yardley PA: Westholme Press, 2024), 4.
5. Oller, *Swamp Fox*, 146.
6. Robert Bass, *Swamp Fox: The Life and Campaigns of General Francis Marion* (Orangeburg, SC: Sandlapper Publishing, 2000), 171.
7. Oller, *Swamp Fox*, 147.
8. Ibid., 147; Bass, *Swamp Fox*, 171.
9. Oller, *Swamp Fox*, 149.
10. Oller, *Swamp Fox*, 8.
11. Ibid., 149–50 and Bass, *Swamp Fox*, 177.
12. Edward McCrady, *The History of South Carolina in the Revolution, 1780–1783*, Volume 4 (New York, NY: MacMillan, 1902), 175.
13. Hugh F. Rankin, *Francis Marion: The Swamp Fox* (NY: Thomas Y. Crowell, 1973), 188–89.
14. Bass, *Swamp Fox*, 178.
15. Oller, *Swamp Fox*, 150, and Rankin, 189.
16. William Gilmore Simms, *The Life of Francis Marion: The "Swamp Fox"* (New York, NY: G. F. Cooledge & Brother, 1844), 232.
17. See Michael Morgan for information about the version of Maham's Tower at Vicksburg, "America's Civil War: Digging to Victory at Vicksburg," HistoryNet, available https://www.historynet.com/americas-civil-war-digging-to-victory-at-vicksburg/. Accessed July 10, 2024.
18. Aiken, *Swamp Fox*, 166.
19. James Kouzes and Barry Posner, *The Leadership Challenge* (San Francisco, CA: Jossey-Bass, 2012), 173.
20. Peter Northouse, *Leadership Theory and Practice* (Thousand Oaks, CA: Sage Publications, 2004), 10.
21. Kouzes and Posner, *Leadership Challenge*, 209.
22. Ibid., 182. See also 160.

23. Quoted in Kevin Dougherty, *The Campaigns for Vicksburg, 1862–1863* (Philadelphia, PA: Casemate, 2011), 166.
24. Kouzes and Posner, *Leadership Challenge*, 188.
25. Aiken, *Swamp Fox*, 48.
26. Henry Lee, *Memoirs of the War in the Southern Department of the United States* (Washington: Peter Force, 1827), 218.
27. Kouzes and Posner, *Leadership Challenge*, 220.

Rebecca Motte and Leadership by Example

1. Walter B. Edgar and N. Louise Bailey, *Biographical Directory of the South Carolina House of Representatives, Volume II, The Commons House of Assembly 1692–1775* (Columbia: University of South Carolina Press, 1974), 480–81.
2. Elise Pinckney, "Letters of Eliza Lucas Pinckney, 1768–1782," *South Carolina Historical Magazine*, 76(3), 1975: 145, 165; Anne B. L. Bridges and Roy Williams, III, *St James Santee Plantation Parish: History and Records, 1685–1925* (Spartanburg, SC: The Reprint Company, 1997), 56; Margaret F. Pickett, *Rebecca Brewton Motte: American Patriot and Successful Rice Planter* (Charleston, SC: Evening Post Books, 2022), 22.
3. Edgar and Bailey, *Biographical Directory*, 95–97.
4. Ibid., 96.
5. Richard N. Côté, *Mary's World: Love, War, and Family Ties in Nineteenth-Century Charleston* (Mount Pleasant, SC: Corinthian Books, 2001), 16; Alexander Salley, "Col. Miles Brewton and Some of His Descendants," *South Carolina Historical Magazine*, 2(2), 1901: 130–131, 142–44, 148–50.
6. Mrs. O. J. Weslin and Miss Agnes Irwin, *Worthy Women of Our First Century* (Philadelphia: J. B. Lippenwith Co., 1877), 264.
7. Margaret Hayne Harrison, *A Charleston Album* (Ringe, NH: Richard R. Smith Publications, Inc., 1953), 36–43.
8. John W. Gordon, *South Carolina and the American Revolution: A Battlefield History* (Columbia: University of South Carolina Press, 2003), 151.
9. Ibid., 150–51.
10. Steven D. Smith, *The Battles of Fort Watson and Fort Motte* (Yardley, PA: Westholme Press, 2004), 22–23.
11. Marion to Greene, May 6, 1781, Dennis Conrad, Dennis, ed., *The Papers of Nathanael Greene*, Volume 8 (Chapel Hill: The University of North Carolina Press, 1995), 214; Robert K. Wright, Jr., *The Continental Army* (Washington, DC: Center of Military History, United States Army, 1983), 161.
12. Hugh F. Rankin, *The North Carolina Continentals* (Chapel Hill: The University of North Carolina Press, 1971), 329–331.
13. Marion to Greene, May 12, 1781, in *GP*, Volume 8, 246.
14. Smith, *Battles*, 48–49.

15. Alexander Garden, *Anecdotes of the Revolutionary War in America: With Sketches of Character of Persons the Most Distinguished, In the Southern States, For Civil and Military Service* (Charleston, SC: A. E. Miller, 1822), 231.
16. Lee, Robert E., ed. *The Revolutionary War Memoirs of General Henry Lee*. New York, NY: De Capo Press, 1998), 346–47.
17. Peter Horry and Parson M. L. Weems, *The Life of General Francis Marion: A Celebrated Partisan Officer, in the Revolutionary War, against the British and Tories in South Carolina and Georgia* (Philadelphia, PA: J. P. Lippincott, 1854 Reprint, Winston-Salem, NC: John F. Blair, 2000), 208.
18. Lee, *Memoirs*, 347.
19. Ibid., 347.
20. Roderick Mackenzie, *Strictures of Lt. Col. Tarleton's History of the Campaigns of 1780 and 1781* (London: 1787), 151–52.
21. Lee, *Memoirs*, 348.
22. Smith, *Battles*, 73–75.
23. John Gordon, *South Carolina and the American Revolution* (Columbia: The University of South Carolina Press, 2003), 152.
24. Lee, *Memoirs*, 348.
25. Alexia Jones Helsley, "Rebecca Motte," in *South Carolinians in the War for American Independence* (Columbia: South Carolina Department of Archives and History, 2000), 65–69.
26. James Kouzes and Barry Posner, *The Leadership Challenge* (San Francisco, CA: Jossey-Bass, 2012), 17 and 74.
27. Ibid., 37.
28. Ibid., 37.
29. Horry and Weems, *Life of Marion*, 208.
30. Kouzes and Posner, *Leadership Challenge*, 40.
31. Helsley, "Rebecca Motte," 121.
32. Joseph Badaracco, *Questions of Character: Illuminating the Heart of Leadership Through Literature* (Boston, MA: Harvard Business Review Press, 2006), 55.
33. Horry and Weems, *Life of Marion*, 209.

William Moultrie and Servant Leadership

1. C. L. Bragg, *Cresent Moon over Carolina: William Moultrie and American Liberty* (Columbia: The University of South Carolina Press, 2013), 7.
2. Ibid., 9 and 14.
3. Ibid., 16.
4. Ibid., 22.
5. Ibid., 22.
6. Ibid., 37.
7. Ibid., 53–55.

8. Carl P. Borick, *A Gallant Defense: The Siege of Charleston, 1780* (Columbia: University of South Carolina Press, 2003), 28; David K. Wilson, *The Southern Strategy: Britain's Conquest of South Carolina and Georgia, 1775–1780* (Columbia: University of South Carolina Press, 2005), 198–99.
9. Bragg, *Crescent Moon*, 182.
10. Ibid., 184–85.
11. Ibid., 185.
12. William Moultrie, *Memoirs of the American Revolution* (New York, NY: David Longworth, 1802), 118.
13. Ibid., 113.
14. Bragg, *Crescent Moon*, 186–87.
15. Moultrie, *Memoirs*, 119.
16. Ibid., 119.
17. Ibid., 123–24.
18. Ibid., 131.
19. Ibid., 132–33.
20. Ibid., 133–35.
21. Ibid., 252.
22. Bragg, *Crescent Moon*, 189.
23. Ibid., 189.
24. Ibid., 190–91.
25. Moultrie, *Memoirs*, 166–67.
26. Ibid., 169.
27. Bragg, *Crescent Moon*, 192–94.
28. Moultrie, *Memoirs*, 172.
29. Ibid., 173–74.
30. Bragg, *Crescent Moon*, 198.
31. Ibid., 199.
32. Ibid., 200.
33. Ibid., 205.
34. James Hunter, *The Servant: A Simple Story About the True Essence of Leadership* (New York, NY: Crown Currency, 1998), 125.
35. James Swipe and Don Frick, *Seven Pillars of Servant Leadership* (New York, NY: Paulist Press, 2009), xvi.
36. Ibid., 4–6.
37. Ibid., 20.
38. Ibid., 25.
39. Ibid., 34.
40. Ibid., 45.
41. Ibid., 77.
42. Ibid., 104.
43. Ibid., 130.

44. Ibid., 155.
45. "Executive Order 10631—Code of Conduct for members of the Armed Forces of the United States," National Archives, available https://www.archives.gov/federal-register/codification/executive-order/10631.html. Accessed October 7, 2024.
46. "The US Fighting Man's Code," (Washington, DC: Office of Armed Forces Information and Education, Department of Defense, 1955), 42–44.

Andrew Pickens and Personal Leadership

1. Rod Andrew, *The Life and Times of General Andrew Pickens: Revolutionary War Hero, American Founder* (Chapel Hill: University of North Carolina Press, 2017), 18.
2. Ibid., 19.
3. Ibid., 24.
4. Ibid., 34 and 42–43.
5. Ibid., 48–51.
6. Ibid., 53–68.
7. Ibid., 88–89.
8. Ibid., 162.
9. Samuel K. Fore, "Pickens, Andrew," in Walter Edgar, ed., *The South Carolina Encyclopedia* (Columbia: The University of South Carolina Press, 2006), 721; Andrew, *Life and Times of Pickens*, 309.
10. Andrew, *Life and Times of Pickens*, 165.
11. Gene Klann, "The Application of Power and Influence in Organizational Leadership," in *Book of Readings* (Fort Leavenworth, KS: US Army Command and General Staff College, August 2011), 62.
12. Peter Northouse, *Leadership Theory and Practice* (Thousand Oaks, CA: Sage Publications, 2004), 6.
13. Andrew, *Life and Times of Pickens*, 54.
14. Robert Wright and Morris MacGregor, *Soldier-Statesmen of the Constitution* (Washington, DC: US Army Center of Military History, 1987), 168.
15. Andrew, *Life and Times of Pickens*, 54.
16. Andrew, *Life and Times of Pickens*, 164.
17. Klann, "Application of Power," 62.
18. Ibid., 63–64.
19. Andrew, *Life and Times of Pickens*, 95.
20. Klann, "Application of Power," 63–64.
21. Ibid., 54.
22. Northouse, *Leadership*, 6.
23. Robert Greenleaf, *Servant Leadership* (Mahwah, NJ: Paulist, 2002), 23–24.
24. Andrew, *Life and Times of Pickens*, 309.
25. Ibid., 307.
26. Ibid., 288.

27. Ibid., 165.
28. Klann, "Application of Power," 64.
29. Andrew, *Life and Times of Pickens*, 165.
30. Ibid., 165.

Conclusion

1. Maurice Matloff, *American Military History* (Washington, DC: Office of the Chief of Military History, United States Army, 1969), 100.
2. Peter Northouse, *Leadership: Theory and Practice* (Thousand Oaks, CA: Sage Publications, 2004), 3.
3. Ibid., 7.
4. John Buchanan, *The Road to Charleston: Nathanael Greene and the American Revolution* (Charlottesville, University of Virginia Press, 2019), 67–69.
5. Bob Chapman and Raj Sisodia, *Everybody Matters* (New York, NY: Portfolio/Penguin, 2015), 175.

Bibliography

Aiken, Scott. *The Swamp Fox: Lessons in Leadership from the Partisan Campaigns of Francis Marion*. Annapolis, MD: Naval Institute Press, 2012.

Alderman, Pat. *One Heroic Hour at King's Mountain*. Johnson City, TN: The Overmountain Press, 1968.

Alger, John. *Definitions and Doctrine of the Military Art*. West Point, NY: Department of History, United States Military Academy, 1979.

American Battlefield Trust. "Dills Bluff Battle of James Island." Accessed May 17, 2024. https://www.battlefields.org/learn/revolutionary-war/battles/dills-bluff.

Andrew, Rod. *The Life and Times of General Andrew Pickens*. Chapel Hill: The University of North Carolina Press, 2017.

Appletons' Cyclopaedia of American Biography, Volume 6. New York, NY: D. Appleton & Sons, 1889.

Babits, Lawrence. *A Devil of a Whipping: The Battle of Cowpens*. Chapel Hill: The University of North Carolina Press, 1998.

Badaracco, Joseph. *Questions of Character: Illuminating the Heart of Leadership Through Literature*. Boston, MA: Harvard Business Review Press, 2006.

Baker, Robert, and Paul Craven. *History of the First Baptist Church of Charleston: 1682–2007*. Springfield, MO: Particular Baptist Press, 2007.

Bass, Robert. *Swamp Fox: The Life and Campaigns of General Francis Marion*. Orangeburg, SC: Sandlapper Publishing Co., 1982.

"The Battle of the Rice Boats." Accessed April 12, 2024. https://revolutionarywar.us/year-1776/battle-of-rice-boats/.

Bauman, Sam. "The True Story Behind the Sgt. Jasper Ceremony." *WTOC11*, March 17, 2021. https://www.wtoc.com/2021/03/17/true-story-behind-sgt-william-jasper-ceremony/.

Bearss, Edwin. *The Battle of the Cowpens: A Documented Narrative & Troop Movement Maps*. Washington, DC: Office of Archeology and Historic Preservation, US Department of the Interior, 1967.

Boatner, Mark. *Encyclopedia of the American Revolution*. New York, NY: David McKay Company Inc., 1963.

Boddie, William. *Traditions of the Swamp Fox: William Willis Boddie's Francis Marion*. Spartanburg, SC: The Reprint Company for the Williamsburgh Historical Society, 2000.

Borick, Carl P. *A Gallant Defense: The Siege of Charleston, 1780.* Columbia: University of South Carolina Press, 2003.

Bragg, C. L. *Crescent Moon over Carolina: William Moultrie & American Liberty.* Columbia: The University of South Carolina Press, 2013.

Bridges, Anne B. L., and Roy Williams, III, *St James Santee Plantation Parish: History and Records, 1685–1925.* Spartanburg, SC: The Reprint Company, 1997.

Brown, Robert. *Kings Mountain and Cowpens Our Victory Was Complete* Charleston, SC: The History Press, 2009.

Buchanan, John. *The Road to Guilford Courthouse: The American Revolution in the Carolinas.* New York, NY: John Wiley & Sons, 1997.

———. *The Road to Charleston: Nathanael Greene and the American Revolution.* Charlottesville: University of Virginia Press, 2019.

———. *The Battle of Musgrove's Mill.* Yardley, PA: Westholme Press, 2022.

Butler, Nic. "Who was Sgt. William Jasper?" *Weblog for the Mayor's "Walled City" Task Force*, June 22, 2015. Accessed September 30, 2024. https://walledcitytaskforce.org/2015/06/22/who-was-sgt-william-jasper/.

Chapman, Bob, and Raj Sisodia. *Everybody Matters.* New York, NY: Portfolio/Penguin, 2015.

Coleman, Kenneth. "Georgia in the American Revolution, 1775–1782." In *A History of Georgia.* 2nd ed., edited by Kenneth Coleman. Athens: The University of Georgia Press, 1991.

———. *The American Revolution in Georgia, 1763–1789.* Athens: University of Georgia Press, 1958. Reissued 2021, online. Accessed January 25, 2024. https://ugapress.manifoldapp.org/read/the-american-revolution-in-georgia-1763–1789/section/591084e9–4ca1–4d65–98dc-abd3bc1334a7.

Collins, James. *Good to Great.* New York, NY: Harper Business, 2001.

Commager, Henry Steele and Richard B. Morris, eds. *The Spirit of 'Seventy-Six: The History of the American Revolution as Told by Participants.* Edison, NJ: Castle Books, 2002.

Conger, Jay. *The Charismatic Leader: Behind the Mystique of Exceptional Leadership.* San Francisco, CA: Jossey-Bass, 1989.

Conway, Stephen. "British Governments and the Conduct of the American War." In *Britain and the American Revolution*, edited by H. T. Dickinson. London: Addison Wesley Longman Limited, 1998.

———. *The British Army 1714–1783: An Institutional History.* Philadelphia, PA: Pen & Sword Press, 2021.

Conrad, Dennis, Roger N. Parks, Martha King Richard Showman, eds. *The Papers of Nathanael Greene*, Volume 8. Chapel Hill: The University of North Carolina Press, 1995.

Côté, Richard N. *Mary's World: Love, War, and Family Ties in Nineteenth-Century Charleston.* Mount Pleasant, SC: Corinthian Books, 2001.

Covey, Stephen. *The 7 Habits of Highly Effective People.* New York, NY: Simon and Schuster, 1989.

Dameron, J. David. *King's Mountain: The Defeat of the Loyalists, October 7, 1780*. Cambridge, MA: Da Capo Press, 2003.

Davies, K. G., ed. *Documents of the American Revolution 1770–1783*, Volume 15. Dublin: Irish Academic Press, 1976.

———. *Documents of the American Revolution 1770–1783*, Volume 20. Dublin: Irish Academic Press, 1978.

———. *Documents of the American Revolution 1770–1783*, Volume 21. Dublin: Irish Academic Press, 1981.

Dougherty, Kevin. *The Campaigns for Vicksburg, 1862–1863*. Philadelphia, PA: Casemate, 2011.

Dougherty, Kevin, and Steven D. Smith. *Leading Like the Swamp Fox: The Leadership Lessons of Francis Marion*. Philadelphia, PA: Casemate Publishers, 2022.

Draper, Lyman C. *King's Mountain and Its Heroes: History of the Battle of King's Mountain*. Johnson City, TN: The Overmountain Press, 1881. Reprint 1996.

Dunkerly, Robert. *The Battle of Kings Mountain: Eyewitness Accounts*. Charleston, SC: History Press, 2007.

Dunkerly, Robert, and Eric K. Williams. *Old Ninety Six: A History and Guide*. Charleston, SC: The History Press, 2006.

Edgar, Walter. *South Carolina: A History*. Columbia: University of South Carolina Press, 1998.

———. *Partisans and Redcoats: The Southern Conflict That Turned the Tide of the American Revolution*. Columbia, SC: Harper Collins, 2001.

Edgar, Walter, and N. Louise Bailey. *Biographical Directory of the South Carolina House of Representatives*, Volume 2, The Commons House of Assembly 1692–1775. Columbia: University of South Carolina Press, 1974.

"Executive Order 10631—Code of Conduct for members of the Armed Forces of the United States." National Archives. Accessed July 11, 2024. https://www.archives.gov/federal-register/codification/executive-order/10631.html.

FM 100–5, *Operations*. Washington, DC: Headquarters, Department of the Army, 1993.

Foner, Philip. *Blacks in the American Revolution*. Westport, CT: Greenwood Press, 1976.

Ford, William Chauncey, ed. *The Writings of George Washington*, Volume 9. New York, NY: Putman's Sons, 1890.

Fore, Samuel K. "Pickens, Andrew." In *The South Carolina Encyclopedia*, edited by Walter Edgar. Columbia: The University of South Carolina Press, 2006.

Garden, Alexander. *Anecdotes of the Revolutionary War in America: With Sketches of Character of Persons the Most Distinguished, In the Southern States, For Civil and Military Service*. Charleston, SC: A. E. Miller, 1822.

Goldsmith, Marshall. *What Got You Here Won't Get You There: How Successful People Become Even More Successful*. New York, NY: Hyperion, 2007.

Goleman, Daniel. "What Makes a Leader?" *Harvard Business Review*, Volume 82, 2004: 82–91.

Golway, Terry. *Washington's General: Nathanael Greene and the Triumph of the American Revolution*. New York, NY: Henry Holt and Company, 2005.

Gordon, John W. *South Carolina and the American Revolution.* Columbia: The University of South Carolina Press, 2003.

Gregorie, Anne King. *Thomas Sumter.* Columbia, SC: The R.L. Bryan Company, 1931.

Greene, Jerome. *Historic Resource and Historic Structure Report, Ninety Six: A Historical Narrative.* Denver, CO: Denver Service Center, National Park Service, 1979.

Greenleaf, Robert. *Servant Leadership.* Mahwah, NJ: Paulist, 2002.

Haiman, Miecislaus. *Kosciuszko in the American Revolution.* New York, NY: Polish Institute of Arts and Science in America, 1943.

Hairr, John. *Colonel David Fanning: The Adventures of a Carolina Loyalist.* Erwin, NC: Averasboro Press, 2000.

Haller, Stephen E. *William Washington: Cavalryman of the Revolution.* Bowie, MD: Heritage Books, Inc., 2001.

Harrison, Margaret Hayne. *A Charleston Album.* Ringe, NH: Richard R. Smith Publications, Inc., 1953.

Haw, James. "Every Thing here Depends on Opinion: Nathanael Greene and Public Support in the Southern Campaign of the American Revolution." *The South Carolina Historical Magazine,* No. 3 (July 2008): 212–231.

Helsley, Alexia Jones. *South Carolinians in the War for American Independence.* Columbia: South Carolina Department of Archives and History, 2000.

———. "Rebecca Motte." In *South Carolina Women: Their Lives and Times,* Volume 1, edited by Marjorie Julian Spruill, et al. Athens: University of Georgia Press, 2009.

Heracleous, Loizos, and Laura Alexa Klaering. "Charismatic Leadership and Rhetorical Competence: An Analysis of Steve Jobs's Rhetoric." *Group & Organization Management,* No. 2 (2014): 131–161.

Horry, P., and Parson M. L. Weems. *The Life of General Francis Marion: A Celebrated Partisan Officer, in the Revolutionary War, against the British and Tories in South Carolina and Georgia.* Philadelphia, PA: J. P. Lippincott, 1854. Reprint, Winston-Salem, NC: John F. Blair, 2000.

Hunter, James. *The Servant: A Simple Story About the True Essence of Leadership.* New York, NY: Crown Currency, 1998.

Johansen, Bob. *Leaders Make the Future: Ten New Leadership Skills for an Uncertain World.* Oakland, CA: Berrett-Koehler Publishers, 2009.

Joint Publication 5–0. *Joint Planning.* Washington, DC: Office of the Joint Chiefs of Staff, 2020.

Jones, Charles, Jr. *Sergeant William Jasper. An Address Delivered before the Georgia Historical Society, in Savannah, Georgia, on the 3rd of January, 1876.* Albany, GA: J. Munsell, printer, 1876.

Jong, Rob-Jan de. *Anticipate: The Art of Leading by Looking Ahead.* New York, NY: AMACOM, 2015.

Keegan, John. *The Mask of Command.* New York, NY: Elisabeth Sifton Books, 1987.

Kerrissey, Michaela, and Amy Edmondson. "Leading Through a Sustained Crisis Requires a Different Approach." *Harvard Business Review,* June 20, 2023. Accessed

September 30, 2024. https://hbr.org/2023/06/leading-through-a-sustained-crisis-requires-a-different-approach.

Klann, Gene. "The Application of Power and Influence in Organizational Leadership." In *Book of Readings*. Fort Leavenworth, KS: US Army Command and General Staff College, August 2011.

Kotter, John. *Leading Change*. Boston, MA: Harvard Business School Press, 1996.

Kouzes, James, and Barry Posner. *The Leadership Challenge*. San Francisco, CA: Jossey-Bass, 2012.

Krawczynski, Keith. *William Henry Drayton: South Carolina Revolutionary Patriot*. Baton Rouge: Louisiana State University Press, 2001.

Lancaster, Bruce. "'Heroic Huguenot' Review of The Swamp Fox" *Saturday Review* (January 31, 1959): 32–33.

Landrum, J. B. O. *Colonial and Revolutionary History of Upper South Carolina*. Greenville, SC: Shannon & Co., 1897.

Lee, Henry. *The Campaign of 1781 in the Carolinas: With Remarks, Historical and Critical on Johnson's Life of Greene*. Philadelphia, PA: E. Littell, 1824.

Lee, Robert E., ed. *The Revolutionary War Memoirs of General Henry Lee*. New York, NY: De Capo Press, 1998.

Lipscomb, Terry. *South Carolina Becomes a State: The Road from Colony to Independence*. Columbia: South Carolina Department of Archives and History, 1976.

———. *Battles, Skirmishes, and Actions Which Took Place In South Carolina During the American Revolution*. Columbia: South Carolina Department of Archives and History, c. 1991.

Lowney, Chris. *Heroic Leadership: Best Practices from a 450-Year-Old Company That Changed the World*. Chicago, IL: Loyola Press, 2005.

Lykke, Arthur F., Jr., "Defining Military Strategy = E + W + M." *Military Review* 69, No. 5, 1989.

MacKenzie, Roderick. *Strictures on Lt. Col. Tarleton's History of the Campaigns of 1780 and 1781, in the Southern Provinces of North America*. London: R. Faulder, 1787.

Magee, Roger, ed. *Strategic Leadership Primer*. Carlisle, PA: US Army War College, 1998.

Massey, Gregory D. *John Laurens and the American Revolution*. Columbia: University of South Carolina Press, 2000.

Massey, Gregory and Jim Piecuch. *General Nathanael Greene and the American Revolution in the South*. Columbia: University of South Carolina Press., 2012.

Matloff, Maurice. *American Military History*. Washington, DC: Office of the Chief of Military History, US Army, 1969.

Mattern, David. *Benjamin Lincoln and the American Revolution*. Columbia: University of South Carolina Press, 1998.

Maxwell, John. *The 17 Indisputable Laws of Teamwork*. Nashville, TN: Thomas Nelson, Inc., 2001.

McCrady, Edward. *The History of South Carolina in the Revolution, 1780–1783*, Volume 4. New York, NY: MacMillan, 1902.

Middlekauff, Robert. *The Glorious Cause: The American Revolution, 1763–1789*. New York, NY: Oxford University Press, 1982.

Millet, Allan and Peter Maslowski. *For the Common Defense: A Military History of the United States of America*. New York, NY: The Free Press, 1984.

Moncure, John. *The Cowpens Staff Ride and Battlefield Tour*. Fort Leavenworth, KS: US Army Command and General Staff College, 1996.

Morgan, Michael. "America's Civil War: Digging to Victory at Vicksburg." HistoryNet. June 12, 2006. Accessed July 10, 2024. https://www.historynet.com/americas-civil-war-digging-to-victory-at-vicksburg/.

Morrill, Dan L. *Southern Campaigns of the American Revolution*. Baltimore, MD: The Nautical & Aviation Publishing Company of America, 1993.

Moultrie, William. *Memoirs of the American Revolution so far as it Related to the States of North and South Carolina, and Georgia*. New York, NY: David Longworth, 1802.

Myers, Theodorus Bailey, ed. *Cowpens Papers: Being Correspondence of General Morgan and the Prominent Actors*. Charleston, SC: The News and Courier, 1881.

Northouse, Peter. *Leadership: Theory and Practice*. Thousand Oaks, CA: Sage Publications, 2004.

Oller, John. *The Swamp Fox: How Francis Marion Saved the American Revolution*. New York, NY: Da Capo Press, 2016.

Pancake, John S. *This Destructive War: The British Campaign in the Carolinas*. Tuscaloosa: The University of Alabama Press, 1985.

"Papers of the First Council of Safety of the Revolutionary Party in South Carolina, June–November, 1775 (Continued)." *The South Carolina Historical and Genealogical Magazine*, Vol. 1, No. 1 (Jan., 1900): 41–75.

Pickett, Margaret, *Rebecca Brewton Motte: American Patriot and Successful Rice Planter*. Charleston, SC: Evening Post Books, 2022.

Piecuch, Jim. *The Battle of Camden: A Documentary History*. Charleston: The History Press, 2006.

———. *Three Peoples, One King: Loyalists, Indians, and Slaves in the Revolutionary South, 1775–1782*. Columbia: University of South Carolina Press, 2008.

———. *South Carolina Provincials: Loyalists in British Service During the American Revolution*. Yardley, PA: Westholme Publishing, 2023.

Pinckney, Eliza. "Letters of Eliza Lucas Pinckney, 1768–1782." *South Carolina Historical Magazine*, 76 (3) 1975: 143–70.

Pratt, Fletcher. *Eleven Generals; Studies in American Command*. New York, NY: William Sloane, 1949.

Quarles, Benjamin. *The Negro in the American Revolution*. Chapel Hill: The University of North Carolina Press, 1996.

Rankin, Hugh F. "Charles Lord Cornwallis: Study in Frustration." In *George Washington's Opponents*, edited by George Athan Billias, 193–232. New York, NY: William Morrow and Company, Inc., 1969.

———. *The North Carolina Continentals*. Chapel Hill: The University of North Carolina Press, 1971.

———. *Francis Marion: The Swamp Fox*. New York, NY: Thomas Y. Crowell, 1973.

Reagan, Ronald. "Speech for Commencement by Ronald Reagan, May 15, 1993." The Citadel Archives Digital Collections. Accessed October 3, 2024. https://citadeldigitalarchives.omeka.net/items/show/1075.

Resolution of the South Carolina General Assembly, February 16, 2007. Accessed July 10, 2024. https://www.scstatehouse.gov/sess117_2007–2008/sj07/20070216.htm.

Rogers, James. *Richard Furman: Life and Legacy.* Augusta, GA: Mercer University Press, 1985.

Rosenthal, Jack. "A Terrible Thing to Waste." *New York Times,* July 30, 2009. Accessed October 2, 2024. https://www.nytimes.com/2009/08/02/magazine/02FOB-on-language-t.html.

Rowland, Lawrence S., Alexander Moore, and George C. Rogers, Jr. *The History of Beaufort County, South Carolina, Volume 1, 1514–1861.* Columbia: University of South Carolina Press, 1996.

Saberton, Ian, ed. *The Cornwallis Papers: The Campaigns of 1780 and 1781 in The Southern Theatre of the American Revolution,* Volumes 1 and 5. East Sussex: The Naval & Military Press Ltd., 2010.

Salley, Alexander. "Col. Miles Brewton and Some of His Descendants," *South Carolina Historical Magazine,* 2(2), 1901: 125–52.

Scheer, George F., and Hugh F. Rankin. *Rebels and Redcoats: The American Revolution Through the Eyes of Those Who Fought and Lived It.* New York, NY: Da Capo Press, Reprint, 1957.

Scoggins, Michael C. *The Day It Rained Militia: Huck's Defeat and the Revolution in the South Carolina Backcountry, May–July 1780.* Charleston, SC: The History Press, 2005.

Selesky, Harold, ed. *Encyclopedia of the American Revolution,* 2 Volumes. New York, NY: Thomson Gale, 2006.

Sgt. William Jasper Memorial Ceremony Honors Military. Savannah St. Patrick's Day Parade Committee. Accessed July 10, 2024. https://savannahsaintpatricksday.com/sgt-william-jasper-memorial-ceremony-honors-military/.

Scarborough, William. *The Allstons of Chicora Wood.* Baton Rouge: Louisiana State University Press, 2011.

Schelhammer, Michael. "10 Fateful Hits and Misses," online *Journal of the American Revolution,* September 19, 2013. Accessed November 17, 2020. https://allthingsliberty.com/2013/09/10-fateful-hits-misses/.

Sherman, William. *Calendar and Record of the Revolutionary War in the South, 1780–1781.* 10th edition. Seattle, WA: Gun Jones Publishing, 2018.

Showman, Richard, gen. ed. *The Papers of Nathanael Greene,* Volume 6. Chapel Hill: The University of North Carolina Press, 1991.

———. *The Papers of Nathanael Greene,* Volume 7. Chapel Hill: The University of North Carolina Press, 1994.

Simms, William Gilmore. *The Life of Francis Marion: The "Swamp Fox."* New York, NY: G. F. Cooledge & Brother, 1844.

Smith, Steven D. *Archaeological Evaluation of Wadboo Plantation, 38BK464*. Columbia: South Carolina Institute of Archaeology and Anthropology, 2008.

———. *Francis Marion and the Snow's Island Community: Myth, History, and Archaeology*. Asheville, NC: United Writers Press, Inc., 2021.

———. *The Battles of Fort Watson and Fort Motte, 1781*. Yardley, PA: Westholme Press, 2024.

Smith, Steven, and James Legg. *Running the Gauntlet: Locating the Battle of Parkers Ferry, South Carolina August 30, 1781*. Columbia: South Carolina Institute of Archaeology and Anthropology, 2019.

Smith, Steven, James B. Legg, and Tamara S. Wilson. *The Archaeology of the Camden Battlefield: History, Private Collections, and Field Investigations*. Columbia: South Carolina Institute of Archaeology and Anthropology, 2008.

Storozynski, Alex. *The Peasant Prince: Thaddeus Kosciuszko and the Age of Revolution*. New York, NY: Thomas Dunne Books, 2009.

Sun Tzu. *The Art of War*, trans. Thomas Cleary. Boston, MA: Shambhala Publications, 1988.

Swipe, James and Don Frick. *Seven Pillars of Servant Leadership*. New York, NY: Paulist Press, 2009.

Thayer, Theodore. *Nathanael Greene: Strategist of the American Revolution*. New York, NY: Twayne Publishers, 1960.

"The US Fighting Man's Code." Washington, DC: Office of Armed Forces Information and Education, Department of Defense, 1955.

Wallace, David Duncan. *The Life of Henry Laurens*. New York, NY: Russell and Russell, 1915.

Waters, Andrew. *To the End of the World: Nathanael Greene, Charles Cornwallis, and the Race to the Dan*. Yardley, PA: Westholme Publishing, 2020.

Weigley, Russell. *The American Way of War: A History of United States Military Strategy and Policy*. Bloomington: Indiana University Press, 1977.

Weslin, Mrs. O. J., and Miss Agnes Irwin. *Worthy Women of Our First Century*. Philadelphia, PA: J. B. Lippenwith Co., 1877.

White, Katherine. *The King's Mountain Men: The Story of the Battle, with Sketches of the American Soldiers who Took Part*. Reprint: Baltimore, MD: Clearfield Company, 2001.

Wilcox, William B., ed. *The American Rebellion: Sir Henry Clinton's Narrative of His Campaigns, 1775–1782*. New Haven, CN: Yale University Press, 1954.

Wills, Gary. *Certain Trumpets: The Nature of Leadership*. New York, NY: Simon & Schuster, 1994.

Wilson, David K. *The Southern Strategy: Britain's Conquest of South Carolina and Georgia, 1775–1780*. Columbia: University of South Carolina Press, 2005.

Wood, Peter. *Black Majority; Negroes in Colonial South Carolina from 1670 through the Stono Rebellion*. New York, NY: Knopf, 1974.

Woodward, Joel. "A Comparative Evaluation of British and American Strategy in the Southern Campaign of 1780–1781," master's thesis. Fort Leavenworth, KS: US Army Command and Staff College, 2002.

Wright, Robert K. Jr. *The Continental Army*. Washington, DC: Center of Military History, United States Army, 1983.

Wright, Robert, and Morris MacGregor. *Soldier-Statesmen of the Constitution*. Washington, DC: US Army Center of Military History, 1987.

Index

Alexander the Great, 94–95
Arbuthnot, Marriott, 98, 173
Arnold, Benedict, 41, 140, 174
Augusta, Georgia, 9–10, 14, 17, 19, 27, 33, 36, 43, 48, 50, 53, 134, 152, 160, 181

Ball, John Coming, 114
Bee, Thomas, 75, 76, 98
Black Mingo, South Carolina, battle of, 25–6, 114
Black soldiers, various efforts to raise and service of, 6–7, 14, 65, 66, 68
Blackstock's Plantation, South Carolina, battle of, 30, 32, 43, 105
Blue Savannah, South Carolina, battle of, 25–6, 115–7
branches, as a part of operational planning, 148
Bratton, William, 20, 30
Brewerton, Miles, 75, 163–4
Brown, Thomas, 5, 50, 180
Buford, Abraham, 17, 112

Camden, South Carolina, 17, 22, 28, 38, 41, 43, 46, 47, 48, 51, 53, 61, 123, 134, 147, 152, 164
  battle of, 21–5, 26, 27, 111, 113, 121, 136, 141, 144, 149
Campbell, Archibald, 9–10
  at Kings Mountain, 27, 124, 127
Campbell, William, 122

Carrington, Edward, 31, 146
Catawba River, 32, 35–7, 140, 146, 148
charismatic leadership, 89–90, 187
Charleston, South Carolina, 19, 36, 38, 41, 46, 51, 53, 55, 56, 57, 60, 61, 63, 64, 66, 67, 68–9, 73, 74, 79, 83–5, 94, 96, 103, 134, 147, 157, 163, 164
  1776 battle for, 3–5, 80, 91–4, 170, 172, 175, 180
  1780 battle for, 8–9, 12–18, 21, 22, 88, 99, 105, 111, 121, 170–1, 180, 187
Charlotte, North Carolina, 27, 28, 31, 36, 100, 101, 129, 137
Cheraw, South Carolina, 100, 133, 137, 146, 189
Cherokee Indians, 2, 5, 6, 73–4, 80, 83–4, 86, 111, 113, 169, 180, 181, 183
Chronicle, William, 122, 127–8
Clarke, Elijah, 19, 27, 30, 43, 50, 123, 181
  at Musgrove's Mill, 26, 122
Cleveland, Benjamin, 122, 124, 127
Clinton, Henry, 2–4, 7–9, 35, 60, 61, 65, 91, 112, 121, 129
  and the 1780 battle for Charleston, 12–13, 98–9, 180
  June 13, 1780 proclamation of, 18–19
Coates, James, 54–5

Cornwallis, Charles, 13, 18–19, 27, 28, 32, 40–1, 46, 68, 87, 121, 124, 125, 128, 133, 134, 135, 136, 140, 148, 149, 152, 173, 174
  and the Race to the Dan, 35–8
  at the battle of Camden, 22–5
  at the battle of Yorktown, 60–2
Council of Safety, 1, 76–81, 86, 187
Cowpens, South Carolina, 27, 124
  battle of, 33–34, 40, 136, 140–4, 149, 152, 181
Craig, James, 40, 63
crisis leadership, 98, 103
Cruger, John, 43, 48–50, 53, 58
Cunningham, Patrick, 2, 80, 85–7, 179
Cunningham, Robert, 85, 86
Cunningham, William, 124–5

d'Estaing, Charles Hector, 12
Dan River, 31–2, 35, 37–8, 133, 146
Davidson, William Lee, 37, 124
Davie, William, 21
DePeyster, Abraham, 127–8
de Kalb, Johann, 22, 23–5
Doyle, Welbore Ellis, 42, 43, 152, 157
Drayton, William, 1–2, 7, 75, 76, 79, 86

Elliott, Benjamin, 75
emotional intelligence, 111, 144
empathy, 117
Eutaw Springs, South Carolina, battle of, 57–60, 134, 143, 181

Fanning, David, 5, 26, 63–4
Ferguson, Patrick, 27–8, 121–8
Ferguson, Thomas, 75
Fishdam, South Carolina, battle of, 30
Fishing Creek, South Carolina, battle of, 26, 27, 105
Fletchall, Thomas, 2, 79
Fort Granby, South Carolina, battle of, 43, 46–8, 53, 106, 152–6
Fort Johnson, South Carolina, 8, 14, 69, 119, 170

Fort Motte, South Carolina, battle of, 46–7, 53, 134, 152, 154, 164–7
Fort Moultrie, South Carolina, 5, 14–16, 92–4, 96, 170, 173, 187
Fort Sullivan, South Carolina; see Fort Moultrie, South Carolina
Fort Watson, South Carolina, battle of, 42, 44, 46, 47, 49, 50–1, 53, 134, 152, 157–60
Furman, Robert, 1, 84
  and charismatic leadership, 89–90
  mission to South Carolina backcountry, 83–90, 187

Gadsden, Christopher, 98, 169, 173
Gates, Horatio, 124, 145, 163
  and Francis Marion, 111, 113, 132
  at battle of Camden, 22–5, 46, 100
  takes command of Second Continental Army, 22, 99
Georgetown, South Carolina, 26, 41, 42, 46, 47, 106, 134, 152, 157
Germain, George, 7–8, 61, 62, 65
Gervais, John Lewis, 98
Gilbert Town, North Carolina, 27, 43, 121, 124
Giles, Edward, 33, 141
Golden Rule, Marshall Goldsmith version of, 117–18
Grant, James, 74, 111, 169, 179, 183
Great Britain, strategy of
  assumption of Loyalist support in the South, 1, 8, 18
  emphasis on the Southern colonies, 1, 7, 8
Greenleaf, Robert, 175, 184
Greene, Nathanael, 44–6, 49, 51–3, 56, 61, 68, 69, 140, 146, 151–2, 157, 158, 160, 164, 175, 189
  and Thaddeus Kosciuszko, 145–9
  and the Race to the Dan, 35–8
  as quartermaster, 132
  as strategist, 134–7, 189
  at the battle of Eutaw springs, 57–60

foresight of, 31–2, 146–9
pre-Revolutionary War life of, 131
relationship with Francis Marion, 32
relationship with John Rutledge, 101–2, 103–4
relationship with Thomas Sumter, 32
returns to South Carolina, 40–1
takes command of Sothern Theater, 31, 101
Guilford Court House, North Carolina, battle of, 34, 38–40, 60, 101, 133, 143, 152
Gunby, John, 45

Hambright, Frederick, 124, 127–8
Hampton, Andrew, 124
Hanging Rock, South Carolina, battle of, 20–1, 24, 105
Hart, Oliver, 1, 79, 83, 86, 88
Hayne, Isaac, 18
heroic leadership, 91, 94–6
Heyward, Thomas, 75, 76, 173
Hill, William, 20, 27, 30
Hillsborough, North Carolina, 31, 36, 38, 63, 100, 113, 146
Hobkirk's Hill, South Carolina, battle of, 44, 134, 164
Howard, John Edward, 66, 142
Huck, Christian, 20, 113
Huger, Daniel, 198
Huger, Isaac, 18, 37, 169, 183
Huger, John, 75, 76

Innes, Alexander, 18, 26, 122

Jasper, William
 at battle of Savannah, Georgia, 13, 92, 94
 at battle of Sullivan's Island, 4–5, 92–6, 188

Kettle Creek, Georgia, battle of, 9–10, 180
Kings Mountain, South Carolina, battle of, 27–8, 124–30

Kirkwood, Robert, 57
Kosciuszko, Thaddeus, 145
 at Dill's Bluff, 69
 at Ninety Six, 49, 51
 performing reconnaissance and boat-building for Nathanael Greene, 145–9, 189
Kotter, John, eight-step change process of, 75–81, 187

Lacy, Edward, 20, 27, 30, 127
Lafayette, Marquis de, 61
Laurens, Henry, 1, 6–7, 86, 169, 179, 183
 and creating change through the Council of Safety, 75–81, 187
 pre-Revolutionary War life of, 73–5
Laurens, John, 6, 65, 66, 67
"law of the niche," 143–4
leadership, definition and description of, 187
"leadership by example," description of, 167–8
Lee, Charles, 3, 97–8
Lee, Henry, 38, 41–3, 46, 49, 50, 52, 53, 54, 60, 61, 67, 100, 113, 117, 133, 134, 137, 151, 181
 and negotiation, 153–6
 at Fort Granby, 46–8, 152–6, 189
 at Fort Motte, 164–8
 at Fort Watson, 44, 157, 159
 at Guilford Court House, 39
 at Shubrick's Plantation, 55
Lenud's Ferry, South Carolina, battle of 16
Leslie, Alexander, 35, 61, 68
Lincoln, Benjamin, 22
 and the defense of Charleston, 9–17, 98, 170–1
Lowndes, Rawlins, 75, 76
Lyttelton, William Henry, 74, 169

magis leadership, 95–6
Maham, Hezekiah, 44, 158–61, 190
"Maham's Tower," 44, 50–1, 159–61, 165
Majoribanks, John, 59

Mao Tse-tung, 136
Marion, Francis, 13, 14, 41–3, 46, 49, 51–2, 60, 61, 66, 67, 68, 87, 93, 95, 100, 101, 103, 106, 108, 134, 136, 137, 144, 151–2, 164, 169, 188
  and the "conniving lieutenant," 119–20
  and emotional intelligence, 111–20
  and the "sweet potato dinner," 109–10
  at Black Mingo Creek, 114–15
  at Blue Savannah, 115–17
  at Fort Motte, 165–7
  at Fort Watson, 44, 157–61, 190
  at Parker's Ferry, 56–7
  at Shubrick's Plantation, 55
  at Sullivan's Island, 5
  relationship with Nathanael Greene, 32, 101
  takes command of partisan force, 25–6
Martin, Josiah, 2
Matthews, John, 101
Maxwell, Andrew, 152–4, 156
McDowell, Charles, 122, 127
Middleton, Arthur, 75, 76
military crest, 125
militiaman, idiosyncrasies of, 118, 141, 188, 189
Monck's Corner, South Carolina, 15, 46, 48, 51, 54, 60, 67, 99
Money, John, 30
Moore, John, 19
Moore's Creek Bridge, North Carolina, battle of, 2, 19
Morgan, Daniel, 32, 124, 132, 137, 181, 183
  at the battle of Cowpens, 33–5, 133, 136, 147–8, 189
  during the Race to the Dan, 35–7
  health issues of, 37
  Patriot replication of his Cowpens tactics, 34, 39–40, 57, 142–3
  pre-Revolutionary War life of, 140
Motte, Rebecca, 163–8, 190

"Moultrie Flag," 91, 94, 95, 170
Moultrie, William, 10, 103, 120, 170, 183
  as a prisoner of war, 171–7, 190
  at the battle of Sullivan's Island, 3, 5, 91–2, 95, 98
Musgrove's Mill, South Carolina, battle of, 26–7, 122

Nelson's Ferry, South Carolina, 48, 57, 105, 157, 164
Ninety Six, South Carolina, 2, 17, 19, 28, 32, 36, 41, 43, 46, 77, 87, 123, 133, 137, 152, 179, 180, 182
  siege of, 48–53, 58, 80, 134, 160, 181
North, Frederick Lord, 63

Orangeburg, South Carolina, 47, 53, 54, 134
"Overmountain Men," 27, 121–3, 188

Parker, Peter, 2–3, 91–2
Parker's Ferry, South Carolina, battle of, 56–7
partisan warfare, importance of to Nathanael Greene, 133, 136–7, 147, 189
Pearson, James, 75, 76
Pee Dee River, 25, 26, 32, 35, 42, 80, 116–17, 146, 147, 148
personal power, as a component of leadership, 182–5, 190
Pickens, Andrew, 18, 19, 41–2, 43, 50, 51, 53, 66, 100, 103, 134, 169, 179
  and personal power, 182–5, 190
  at Cowpens, 33–4, 141–2, 181
  at Eutaw Springs, 57, 59, 181
  at Kettle Creek, 9–10
  at the "Ring Fight," 6, 180
  political career of, 182
Pinckney, Charles Cotesworth, 75, 76, 98, 171, 175
Prevost, Augustine, 8, 9–11, 12

Prevost, Mark, 11
Purrysburg, South Carolina, 8, 9, 10
"Pyle's Massacre," 38

"Race to the Dan," 35–8, 40, 41, 102, 148, 152
Ramsour's Mill, North Carolina, battle of, 19, 35
Rawdon, Francis, 19, 22–4, 35, 41–2, 44–5, 46, 48, 51–3, 54, 57, 61, 134, 153–5, 164–5
Reagan, Ronald, 96
"Regulators," 84–5, 170
"responsible freedom," 190
Richardson, Richard, 2, 80, 86
Rocky Mount, South Carolina, battle of, 20–1, 105
Rugeley's Mill, South Carolina, battle of, 22–3, 32, 46, 152
Rutledge, John, 26, 55–6, 65, 87, 93, 97, 106, 108, 112, 183
  and crisis leadership, 103–4, 187
  and restoration of civil government, 102–3, 187
  resolve of to defend Sullivan's Island, 3, 97–8, 170

Salisbury, North Carolina, 31, 37, 99, 100
Saratoga, New York, battle of, 7, 22, 37, 49, 140, 145
Savannah, Georgia, 5, 8, 11, 43, 53, 60, 63, 65, 94, 99, 170
  siege of, 12–13
self-awareness, 114–15
sequels, as part of operational planning, 149
servant leadership, description of, 175–7
Sevier, John, 27, 122, 124, 127
Shelby, Isaac, 50
  at Kings Mountain, 27, 121–30, 188
  at Musgrove's Mill, 26
Shubrick's Plantation, South Carolina, battle of, 55

Snow's Island, South Carolina, 25, 32, 42–3
social skill, 119
South Carolina "backcountry," competition for loyalty of, 1, 5, 19–20, 79, 80, 83–8, 180–2, 187
St. Augustine, Florida, 5, 7, 8, 19
Stevens, Edward, 22, 31, 146
Stewart, Alexander, 53, 58–9, 60
Strategy, "ends, ways, and means" as an understanding of, 134–7, 189
Stuart, John, 18
Sullivan's Island, South Carolina, 3
  battle of 80, 91–94, 171. *See also* Charleston, South Carolina, 1776 battle for
"Sumter's Law," 55–6, 106–7, 110
Sumter, Thomas, 28, 47, 51, 66, 87, 100, 101, 103, 113, 134, 157, 188
  as a transactional leader, 107–8. *See also* "Sumter's Law"
  at Blackstock's Plantation, 30–1, 43, 105
  at Fishdam, 28–30
  at Fishing Creek, 26, 105
  at Fort Granby, 43, 106, 152, 155
  at Hanging Rock, 20–1, 105
  at Rocky Mount, 20–1, 105
  at Shubrick's Plantation, 54–5
  takes command of militia, 26, 100
Sun Tzu, 154–6

Tarleton, Banastre, 15–16, 20, 26, 31, 120, 128, 137, 151, 180
  at Blackstock's Plantation, 30, 32
  at Camden, 22–4
  at Cowpens, 33–5, 133, 140–4
  at Guilford Court house, 38–40
  at Waxhaws, 17, 112
  during the Race to the Dan, 37
Taylor, Thomas, 55
Tennent, William, 1, 79, 86
Thomas, John, 79

Thompson, Benjamin, 66–7
Thomson, William, 2, 4
topographical crest, 125
transactional leadership, 105, 107–10, 156, 188
transformational leadership, 108, 109, 111, 188
Turnbull, George, 19–20

"unity of effort," description of, 129–30

"War of the Posts," 102, 134, 152, 157, 181
Washington, George, 21, 31, 62, 93, 99, 132, 133, 135, 147, 151, 174
Washington, William, 45, 57, 59, 152
    at Cowpens, 32–4, 141–2
    at Guilford Court House, 39
Watson, John, 41–2, 44, 46, 110, 157
Waxhaws, South Carolina, battle of, 17, 33, 112

Wayne, Anthony, 61, 66, 69
Weems, Mason Locke, 93, 109–10, 114–15, 119–20, 168
Wemyss, James, 118
Whipple, Abraham, 14–15
Williams, Arland, 96
Williams, James, 26, 122–4, 127
Williams, Ortho, 37, 57, 66
Williamson, Andrew, 6, 10, 18, 19, 77, 80, 87, 179, 180
Williamson, William, 75
Wilmington, North Carolina, 40, 46, 60, 63, 133
Winn, Richard, 20
Winston, Joseph, 122, 124, 127

Yadkin River, 31–2, 37
Yorktown, Virginia, battle of, 18, 48, 60–2, 63, 65, 136, 181